My First Catholic Bible

Illustrations by Natalie Carabetta

NEW REVISED STANDARD VERSION

THOMAS NELSON PUBLISHERS
Nashville

About the Illustrator

Natalie Carabetta was born in Meriden, Connecticut, in 1963. She graduated from the Philadelphia College of Art in 1985 and has been illustrating books for children since 1990. Presently, Natalie lives in Perkasie, Pennsylvania, with her daughter, Grace.

A Special Letter to Children
from
Mother Teresa of Calcutta

+LDM

6 May 1997

My dear Children

God loved the world so much that He sent us His only Son to
save us from sin. And Jesus brought us the Good News that
God loves each one of us with a most tender love. We are
precious to Him. He has carved us in the palm of His hand.
And we are created for greater things: to love and to be loved.

It is so important for us to know the Word of God. Because if
we know it, we will love it; and if we love it, we will keep it
and live it. Let us ask Mary, the Mother of Jesus and our
Mother, for the grace to imitate her. She kept the Word of
God and pondered it in her heart. And to be able to do that,
we must pray. Prayer gives a clean heart, and a clean heart
can see God and know His will for us.

Jesus tells us, "Love one another as I have loved you."
And how do we do that? Love begins in the family. I begin
by loving my father and my mother, my brothers and sisters;
my friends in the neighbourhood and at school and all those
I meet in my town or city. Love to be true must hurt, must
cost us something. When we love like that, ready to make a
sacrifice, we will find peace and joy.

Look around and see if there is anyone around you who is sick,
poor, lonely, or feeling unloved or unwanted. We don't have
to do big things. What counts is that we do small things with
great love - giving a smile, a kind word, a helping hand,
bringing a glass of water, sharing a sweet. Remember that we
do it to Jesus because He said, "Whatever you do to the least,
you do it to Me." So let us pray much that we may be the
sunshine of God's love to all we meet.

Let us pray.

God bless you
M Teresa mc

Learn to Pray the Rosary

Now that you have your very own Bible, you can use it not only to learn the stories and memory verses, you can also use it to learn the Our Father and the Hail Mary. Then you will be able to pray the Rosary every day.

Below, you'll see that we have divided the prayers of the Rosary. Ask your parents or someone from your church to teach you how to use a Rosary and soon you will be able to pray it every day.

First, you can memorize one line each day for five days. Try doing this every morning while you eat breakfast or in the afternoons after school. You could even work on them while you're going to sleep at night. Some people seem to think better at certain times of the day, so just pick the time you're most alert and use it to memorize a line of a prayer.

Or, if you need to take a little longer, spend five days learning each line by breaking them into small sections and memorize a few words at a time.

Pretty soon, you'll be able to pray the Rosary all by yourself.

Our Father

Our Father who art in heaven, hallowed be thy name.

Thy kingdom come. Thy will be done on earth, as it is in heaven.

Give us this day our daily bread,

and forgive us our trespasses, as we forgive those
who trespass against us,

and lead us not into temptation, but deliver us from evil. Amen.

Hail Mary

Hail Mary, full of grace! The Lord is with thee,

blessed art thou among women,

and blessed is the fruit of thy womb, Jesus.

Holy Mary, Mother of God,

pray for us sinners, now and at the hour of our death. Amen.

Glory Be to the Father

Glory be to the Father,

to the Son, and to the Holy Spirit.

As it was in the beginning,

is now, and ever shall be,

World without end. Amen.

Contents

The Devotionals
(Use the boxes to the left of the Devotionals to check off the ones you've read.)

CONTENTS

CONTENTS

Introduction

Looking for a Best Friend?

We all need one. Someone we can share our secrets with. Someone who likes us. Someone who's fun to be around. We need somebody like that to talk to every day.

My First Catholic Bible will help you become best friends with the *best* Best Friend of all—the wonderful God, creator of heaven and earth. God knows all about you, and he likes you very much. He loves you deeply. He's a joy to be with. You can tell him all your secrets. And you can spend time with him every day—for the rest of your life.

God becomes our Best Friend . . .

- when we ask Jesus Christ, his Son, to forgive our sins and to give us everlasting life, and . . .
- when we begin reading our Bibles and praying every day.

Daily Bible reading and praying is like talking with God himself. He speaks to us when we read his book, the Bible. And we speak to him when we pray. These daily times of Bible study and prayer make us more and more devoted to God, which is why we call them—daily devotions.

Here are seven ways to get the most from *My First Catholic Bible:*

1. Use it about the same time each day—maybe in the morning before school or at night just before going to bed.

2. Think of each day's Scripture as a special message from God just for you.

3. Study the pictures. Each has been drawn to accurately show something about the words you're reading.

4. Use the prayer starters to . . . well, to start your prayers. Then go on to tell God whatever you'd like. Learn to talk to him naturally, just like talking to a friend.

5. Work hard on the memory verses. Collect all of them in your mind.

6. Use weekends to look over Scriptures you've previously read and to review verses you've already learned.

7. If you *do* occasionally skip a day, make sure you don't miss the next one. Make your daily devotions a habit, and stick to them.

No matter how many—or how few—friends you have, you've got one Best Friend who will never leave you or let you down. And he's waiting for you to get to know him better . . . just as soon as you turn to page one.

A Word for Parents

Deuteronomy 6.5-7 tells parents how to help their children get established in a lifestyle of daily prayer and Scripture reading. The order established in that passage is important. First, parents should love the Lord with all their hearts. Next we're to memorize his Word, his laws. Then we are to talk about them all the time to our children.

My First Catholic Bible can help.

- For younger children, use this as a read-to-me picture book of daily devotions.

- For older children, gently monitor their use of this book and help them build the "daily devotional" habit into their routine.

- Keep your own copy of *My First Catholic Bible* (you can use it for your devotions, too) so you can talk more easily about the Scripture wherever you are and whatever you're doing.

- Provide a full copy of the Bible so your children can look up surrounding passages for further study.

- Help your child learn the memory verses. John Ruskin, English social critic, said the verses his mother helped him memorize in childhood "set my soul for life." Use charts, stars, incentives, and rewards. Make it a family project.

- Involve your family in a good church with a strong youth ministry.

- Be a spiritual model for your children. The best way to entice your kids into the daily devotional habit is to let them see you enjoying yours.

Our spiritual vitality depends on two aspects of victorious Christian living: conversion and conversation. The first is a matter of heart; the second, of habit. When we meet Christ at the cross, that's *conversion.* When we meet with him behind the closed door, that's *conversation.*

*The message about **the cross** is foolishness to those who are perishing, but to us who are being saved it is the power of God (1 Corinthians 1.18).*

*Whenever you pray, go into your room and **shut the door** and pray to your Father who is in secret; and your Father who sees in secret will reward you (Matthew 6.6).*

We're converted to Jesus Christ when we trust him as Savior, confessing our sins to him, asking him for eternal life, and committing ourselves to him as Lord and Master. Then the friendship starts. The God of the Universe wants to meet us each day over an old Book at the kitchen table. It's beyond comprehension.

God is both infinite and intimate! He delights in being with his people, hearing us pray and talking to us through his Word. The Master, it seems, occupies two addresses: in the highest heavens and with the humblest hearts.

The heavenly Father wants our earthly friendship. Could anything be more astonishing than that?

x

Only one: Many of us can't find time for him. We're too busy for Bible study, and too pooped for prayer.

We rush into each day, bolting from bed like a thoroughbred from the gate. We gulp down our coffee, throw on designer labels, then veer onto the fast lane. We whirl through our daily tasks like a spinning top, then drive by the restaurant on the way home so they can throw food to us through the window. We drag ourselves to the couch for an hour of video violence, then stagger to be bed for six hours of sleep. Whatever happened to green pastures and still waters? We're too frazzled to find them!

But suppose you do go to bed at a reasonable hour and get up a half hour earlier to meet God the next morning—what do you do with those thirty minutes? I'd like to suggest a sequence called *JARS and Rs*.

J=Jot

J stands for "jot." You'll need a notebook for this, but any kind will do. At the top of the page, jot the date. You can then write anything you want about your feelings, your moods, or the circumstances of your life. Or, just use the margin of your Bible to jot down the date and any useful information.

After you've written everything you want to remember, you're ready for the next step.

A=Ask

Take a moment to ask God to speak to you through his Word. Though some people read the Bible only as a textbook, it's primarily a love letter between the Lord and his people. It's designed to transform and invigorate our lives as the Holy Spirit applies it to our hearts. Ask God to open your mind to what he wants to teach you, and ask him to help you know what he wants you to do.

R=Read

Then read your Bible. Begin each day where you left off the day before. Underline significant phrases. Study cross-references. Diagram sentences. Outline chapters. Check key words in a dictionary. Dig into the text, looking for contrasts and comparisons. Rewrite verses in your own words in your notebook. There are no rules for where or how much to read. The important thing is remembering as you read that God is talking to you as one talks to a friend.

S=Select

As you study the Bible, look for one verse to select as your *verse-for-the-day*—a verse that really hammers at your heart. When you find it, copy it in your journal and perhaps on a scrap of paper to carry with you all day. I know one man who writes his verse on the back of a business card that he props on his desk. Another friend jots hers on a sticky note to post on her dashboard. She memorizes it as she drives to work.

Find your verse-for-the-day in the morning, carry it in your heart all day, and at night meditate on it as you fall asleep.

Then having listened to the Lord, it's time to speak to him. The last half of your quiet time centers around the three *Rs* of prayer.

R=Rejoice

Begin by rejoicing, praising, and thanking God for his grace and generosity. A good place to start is with your verse-for-the-day. Usually when engaged in conversation, I respond and react to the words of the one speaking to me. If he's talking about football, I don't abruptly begin a discourse on the excavations of Crocodilopolis. I follow the flow of the conversation.

If your verse-for-the-day is Matthew 22.37—*Love the Lord your God with all your heart . . .*—tell God how much you love him and thank him for his love for you. Rejoice that you have a love-based relationship with the Almighty.

R=Repent

As you worship the Lord, you may begin to feel inadequate, like Peter in Luke 5.8, who, amazed at Christ's miracle of fish, fell at his knees saying, *"Go away from me, Lord, for I am a sinful man!"*

So we move naturally from rejoicing to repenting. We admit to God faults and failures we've knowingly allowed to mar our lives since we last prayed.

R=Request

Then we're ready to obey Philippians 4.6: *With thankgiving let your requests be made known to God.* The Lord promises to answer our prayers if we sincerely ask in the name of the Lord Jesus—with one condition inserted for our protection: He only promises to grant us those things that are good for us, that are according to his will (1 John 5.14-15).

So pray with confidence, using your journal to record your requests and to note God's answers. Pray aloud when you can, and talk to God naturally, as though speaking with a friend. Because you are.

Don't grow discouraged if sometimes you don't feel like praying. Pray anyway. Don't quit on mornings when you don't enjoy your Bible reading. Read anyway. Don't despair if you miss a day. Start again the next.

Develop the habit, then the habit will develop you. Cultivate the friendship, and your Friend will stick closer than a brother.

The impact on your children will be for keeps.

People You'll Meet in
My First Catholic Bible

Who in the world is Mephibosheth? Jehoshaphat? Nebuchadnezzar? Ever heard of Ananias and Sapphira?

These hard-to-say names belong to some very interesting people you'll meet in *My First Catholic Bible*. The following list can help you get to know them. Beside every name is a helpful guide to pronouncing it correctly, and a description of the person's identity. At the end of each entry you'll find the page number first mentioning that character.

Adam *(ADD um)* **and Eve** *(eev)* - the first man and woman, created by God and placed in the Garden of Eden (p. 2)

Cain *(kane)* **and Abel** *(A buhl)* - Adam and Eve's first two sons (p. 6)

Noah *(NOE uh)* - the man who trusted and obeyed God by building a big boat (p. 8)

Abram/Abraham *(A bruhm/AY bruh ham)* - the man who received God's promise to make his descendants into a great nation (p. 15)

Sarai/Sarah *(SAR eye/SAR uh)* - Abraham's wife; she had her first son when she was 90 years old and Abraham was 100 years old (p. 15)

Lot *(laht)* - Abraham's nephew who traveled with him to the land of Canaan (p. 15)

Isaac *(EYE zik)* - the son of Abraham and Sarah through whom God fulfilled his promise to Abraham (p. 24)

Hagar *(HAY gahr)* - Sarah's Egyptian slave woman (p. 24)

Ishmael *(IHSH may ell)* - the son of Abraham and Hagar (p. 24)

Rebekah *(ruh BEK uh)* - Isaac's wife who was promised and chosen by God (p. 28)

Esau *(EE saw)* - Isaac and Rebekah's son who sold his birthright to his twin brother Jacob (p. 30)

Jacob *(JAY cub)* - Isaac and Rebekah's son who received his father's blessing in place of his twin brother Esau (p. 30)

Laban *(LAY bihn)* - Rebekah's wealthy brother for whom Jacob worked for over 14 years (p. 32)

Leah *(LEE uh)*-Laban's oldest daughter who became Jacob's wife through deceit (p. 32)

Rachel *(RAY chuhl)* - Leah's sister who became Jacob's wife after he had worked 14 years for her father Laban (p. 32)

Joseph *(JOE zeph)* - the second youngest of the twelve sons of Jacob; he became the governor of all Egypt (p. 36)

Moses *(MOE zez)* - the man God used to deliver the children of Israel from Egyptian bondage (p. 42)

Miriam *(MER eh um)* - Moses' older sister who saved his life when he was just a baby (p. 42)

Aaron *(EHR un)* - the older brother of Moses who became his spokesman; he and his sons were the first priests of Israel (p. 46)

Balaam *(BAY lum)* - A magician in Mesopotamia whose donkey was enabled by God to talk (p. 63)

Joshua *(JAHSH oo uh)* - the man who became the leader of Israel following the death of Moses, and who led the nation into the Promised Land (p. 64)

Deborah *(DEB uh rah)* - a prophetess and leader of Israel who was used by God to defeat the enemies of Israel (p. 76)

Barak *(BAR ack)* - the leader of Israel's army who, along with Deborah, defeated the army of Sisera (p. 76)

Gideon *(GIDD ee un)* - the leader God used to rescue Israel from the Midianites with only 300 soldiers (p. 79)

Samson *(SAM suhn)* - a leader of Israel who had great strength when the Holy Spirit came upon him (p. 80)

Delilah *(dih LIE lah)* - the Philistine woman who tricked Samson, causing him to lose his great strength (p. 80)

Naomi *(nay OH mee)* - a woman whose family moved to Moab after a famine in their hometown of Bethlehem (p. 84)

Ruth *(rooth)* - the daughter-in-law of Naomi who returned with Naomi to Bethlehem after the death of both of their husbands (p. 84)

Boaz *(BOE az)* - a wealthy man from Bethlehem, a relative of Naomi's husband, who married Ruth and became an ancestor of David and Jesus (p. 86)

Hannah *(HAN nuh)* - the wife of Elkanah who prayed for a son and dedicated him to God before his birth (p. 88)

Eli *(EE lie)* - a priest and judge of Israel (p. 88)

Elkanah *(el KAY na)* - a Levite who was the husband of Hannah and the father of Samuel (p. 89)

Samuel *(SAM yoo uhl)* - a Hebrew prophet who, as a child, ministered to the Lord by helping Eli the priest (p. 89)

Saul *(sawl)* - the man who was anointed by Samuel as the first king of Israel (p. 92)

David *(DAY vid)* - a musician and warrior for Saul who eventually became king of Israel in Saul's place (p. 95)

Goliath *(goe LIE ahth)* - the gigantic Philistine whom David killed with a slingshot and stone (p. 97)

Jonathan *(JAHN uh thuhn)* - Saul's son and David's best friend (p. 101)

Mephibosheth *(meh FIB oh shehth)* - the son of Jonathan and grandson of Saul; David showed kindness to him for the sake of Jonathan (p. 109)

Solomon *(SAHL uh mun)* - David's son who became king of Israel; he was given special wisdom from God (p. 110)

Ahab *(A hab)* - a wicked king of Israel who built altars to Baal (p. 114)

Elijah *(ee LIE juh)* - a prophet of God during the reign of King Ahab (p. 115)

Elisha *(ee LIE shuh)* - the prophet of God who came after Elijah; he was given twice as much power as the other prophets (p. 119)

Naaman *(NAY a man)* - the commander of the Syrian army who was healed of leprosy (p. 121)

Jezebel *(JEZ uh bel)* - the evil wife of King Ahab and a worshiper of the false god Baal (p. 125)

Hezekiah *(hez uh KIGH uh)* - a king of Judah who trusted in the Lord for defeat of his enemies (p. 127)

Isaiah *(eye ZAY uh)* - a prophet of Judah during the reigns of four kings, including Hezekiah (p. 129)

Josiah *(joe SIGH uh)* - a godly king of Judah who took the throne when he was only eight years old (p. 131)

Jehoshaphat *(juh HAH shuh fat)* - a king of Judah who obeyed and worshiped the Lord; the Lord helped him keep control of his kingdom (p. 134)

Joash *(JOE ash)* - the king of Judah during the time when the temple was repaired (p. 135)

Uzziah *(you ZIE uh)* - the king of Judah who was struck with leprosy as a punishment from the Lord (p. 137)

Ahaz *(A haz)* - a wicked king of Judah who offered sacrifices to Baal (p. 138)

Nehemiah *(knee uh MY ah)* - a Jewish servant of the king of Persia who led in the rebuilding of the walls of Jerusalem (p. 139)

Tobit *(TOB it)* - a good man who was blinded after hearing of evil in Israel. He was later healed by his son Tobias (p. 141)

Judith *(JUDE ith)* - a wealthy widow who killed the Assyrian king and led Israel to praise God (p. 146)

Esther *(ESS ter)* - the Jewish wife of King Xerxes and the queen of Persia who risked her life to save her people (p. 149)

Mordecai *(MAWR deh kie)* - the cousin of Esther and a palace official in Persia (p. 149)

Haman *(HAY mun)* - evil officer in Persia who wanted to destroy all the Jews in the world (p. 150)

Judas *(JU das)* - A mighty warrior who led the Israelites to defeat the Gentiles and then cleansed the temple (p. 156)

Heliodorus *(HE li o door us)* - a foreign official who planned to rob the temple but was struck by God's power (p. 159)

Job *(jobe)* - a worshiper of God who trusted the Lord even when tested with the loss of all his possessions (p. 162)

Jeremiah *(jer uh MIGH uh)* - a priest and prophet of God who warned the people of their disobedience to God (p. 194)

Nebuchadnezzar *(neb you kad NEZ ur)* - the king of Babylonia who led his army in an attack on Jerusalem that captured the city (p. 198)

Ezekiel *(ih ZEEK e uhl)* - a priest and prophet of God before and after the fall of Jerusalem (p. 203)

Daniel *(DAN yuhl)* - a young Jew taken captive by the Babylonians who remained completely faithful to the Lord (p. 206)

Belshazzar *(bel SHAZ zur)* - the last king of Babylon whose evil ways caused the Lord to write a message of doom on the wall of his banquet room (p. 209)

Hosea *(hoe ZAY uh)* - a prophet in Israel for over 40 years (p. 214)

Joel *(JOE uhl)* - a prophet in Israel who used swarms of locusts to describe how God was going to destroy Israel (p. 215)

Amos *(AIM us)* - a man who left his hometown in Judah and went to the northern kingdom of Israel to deliver God's message to the people (p. 216)

Jonah *(JOE nuh)* - a prophet whose disobedience led to his being swallowed by a great fish, but he repented and was sent to preach in Nineveh (p. 218)

Micah *(MIE kuh)* - a prophet who gave messages from the Lord especially to the cities of Samaria and Jerusalem (p. 220)

Nahum *(NAY hum)* - a prophet who told of justice and punishment to come upon Assyria (p. 222)

Habakkuk *(huh BAK uhk)* - a prophet of Judah who praised the Lord's power and glory (p. 223)

Zechariah *(zeck ah RIE a)* - a priest and prophet whose visions were used by God to help the people of Jerusalem rebuild the temple (p. 224)

Malachi *(MAL ah kie)* - a prophet who reminded the people of Israel to give to God what belonged to him (p. 227)

Jesus *(GEE zus)* - the Son of God, the Savior of the world, who was both God and man (p. 228)

Herod *(HEHR ud)* - the king of Israel when Jesus was born (p. 228)

Mary *(MAIR ee)* - the wife of Joseph and the woman chosen by the Lord as the mother of Jesus (p. 228)

Joseph *(JOE zeph)* - a carpenter from Nazareth; the husband of Mary, mother of Jesus (p. 229)

Simon Peter *(SIGH mun PEE ter)* - a fisherman who was brought to Jesus by his brother Andrew; he became one of Jesus' apostles (p. 235)

James *(jamez)* **and John** *(jahn)* - the sons of Zebedee; fishermen who became apostles of Jesus (p. 238)

Pilate *(PIE lat)* - the Roman governor of Judea during the time of Jesus (p. 243)

Jairus *(jay EYE ruhs)* - a ruler of the Jewish meeting place whose daughter needed healing from Jesus (p. 246)

Pharisees *(FARE uh sees)* - the religious teachers of Jesus' day (p. 249)

Elizabeth *(ee LIZ uh buth)* - the cousin of Mary and the mother of John (p. 256)

John *(jahn)* - the son of Zechariah and Elizabeth; the man God sent to prepare the people to receive Jesus (p. 262)

Judas *(JOO duhs)* - the apostle who betrayed Jesus (p. 278)

Nicodemus *(nick oh DEE mus)* - a Pharisee and Jewish leader who came to Jesus at night (p. 285)

Mary *(MAIR ee)* **and Martha** *(MAR thuh)* - sisters from the town of Bethany; Jesus was a close friend of their family (p. 291)

Lazarus *(LAZ ah russ)* - the brother of Mary and Martha who was raised from the dead by Jesus (p. 291)

Mary Magdalene *(MAIR ee MAG deh leen)* - a woman from Magdala of Galilee who was one of Jesus' most devoted followers (p. 299)

Ananias *(an uh NYE us)* **and Sapphira** *(suh FIGH ruh)* - a husband and wife who were struck dead for lying to the Holy Spirit (p. 312)

Stephen *(STEE vun)* - a man of great faith and filled with God's Spirit who was chosen by the twelve apostles to serve God (p. 318)

Simon *(SIGH mun)* - a man of Samaria who practiced witchcraft, but came to believe in Jesus (p. 321)

Philip *(FILL ihp)* - one of seven men chosen by the apostles to serve God by going from place to place telling the good news (p. 321)

Saul *(sawl)* - a man from the city of Tarsus who hated Christians until he came to know Jesus as his Savior; he later became known as Paul, a great preacher of the gospel (p. 323)

Paul *(pawl)* - a faithful follower of Jesus and an apostle to the Gentiles; he took the gospel throughout all the regions north of the Mediterranean Sea; he was originally known as Saul (p. 331)

Barnabas *(BAR nuh bus)* - a devoted follower of the Lord who sold all his goods to give to the work of Christ; he was known as the son of encouragement (p. 333)

Silas *(SIGH lus)* - a loyal companion and friend of Paul who went with him on one of his missionary trips (p. 338)

Timothy *(TIM uh thih)* - a faithful servant of the Lord who was like a son to Paul and served as his assistant (p. 339)

Aquila *(A kwil uh)* **and Priscilla** *(prih SIL uh)* - a Jewish couple who made tents for their living; followers of the Lord and friends of Paul (p. 346)

Philemon *(fie LEE mun)* - a wealthy man who used his large house for church meetings (p. 389)

The Story of Creation

In the beginning when God created*ᵃ* the heavens and the earth, ²the earth was a formless void and darkness covered the face of the deep, while a wind from God*ᵇ* swept over the face of the waters. ³Then God said, "Let there be light"; and there was light. ⁴And God saw that the light was good; and God separated the light from the darkness. ⁵God called the light Day, and the darkness he called Night. And there was evening and there was morning, the first day.

⁶And God said, "Let there be a dome in the midst of the waters, and let it separate the waters from the waters." ⁷So God made the dome and separated the waters that were under the dome from the waters that were above the dome. And it was so. ⁸God called the dome Sky. And there was evening and there was morning, the second day.

⁹And God said, "Let the waters under the sky be gathered together into one place, and let the dry land appear." And it was so. ¹⁰God called the dry land Earth, and the waters that were gathered together he called Seas. And God saw that it was good. ¹¹Then God said, "Let the earth put forth vegetation: plants yielding seed, and fruit trees of every kind on earth that bear fruit with the seed in it." And it was so. ¹²The earth brought forth vegetation: plants yielding seed of every kind, and trees of every kind bearing fruit with the seed in it. And God saw that it was good. ¹³And there was evening and there was morning, the third day.

¹⁴And God said, "Let there be lights in the dome of the sky to separate the day from the night; and let them be for signs and for seasons and for days and years, ¹⁵and let them be lights in the dome of the sky to give light upon the earth." And it was so. ¹⁶God made the two great lights— the greater light to rule the day and the lesser light to rule the night— and the stars.

ᵃOr when God began to create or In the beginning God created
ᵇOr while the spirit of God or while a mighty wind

Prayer Starter: Thank you, Lord, for stars and sky, for trees and plants, and for making the world so beautiful.

Memory Verse: God made the two . . .   —*Genesis 1.16*

1

Animals and Humans

And God said, "Let the earth bring forth living creatures of every kind: cattle and creeping things and wild animals of the earth of every kind." And it was so. 25God made the wild animals of the earth of every kind, and the cattle of every kind, and everything that creeps upon the ground of every kind. And God saw that it was good.

26Then God said, "Let us make humankind*a* in our image, according to our likeness; and let them have dominion over the fish of the sea, and over the birds of the air, and over the cattle, and over all the wild animals of the earth,*b* and over every creeping thing that creeps upon the earth."

27 So God created humankind*a* in his image,
  in the image of God he created them;*c*
  male and female he created them.

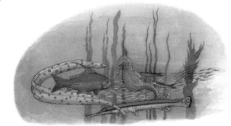

28God blessed them, and God said to them, "Be fruitful and multiply, and fill the earth and subdue it; and have dominion over the fish of the sea and over the birds of the air and over every living thing that moves upon the earth." 29God said, "See, I have given you every plant yielding seed that is upon the face of all the earth, and every tree with seed in its fruit; you shall have them for food. 30And to every beast of the earth, and to every bird of the air, and to everything that creeps on the earth, everything that has the breath of life, I have given every green plant for food." And it was so. 31God saw everything that he had made, and indeed, it was very good. And there was evening and there was morning, the sixth day.

2Thus the heavens and the earth were finished, and all their multitude. 2And on the seventh day God finished the work that he had done, and he rested on the seventh day from all the work that he had done. 3So God blessed the seventh day and hallowed it, because on it God rested from all the work that he had done in creation.

4These are the generations of the heavens and the earth when they were created.

*a*Heb *adam*
*b*Syr: Heb *and over all the earth*
*c*Heb *him*

Prayer Starter: Thank you, Lord, for dogs, cats, fish, and birds. And thank you for men and women and boys and girls—and me.

Memory Verse: God made the two great lights . . .   *—Genesis 1.16*

The First Sin

Now the serpent was more crafty than any other wild animal that the LORD God had made. He said to the woman, "Did God say, 'You shall not eat from any tree in the garden'?" ²The woman said to the serpent, "We may eat of the fruit of the trees in the garden; ³but God said, 'You shall not eat of the fruit of the tree that is in the middle of the garden, nor shall you touch it, or you shall die.'" ⁴But the serpent said to the woman, "You will not die; ⁵for God knows that when you eat of it your eyes will be opened, and you will be like God,ᵃ knowing good and evil." ⁶So when the woman saw that the tree was good for food, and that it was a delight to the eyes, and that the tree was to be desired to make one wise, she took of its fruit and ate; and she also gave some to her husband, who was with her, and he ate. ⁷Then the eyes of both were opened, and they knew that they were naked; and they sewed fig leaves together and made loincloths for themselves.

⁸They heard the sound of the LORD God walking in the garden at the time of the evening breeze, and the man and his wife hid themselves from the presence of the LORD God among the trees of the garden. ⁹But the LORD God called to the man, and said to him, "Where are you?" ¹⁰He said, "I heard the sound of you in the garden, and I was afraid, because I was naked; and I hid myself." ¹¹He said, "Who told you that you were naked? Have you eaten from the tree of which I commanded you not to eat?" ¹²The man said, "The woman whom you gave to be with me, she gave me fruit from the tree, and I ate." ¹³Then the LORD God said to the woman, "What is this that you have done?" The woman said, "The serpent tricked me, and I ate."

²⁰The man named his wife Eve,ᵇ because she was the mother of all living. ²¹And the LORD God made garments of skins for the manᶜ and for his wife, and clothed them.

²²Then the LORD God said, "See, the man has become like one of us, knowing good and evil; and now, he might reach out his hand and take also from

the tree of life, and eat, and live forever"— ²³therefore the Lord God sent him forth from the garden of Eden, to till the ground from which he was taken. ²⁴He drove out the man; and at the east of the garden of Eden he placed the cherubim, and a sword flaming and turning to guard the way to the tree of life.

ᵃOr *gods*
ᵇIn Heb *Eve* resembles the word for *living*
ᶜOr *for Adam*

Prayer Starter: Father, forgive me for times when I disobey you and do things that make you sad. Help me to please you in all I do and say.

Memory Verse: God made the two great lights—the greater light . . .
—*Genesis 1.16*

Cain and Abel

Now the man knew his wife Eve, and she conceived and bore Cain, saying, "I have produced[a] a man with the help of the LORD." ²Next she bore his brother Abel. Now Abel was a keeper of sheep, and Cain a tiller of the ground. ³In the course of time Cain brought to the LORD an offering of the fruit of the ground, ⁴and Abel for his part brought of the firstlings of his flock, their fat portions. And the LORD had regard for Abel and his offering, ⁵but for Cain and his offering he had no regard. So Cain was very angry, and his countenance fell. ⁶The LORD said to Cain, "Why are you angry, and why has your countenance fallen? ⁷If you do well, will you not be accepted? And if you do not do well, sin is lurking at the door; its desire is for you, but you must master it."

⁸Cain said to his brother Abel, "Let us go out to the field."[b] And when they were in the field, Cain rose up against his brother Abel, and killed him. ⁹Then the LORD said to Cain, "Where is your brother Abel?" He said, "I do not know; am I my brother's keeper?" ¹⁰And the LORD said, "What have you done? Listen; your brother's blood is crying out to me from the ground! ¹¹And now you are cursed from the ground, which has opened its mouth to receive your brother's blood from your hand."

[a]The verb in Heb resembles the word for *Cain*
[b]Sam Gk Syr compare Vg: MT lacks *Let us go out to the field*

Prayer Starter: Lord, help us love each other as you love us. Help me be concerned about others and treat them as I want to be treated.

Memory Verse: God made the two great lights—the greater light to rule the day . . .
—*Genesis 1.16*

Noah

The LORD saw that the wickedness of humankind was great in the earth, and that every inclination of the thoughts of their hearts was only evil continually. [6]And the LORD was sorry that he had made humankind on the earth, and it grieved him to his heart. [7]So the LORD said, "I will blot out from the earth the human beings I have created—people together with animals and creeping things and birds of the air, for I am sorry that I have made them." [8]But Noah found favor in the sight of the LORD.

[9]These are the descendants of Noah. Noah was a righteous man, blameless in his generation; Noah walked with God. [10]And Noah had three sons, Shem, Ham, and Japheth.

[11]Now the earth was corrupt in God's sight, and the earth was filled with violence. [12]And God saw that the earth was corrupt; for all flesh had corrupted its ways upon the earth. [13]And God said to Noah, "I have determined to make an end of all flesh, for the earth is filled with violence because of them; now I am going to destroy them along with the earth. [14]Make yourself an ark of cypress[a] wood; make rooms in the ark, and cover it inside and out with pitch. [15]This is how you are to make it: the length of the ark three hundred cubits, its width fifty cubits, and its height thirty cubits. [16]Make a roof[b] for the ark, and finish it to a cubit above; and put the door of the ark in its side; make it with lower, second, and third decks.

¹⁷For my part, I am going to bring a flood of waters on the earth, to destroy from under heaven all flesh in which is the breath of life; everything that is on the earth shall die. ¹⁸But I will establish my covenant with you; and you shall come into the ark, you, your sons, your wife, and your sons' wives with you. ¹⁹And of every living thing, of all flesh, you shall bring two of every kind into the ark, to keep them alive with you; they shall be male and female. ²⁰Of the birds according to their kinds, and of the animals according to their kinds, of every creeping thing of the ground according to its kind, two of every kind shall come in to you, to keep them alive. ²¹Also take with you every kind of food that is eaten, and store it up; and it shall serve as food for you and for them." ²²Noah did this; he did all that God commanded him.

ᵃMeaning of Heb uncertain
ᵇOr *window*

Prayer Starter: Dear Lord, give me good friends who will help me to be a better person. Keep me from the wrong kind of friends.

Memory Verse: God made the two great lights—the greater light to rule the day and the lesser light to rule the night.   —*Genesis 1.16*

The Great Flood

Then the LORD said to Noah, "Go into the ark, you and all your household, for I have seen that you alone are righteous before me in this generation. ²Take with you seven pairs of all clean animals, the male and its mate; and a pair of the animals that are not clean, the male and its mate; ³and seven pairs of the birds of the air also, male and female, to keep their kind alive on the face of all the earth. ⁴For in seven days I will send rain on the earth for forty days and forty nights; and every living thing that I have made I will blot out from the face of the ground." ⁵And Noah did all that the LORD had commanded him.

⁶Noah was six hundred years old when the flood of waters came on the earth. ⁷And Noah with his sons and his wife and his sons' wives went into the ark to escape the waters of the flood. ⁸Of clean animals, and of animals that are not clean, and of birds, and of everything that creeps on the ground, ⁹two and two, male and female, went into the ark with Noah, as God had commanded Noah. ¹⁰And after seven days the waters of the flood came on the earth.

¹¹In the six hundredth year of Noah's life, in the second month, on the seventeenth day of the month, on that day all the fountains of the great deep burst forth, and the windows of the heavens were opened. ¹²The rain fell on the earth forty days and forty nights.

¹⁷The flood continued forty days on the earth; and the waters increased, and bore up the ark, and it rose high above the earth. ¹⁸The waters swelled and increased greatly on the earth; and the ark floated on the face of the waters. ¹⁹The waters swelled so mightily on the earth that all the high mountains under the whole heaven were covered; ²⁰the waters swelled above the mountains, covering them fifteen cubits deep. ²¹And all flesh died that moved on the earth, birds, domestic animals, wild animals, all swarming creatures that swarm on the earth, and all human beings; ²²everything on dry land in whose nostrils was the breath of life died. ²³He blotted out every living thing that was on the face of the ground, human beings and animals and creeping things and birds of the air; they were blotted out from the earth. Only Noah was left, and those that were with him in the ark. ²⁴And the waters swelled on the earth for one hundred fifty days.

Prayer Starter: I know you are a holy God, dear Father. Make me pure and holy like you are. Keep me from sin.

Memory Verse: By faith Noah . . .   —*Hebrews 11.7a*

A New Beginning

But God remembered Noah and all the wild animals and all the domestic animals that were with him in the ark. And God made a wind blow over the earth, and the waters subsided; ²the fountains of the deep and the windows of the heavens were closed, the rain from the heavens was restrained, ³and the waters gradually receded from the earth. At the end of one hundred fifty days the waters had abated; ⁴and in the seventh month, on the seventeenth day of the month, the ark came to rest on the mountains of Ararat. ⁵The waters continued to abate until the tenth month; in the tenth month, on the first day of the month, the tops of the mountains appeared.

⁶At the end of forty days Noah opened the window of the ark that he had made ⁷and sent out the raven; and it went to and fro until the waters were dried up from the earth. ⁸Then he sent out the dove from him, to see if

the waters had subsided from the face of the ground; ⁹but the dove found no place to set its foot, and it returned to him to the ark, for the waters were still on the face of the whole earth. So he put out his hand and took it and brought it into the ark with him. ¹⁰He waited another seven days, and again he sent out the dove from the ark; ¹¹and the dove came back to him in the evening, and there in its beak was a freshly plucked olive leaf; so Noah knew that the waters had subsided from the earth. ¹²Then he waited another seven days, and sent out the dove; and it did not return to him any more.

¹³In the six hundred first year, in the first month, the first day of the month, the waters were dried up from the earth; and Noah removed the covering of the ark, and looked, and saw that the face of the ground was drying. ¹⁴In the second month, on the twenty-seventh day of the month, the earth was dry. ¹⁵Then God said to Noah, ¹⁶"Go out of the ark, you and your wife, and your sons and your sons' wives with you. ¹⁷Bring out with you every living thing that is with you of all flesh—birds and animals and every creeping thing that creeps on the earth—so that they may abound on the earth, and be fruitful and multiply on the earth."

Prayer Starter: Thank you for taking care of all the animals and people you have created. You give us food to eat, water to drink, air to breath. We love you, Father.

Memory Verse: By faith Noah, warned by God . . .　　—*Hebrews 11.7a*

The Rainbow

God blessed Noah and his sons, and said to them, "Be fruitful and multiply, and fill the earth. ²The fear and dread of you shall rest on every animal of the earth, and on every bird of the air, on everything that creeps on the ground, and on all the fish of the sea; into your hand they are delivered."

⁸Then God said to Noah and to his sons with him, ⁹"As for me, I am establishing my covenant with you and your descendants after you, ¹⁰and with every living creature that is with you, the birds, the domestic animals, and every animal of the earth with you, as many as came out of the ark.ᵃ ¹¹I establish my covenant with you, that never again shall all flesh be cut off by the waters of a flood, and never again shall there be a flood to destroy the earth." ¹²God said, "This is the sign of the covenant that I make between me and you and every living creature that is with you, for all future generations: ¹³I have set my bow in the clouds, and it shall be a sign of the covenant between me and the earth. ¹⁴When I bring clouds over the earth and the bow is seen in the clouds, ¹⁵I will remember my covenant that is between me and you and every living creature of all flesh; and the waters shall never again become a flood to destroy all flesh. ¹⁶When the bow is in the clouds, I will see it and remember the everlasting covenant between God and every living creature of all flesh that is on the earth." ¹⁷God said to Noah, "This is the sign of the covenant that I have established between me and all flesh that is on the earth."

¹⁸The sons of Noah who went out of the ark were Shem, Ham, and Japheth. Ham was the father of Canaan. ¹⁹These three were the sons of Noah; and from these the whole earth was peopled.

ᵃGk: Heb adds *every animal of the earth*

Prayer Starter: You made all the colors in the rainbow, dear Lord—green and blue and yellow and red.

Memory Verse: By faith Noah, warned by God about events as yet unseen . . .
—*Hebrews 11.7a*

Abram

When Terah had lived seventy years, he became the father of Abram, Nahor, and Haran.

²⁷Now these are the descendants of Terah. Terah was the father of Abram, Nahor, and Haran; and Haran was the father of Lot. ²⁸Haran died before his father Terah in the land of his birth, in Ur of the Chaldeans. ²⁹Abram and Nahor took wives; the name of Abram's wife was Sarai, and the name of Nahor's wife was Milcah. She was the daughter of Haran the father of Milcah and Iscah. ³⁰Now Sarai was barren; she had no child.

³¹Terah took his son Abram and his grandson Lot son of Haran and his daughter-in-law Sarai, his son Abram's wife, and they went out together from Ur of the Chaldeans to go into the land of Canaan; but when they came to Haran, they settled there. ³²The days of Terah were two hundred five years; and Terah died in Haran.

12Now the LORD said to Abram, "Go from your country and your kindred and your father's house to the land that I will show

you. ²I will make of you a great nation, and I will bless you, and make your name great, so that you will be a blessing. ³I will bless those who bless you, and the one who curses you I will curse; and in you all the families of the earth shall be blessed."*a*

⁴So Abram went, as the LORD had told him; and Lot went with him. Abram was seventy-five years old when he departed from Haran. ⁵Abram took his wife Sarai and his brother's son Lot, and all the possessions that they had gathered, and the persons whom they had acquired in Haran; and they set forth to go to the land of Canaan. When they had come to the land of Canaan, ⁶Abram passed through the land to the place at Shechem, to the oak*b* of Moreh. At that time the Canaanites were in the land. ⁷Then the LORD appeared to Abram, and said, "To your offspring*c* I will give this land." So he built there an altar to the LORD, who had appeared to him. ⁸From there he moved on to the hill country on the east of Bethel, and pitched his tent, with Bethel on the west and Ai on the east; and there he built an altar to the LORD and invoked the name of the LORD. ⁹And Abram journeyed on by stages toward the Negeb.

*a*Or *by you all the families of the earth shall bless themselves*
*b*12:6 Or *terebinth*
*c*12:7 Heb *seed*

Prayer Starter: Dear Lord, I know that you are wise and wonderful, more than anyone else in the universe. Lead me each day in doing what you wish.

Memory Verse: By faith Noah, warned by God about events as yet unseen, respected the warning . . .   —*Hebrews 11.7a*

Lot Chooses

So Abram went up from Egypt, he and his wife, and all that he had, and Lot with him, into the Negeb.

²Now Abram was very rich in livestock, in silver, and in gold. ³He journeyed on by stages from the Negeb as far as Bethel, to the place where his tent had been at the beginning, between Bethel and Ai, ⁴to the place where he had made an altar at the first; and there Abram called on the name of the LORD. ⁵Now Lot, who went with Abram, also had flocks and herds and tents, ⁶so that the land could not support both of them living together; for their possessions were so great that they could not live together, ⁷and there was strife between the herders of Abram's livestock and the herders of Lot's livestock. At that time the Canaanites and the Perizzites lived in the land.

⁸Then Abram said to Lot, "Let there be no strife between you and me, and between your herders and my herders; for we are kindred. ⁹Is not the whole land before you? Separate yourself from me. If you take the left hand, then I will go to the right; or if you take the right hand, then I will go to the left." ¹⁰Lot looked about him, and saw that the plain of the Jordan was well watered everywhere like the garden of the LORD, like the land of Egypt, in the direction of Zoar; this was before the LORD had destroyed Sodom and Gomorrah. ¹¹So Lot chose for himself all the plain of the Jordan, and Lot journeyed eastward; thus they separated from each other. ¹²Abram settled in the land of Canaan, while Lot settled among the cities of the Plain and moved his tent as far as Sodom. ¹³Now the people of Sodom were wicked, great sinners against the LORD.

¹⁴The LORD said to Abram, after Lot had separated from him, "Raise your eyes now, and look from the place where you are, northward and southward and eastward and westward; ¹⁵for all the land that you see I will give to you and to your offspring*ᵃ* forever. ¹⁶I will make your offspring like the dust of the earth; so that if one can count the dust of the earth, your offspring also can be counted. ¹⁷Rise up, walk through the length and the breadth of the land, for I will give it to you." ¹⁸So Abram moved

his tent, and came and settled by the oaks[b] of Mamre, which are at Hebron; and there he built an altar to the LORD.

[a]Heb *seed*
[b]Or *terebinths*

Prayer Starter: Father, I want to be unselfish. Keep me from complaining and bickering and being jealous. May I love others like you do.

Memory Verse: By faith Noah, warned by God about events as yet unseen, respected the warning and built an ark to save his household.
—*Hebrews 11.7a*

Abraham Believed the Lord

After these things the word of the Lord came to Abram in a vision, "Do not be afraid, Abram, I am your shield; your reward shall be very great." ²But Abram said, "O Lord God, what will you give me, for I continue childless, and the heir of my house is Eliezer of Damascus?"ᵃ ³And Abram said, "You have given me no offspring, and so a slave born in my house is to be my heir." ⁴But the word of the Lord came to him, "This man shall not be your heir; no one but your very own issue shall be your heir." ⁵He brought him outside and said, "Look toward heaven and count the stars, if you are able to count them." Then he said to him, "So shall your descendants be." ⁶And he believed the Lord; and the Lord reckoned it to him as righteousness.

17 When Abram was ninety-nine years old, the Lord appeared to Abram, and said to him, "I am God Almighty;ᵇ walk before me, and be blameless. ²And I will make my covenant between me and you, and will make you exceedingly numerous." ³Then Abram fell on his face; and God said to him, ⁴"As for me, this is my covenant with you: You shall be the ancestor of a multitude of nations. ⁵No longer shall your name be Abramᶜ, but your name shall be Abrahamᵈ; for I have made you the ancestor of a multitude of nations. ⁶I will make you exceedingly fruitful; and I will make nations of you, and kings shall come from you. ⁷I will establish my covenant between me and you, and your offspring after you throughout their generations, for an everlasting covenant, to be God to you and to your offspringᵉ after you."

¹⁵God said to Abraham, "As for Sarai your wife, you shall not call her Sarai, but Sarah shall be her name. ¹⁶I will bless her, and moreover I will give you a son by her. I will bless her, and she shall give rise to nations; kings of peoples shall come from her."

ᵃMeaning of Heb uncertain
ᵇTraditional rendering of Heb *El Shaddai*
ᶜThat is *exalted ancestor*
ᵈHere taken to mean *ancestor of a multitude*
ᵉHeb *seed*

Prayer Starter: Father, thank you for Jesus Christ, and for your promise of eternal life. Give me faith in Christ, and may I serve him each day.

Memory Verse: No distrust made him waver . . .   *—Romans 4.20*

Abraham's Guests

The LORD appeared to Abraham[a] by the oaks[b] of Mamre, as he sat at the entrance of his tent in the heat of the day. ²He looked up and saw three men standing near him. When he saw them, he ran from the tent entrance to meet them, and bowed down to the ground. ³He said, "My lord, if I find favor with you, do not pass by your servant. ⁴Let a little water be brought, and wash your feet, and rest yourselves under the tree. ⁵Let me bring a little bread, that you may refresh yourselves, and after that you may pass on—since you have come to your servant." So they said, "Do as you have said." ⁶And Abraham hastened into the tent to Sarah, and said, "Make ready quickly three measures[c] of choice flour, knead it, and make cakes." ⁷Abraham ran to the herd, and took a calf, tender and good, and gave it to the servant, who hastened to prepare it. ⁸Then he took curds and milk and the calf that he had prepared, and set it before them; and he stood by them under the tree while they ate.

⁹They said to him, "Where is your wife Sarah?" And he said, "There, in the tent." ¹⁰Then one said, "I will surely return to you in due season, and your wife Sarah shall have a son." And Sarah was listening at the tent entrance behind him. ¹¹Now Abraham and Sarah were old, advanced in age; it had ceased to be with Sarah after the manner of women. ¹²So Sarah laughed to herself, saying, "After I have grown old, and my husband is old, shall I have pleasure?" ¹³The LORD said to Abraham, "Why did Sarah laugh, and say, 'Shall I indeed bear a child, now that I am old?' ¹⁴Is anything too wonderful for the LORD? At the set time I will return to you, in due season, and Sarah shall have a son."

[a]Heb *him*
[b]Or *terebinths*
[c]Heb *seahs*

Prayer Starter: Heavenly father, you are very great. You know the past, the present, and the future. Thank you for having a plan for my life.

Memory Verse: No distrust made him waver concerning the promise of God . . .
—*Romans 4.20*

Sodom and Gomorrah

The two angels came to Sodom in the evening, and Lot was sitting in the gateway of Sodom. When Lot saw them, he rose to meet them, and bowed down with his face to the ground. ²He said, "Please, my lords, turn aside to your servant's house and spend the night, and wash your feet; then you can rise early and go on your way."

¹²Then the men said to Lot, "Have you anyone else here? Sons-in-law, sons, daughters, or anyone you have in the city—bring them out of the place. ¹³For we are about to destroy this place, because the outcry against its people has become great before the LORD, and the LORD has sent us to destroy it." ¹⁴So Lot went out and said to his sons-in-law, who were to marry his daughters, "Up, get out of this place; for the LORD is about to destroy the city." But he seemed to his sons-in-law to be jesting.

¹⁵When morning dawned, the angels urged Lot, saying, "Get up, take your wife and your two daughters who are here, or else you will be consumed in the punishment of the city." ¹⁶But he lingered; so the men seized him and his wife and his two daughters by the hand, the LORD being merciful to him, and they brought him out and left him outside the city.

²³The sun had risen on the earth when Lot came to Zoar.

²⁴Then the LORD rained on Sodom and Gomorrah sulfur and fire from the LORD out of heaven; ²⁵and he overthrew those cities, and all the Plain, and all the inhabitants of the cities, and what grew on the ground. ²⁶But Lot's wife, behind him, looked back, and she became a pillar of salt.

Prayer Starter: Father, help me to never doubt or question your promises. I know you are faithful. May I trust you more and more.

Memory Verse: No distrust made him waver concerning the promise of God, but he grew strong . . .   —*Romans 4.20*

Hagar's Son

The LORD dealt with Sarah as he had said, and the LORD did for Sarah as he had promised. ²Sarah conceived and bore Abraham a son in his old age, at the time of which God had spoken to him. ³Abraham gave the name Isaac to his son whom Sarah bore him.

⁹But Sarah saw the son of Hagar the Egyptian, whom she had borne to Abraham, playing with her son Isaac*ᵃ*. ¹⁰So she said to Abraham, "Cast out this slave woman with her son; for the son of this slave woman shall not inherit along with my son Isaac." ¹¹The matter was very distressing to Abraham on account of his son. ¹²But God said to Abraham, "Do not be distressed because of the boy and because of your slave woman; whatever Sarah says to you, do as she tells you, for it is through Isaac that offspring shall be named for you. ¹³As for the son of the slave woman, I will make a nation of him also, because he is your offspring." ¹⁴So Abraham rose early in the morning, and took bread and a skin of water, and gave it to Hagar, putting it on her shoulder, along with the child, and sent her away. And she departed, and wandered about in the wilderness of Beer-sheba.

¹⁵When the water in the skin was gone, she cast the child under one of the bushes. ¹⁶Then she went and sat down opposite him a good way off, about the distance of a bowshot; for she said, "Do not let me look on the death of the child." And as she sat opposite him, she lifted up her voice and wept. ¹⁷And God heard the voice of the boy; and the angel of God called to Hagar from heaven, and said to her, "What troubles you, Hagar? Do not be afraid; for God has heard the voice of the boy where he is. ¹⁸Come, lift up the boy and hold him fast with your hand, for I will make a great nation of him." ¹⁹Then God opened her eyes and she saw a well of water. She went, and filled the skin with water, and gave the boy a drink.

²⁰God was with the boy, and he grew up; he lived in the wilderness, and became an expert with the bow. ²¹He lived in the wilderness of Paran; and his mother got a wife for him from the land of Egypt.

ᵃGk Vg: Heb lacks with her son Isaac

Prayer Starter: Lord, many people around the world are hungry and thirsty. Please provide for their needs, and give me what I need each day, too.

Memory Verse: No distrust made him waver concerning the promise of God, but he grew strong in his faith . . .   —*Romans 4.20*

The Test

After these things God tested Abraham. He said to him, "Abraham!" And he said, "Here I am." [2]He said, "Take your son, your only son Isaac, whom you love, and go to the land of Moriah, and offer him there as a burnt offering on one of the mountains that I shall show you." [3]So Abraham rose early in the morning, saddled his donkey, and took two of his young men with him, and his son Isaac; he cut the wood for the burnt offering, and set out and went to the place in the distance that God had shown him.

[6]Abraham took the wood of the burnt offering and laid it on his son Isaac, and he himself carried the fire and the knife. So the two of them walked on together. [7]Isaac said to his father Abraham, "Father!" And he said, "Here I am, my son." He said, "The fire and the wood are here, but where is the lamb for a burnt offering?" [8]Abraham said, "God himself will provide the lamb for a burnt offering, my son." So the two of them walked on together.

[9]When they came to the place that God had shown him, Abraham built an altar there and laid the wood in order. He bound his son Isaac, and laid him on the altar, on top of the wood. [10]Then Abraham reached out his hand and took the knife to kill[a] his son. [11]But the angel of the LORD called to him from heaven, and said, "Abraham, Abraham!" And he said, "Here I am." [12]He said, "Do not lay your hand on the boy or do anything to him; for now I know that you fear God, since you have not withheld your son, your only son, from me." [13]And Abraham looked up and saw a ram, caught in a thicket by its horns. Abraham went and took the ram and offered it up as a burnt offering instead of his son. [14]So Abraham called that place "The LORD will provide";[b] as it is said to this day, "On the mount of the LORD it shall be provided."

[a]Or *to slaughter*
[b]Or *will see*; Heb traditionally transliterated *Jehovah Jireh*

Prayer Starter: Thank you, Lord, for helping me to love you more than anything else in the world. I love you because you first loved me.

Memory Verse: No distrust made him waver concerning the promise of God, but he grew strong in his faith as he gave glory to God.

—*Romans 4.20*

A Wife for Isaac

So the servant put his hand under the thigh of Abraham his master and swore to him concerning this matter. [10]Then the servant took ten of his master's camels and departed, taking all kinds of choice gifts from his master; and he set out and went to Aram-naharaim, to the city of Nahor. [11]He made the camels kneel down outside the city by the well of water; it was toward evening, the time when women go out to draw water. [12]And he said, "O LORD, God of my master Abraham, please grant me success today and show steadfast love to my master Abraham. [13]I am standing here by the spring of water, and the daughters of the townspeople are coming out to draw water. [14]Let the girl to whom I shall say, 'Please offer your jar that I may drink,' and who shall say, 'Drink, and I will water your camels'—let her be the one whom you have appointed for your servant Isaac. By this I shall know that you have shown steadfast love to my master."

[15]Before he had finished speaking, there was Rebekah, who was born to Bethuel son of Milcah, the wife of Nahor, Abraham's brother, coming out with her water jar on her shoulder. [16]The girl was very fair to look upon, a virgin, whom no man had known. She went down to the spring, filled her jar, and came up. [17]Then the servant ran to meet her and said, "Please let me sip a little water from your jar." [18]"Drink, my lord," she said, and quickly lowered her jar upon her hand and gave him a drink. [19]When she had finished giving him a drink, she said, "I will draw for your camels also, until they have finished drinking." [20]So she quickly emptied her jar into the trough and ran again to the well to draw, and she drew for all his camels.

Prayer Starter: You lead those who trust you, Lord. Please be my guide and show me what to do and how to live all my life.

Memory Verse: We know that all things . . .   —*Romans 8.28*

Jacob and Esau

These are the descendants of Isaac, Abraham's son: Abraham was the father of Isaac, [20]and Isaac was forty years old when he married Rebekah, daughter of Bethuel the Aramean of Paddan-aram, sister of Laban the Aramean. [21]Isaac prayed to the LORD for his wife, because she was barren; and the LORD granted his prayer, and his wife Rebekah conceived. [22]The children struggled together within her; and she said, "If it is to be this way, why do I live?"[a] So she went to inquire of the LORD.

[24]When her time to give birth was at hand, there were twins in her womb. [25]The first came out red, all his body like a hairy mantle; so they named him Esau. [26]Afterward his brother came out, with his hand gripping Esau's heel; so he was named Jacob.[b] Isaac was sixty years old when she bore them.

[27]When the boys grew up, Esau was a skillful hunter, a man of the field, while Jacob was a quiet man, living in tents. [28]Isaac loved Esau, because he was fond of game; but Rebekah loved Jacob.

[29]Once when Jacob was cooking a stew, Esau came in from the field, and he was famished. [30]Esau said to Jacob, "Let me eat some of that red stuff, for I am famished!" (Therefore he was called Edom.[c]) [31]Jacob said, "First sell me your birthright." [32]Esau said, "I am about to die; of what

use is a birthright to me?" ³³Jacob said, "Swear to me first."ᵈ So he swore
to him, and sold his birthright to Jacob. ³⁴Then Jacob gave Esau bread
and lentil stew, and he ate and drank, and rose and went his way. Thus
Esau despised his birthright.

ᵃSyr: Meaning of Heb uncertain
ᵇThat is *He takes by the heel* or *He supplants*
ᶜThat is *Red*
ᵈHeb *today*

Prayer Starter: If I have friends who tempt me to do what is wrong, Lord, help
me to say "No." May I always do what pleases you.

Memory Verse: We know that all things work together . . .
—*Romans 8.28*

Jacob and Rachel

Then Jacob went on his journey, and came to the land of the people of the east. ²As he looked, he saw a well in the field and three flocks of sheep lying there beside it; for out of that well the flocks were watered. The stone on the well's mouth was large, ³and when all the flocks were gathered there, the shepherds would roll the stone from the mouth of the well, and water the sheep, and put the stone back in its place on the mouth of the well.

⁴Jacob said to them, "My brothers, where do you come from?" They said, "We are from Haran." ⁵He said to them, "Do you know Laban son of Nahor?" They said, "We do." ⁶He said to them, "Is it well with him?" "Yes," they replied, "and here is his daughter Rachel, coming with the sheep." ⁷He said, "Look, it is still broad daylight; it is not time for the animals to be gathered together. Water the sheep, and go, pasture them." ⁸But they said, "We cannot until all the flocks are gathered together, and the stone is rolled from the mouth of the well; then we water the sheep."

⁹While he was still speaking with them, Rachel came with her

father's sheep; for she kept them. ¹⁰Now when Jacob saw Rachel, the daughter of his mother's brother Laban, and the sheep of his mother's brother Laban, Jacob went up and rolled the stone from the well's mouth, and watered the flock of his mother's brother Laban. ¹¹Then Jacob kissed Rachel, and wept aloud. ¹²And Jacob told Rachel that he was her father's kinsman, and that he was Rebekah's son; and she ran and told her father.

¹³When Laban heard the news about his sister's son Jacob, he ran to meet him; he embraced him and kissed him, and brought him to his house. Jacob*ᵃ* told Laban all these things, ¹⁴and Laban said to him, "Surely you are my bone and my flesh!" And he stayed with him a month.

¹⁵Then Laban said to Jacob, "Because you are my kinsman, should you therefore serve me for nothing? Tell me, what shall your wages be?" ¹⁶Now Laban had two daughters; the name of the elder was Leah, and the name of the younger was Rachel. ¹⁷Leah's eyes were lovely,*ᵇ* and Rachel was graceful and beautiful. ¹⁸Jacob loved Rachel; so he said, "I will serve you seven years for your younger daughter Rachel." ¹⁹Laban said, "It is better that I give her to you than that I should give her to any other man; stay with me." ²⁰So Jacob served seven years for Rachel, and they seemed to him but a few days because of the love he had for her.

²²So Laban gathered together all the people of the place, and made a feast. ²³But in the evening he took his daughter Leah and brought her to Jacob; and he went in to her. ²⁴(Laban gave his maid Zilpah to his daughter Leah to be her maid.)

*ᵃ*Heb *He*
*ᵇ*Meaning of Heb uncertain

Prayer Starter: Thank you for my family. Help us to always take care of each other.

Memory Verse: We know that all things work together for good . . .
—Romans 8.28

> ## Jacob Is Named Israel

Jacob went on his way and the angels of God met him; [2]and when Jacob saw them he said, "This is God's camp!" So he called that place Mahanaim.[a]

[3]Jacob sent messengers before him to his brother Esau in the land of Seir, the country of Edom, [4]instructing them, "Thus you shall say to my lord Esau: Thus says your servant Jacob, 'I have lived with Laban as an alien, and stayed until now; [5]and I have oxen, donkeys, flocks, male and female slaves; and I have sent to tell my lord, in order that I may find favor in your sight.'"

[6]The messengers returned to Jacob, saying, "We came to your brother Esau, and he is coming to meet you, and four hundred men are with him." [7]Then Jacob was greatly afraid and distressed; and he divided the people that were with him, and the flocks and herds and camels, into two companies, [8]thinking, "If Esau comes to the one company and destroys it, then the company that is left will escape."

[16]These he delivered into the hand of his servants, every drove by itself, and said to his servants, "Pass on ahead of me, and put a space between drove and drove." [17]He instructed the foremost, "When Esau my brother meets you, and asks you, 'To whom do you belong? Where are you going? And whose are these ahead of you?' [18]then you shall say, 'They belong to your servant Jacob; they are a present sent to my lord Esau; and moreover he is behind us.'" [19]He likewise instructed the second and the third and all who followed the droves, "You shall say the same thing to Esau when you meet him, [20]and you shall say, 'Moreover your servant Jacob is behind us.'" For he thought, "I may appease him with the present that goes ahead of me, and afterwards I shall see his face; perhaps he will accept me." [21]So the present passed on ahead of him; and he himself spent that night in the camp.

[22]The same night he got up and took his two wives, his two maids, and his eleven children, and crossed the ford of the Jabbok. [23]He took them and sent them across the stream, and likewise everything that he had. [24]Jacob was left alone; and a man wrestled with him until daybreak. [25]When the man saw that he did not prevail against Jacob, he struck him on the hip socket; and Jacob's hip was put out of joint as he wrestled with him. [26]Then he said, "Let me go, for the day is breaking." But Jacob said, "I will not let you go, unless you bless me." [27]So he said to him, "What is your name?" And he said, "Jacob." [28]Then the man[b] said, "You shall no longer be called Jacob, but Israel,[c] for you have striven with God and with humans,[d] and have prevailed." [29]Then Jacob asked him, "Please tell me your name." But he said, "Why is it that you ask my name?" And there he blessed him. [30]So Jacob called the place Peniel,[e] saying, "For I have seen God face to face, and yet my life is preserved." [31]The sun rose upon him as he passed Penuel, limping because of his hip. [32]Therefore to this day the Israelites do not eat the thigh mus-

cle that is on the hip socket, because he struck Jacob on the hip socket at the thigh muscle.

*a*Here taken to mean *Two camps*
*b*Heb *he*
*c*That is The *one who strives with God* or *God strives*
*d*Or *with divine and human beings*
*e*That is *The face of God*

Prayer Starter: May I be strong and cheerful, for I know you give me victory.

Memory Verse: We know that all things work together for good for those who love God . . .   —*Romans 8.28*

Twenty Pieces of Silver

Now his brothers went to pasture their father's flock near Shechem. [13]And Israel said to Joseph, "Are not your brothers pasturing the flock at Shechem? Come, I will send you to them." He answered, "Here I am."

[17]So Joseph went after his brothers, and found them at Dothan. [18]They saw him from a distance, and before he came near to them, they conspired to kill him. [19]They said to one another, "Here comes this dreamer. [20]Come now, let us kill him and throw him into one of the pits; then we shall say that a wild animal has devoured him, and we shall see what will become of his dreams."

[23]So when Joseph came to his brothers, they stripped him of his robe, the long robe with sleeves[a] that he wore; [24]and they took him and threw him into a pit. The pit was empty; there was no water in it.

[25]Then they sat down to eat; and looking up they saw a caravan of Ishmaelites coming from Gilead, with their camels carrying gum, balm, and resin, on their way to carry it down to Egypt. [26]Then Judah said to his brothers, "What profit is it if we kill our brother and conceal his blood? [27]Come, let us sell him to the Ishmaelites, and not lay our hands on him, for he is our brother, our own flesh." And his brothers agreed.

[28]When some Midianite traders passed by, they drew Joseph up, lifting him out of the pit, and sold him to the Ishmaelites for twenty pieces of silver. And they took Joseph to Egypt.

39Now Joseph was taken down to Egypt, and Potiphar, an officer of Pharaoh, the captain of the guard, an Egyptian, bought him from the Ishmaelites who had brought him down there.

[a]Traditional rendering (compare Gk): *a coat of many colors*; Meaning of Heb uncertain

Prayer Starter: Protect me from bad people, Lord. Keep me safe from those who could harm me. And keep me from ever harming another person.

Memory Verse: We know that all things work together for good for those who love God, who are called according to his purpose.—*Romans 8.28*

The King's Dream

After two whole years, Pharaoh dreamed that he was standing by the Nile, ²and there came up out of the Nile seven sleek and fat cows, and they grazed in the reed grass. ³Then seven other cows, ugly and thin, came up out of the Nile after them, and stood by the other cows on the bank of the Nile. ⁴The ugly and thin cows ate up the seven sleek and fat cows. And Pharaoh awoke.

⁸In the morning his spirit was troubled; so he sent and called for all the magicians of Egypt and all its wise men. Pharaoh told them his dreams, but there was no one who could interpret them to Pharaoh.

¹⁴Then Pharaoh sent for Joseph, and he was hurriedly brought out of the dungeon. When he had shaved himself and changed his clothes, he came in before Pharaoh. ¹⁵And Pharaoh said to Joseph, "I have had a dream, and there is no one who can interpret it. I have heard it said of you that when you hear a dream you can interpret it." ¹⁶Joseph answered Pharaoh, "It is not I; God will give Pharaoh a favorable answer.

²⁹"There will come seven years of great plenty throughout all the land of Egypt. ³⁰After them there will arise seven years of famine, and all the plenty will be forgotten in the land of Egypt; the famine will consume the land. ³¹The plenty will no longer be known in the land because of the famine that will follow, for it will be very grievous.

³³"Now therefore let Pharaoh select a man who is discerning and wise, and set him over the land of Egypt. ³⁴Let Pharaoh proceed to appoint overseers over the land, and take one-fifth of the produce of the land of Egypt during the seven plenteous years. ³⁵Let them gather all the food of these good years that are coming, and lay up grain under the authority of Pharaoh for food in the cities, and let them keep it. ³⁶That food shall be a reserve for the land against the seven years of famine that are to befall the land of Egypt, so that the land may not perish through the famine."

³⁷The proposal pleased Pharaoh and all his servants. ³⁸Pharaoh said to his servants, "Can we find anyone else like this—one in whom is the spirit of God?"

Prayer Starter: Thank you for always being at work for Joseph's good—and for mine. May I love you and be chosen for your purpose.

Memory Verse: Do not repay anyone evil . . .   *—Romans 12.17*

Joseph Becomes Governor

So Pharaoh said to Joseph, "Since God has shown you all this, there is no one so discerning and wise as you. [40]You shall be over my house, and all my people shall order themselves as you command; only with regard to the throne will I be greater than you." [41]And Pharaoh said to Joseph, "See, I have set you over all the land of Egypt." [42]Removing his signet ring from his hand, Pharaoh put it on Joseph's hand; he arrayed him in garments of fine linen, and put a gold chain around his neck. [43]He had him ride in the chariot of his second-in-command; and they cried out in front of him, "Bow the knee!"[a] Thus he set him over all the land of Egypt. [44]Moreover Pharaoh said to Joseph, "I am Pharaoh, and without your consent no one shall lift up hand or foot in all the land of Egypt." [45]Pharaoh gave Joseph the name Zaphenath-paneah; and he gave him Asenath daughter of Potiphera, priest of On, as his wife. Thus Joseph gained authority over the land of Egypt.

[46]Joseph was thirty years old when he entered the service of Pharaoh king of Egypt. And Joseph went out from the presence of Pharaoh, and went through all the land of Egypt. [47]During the seven plenteous years the earth produced abundantly. [48]He gathered up all the food of the seven years when there was plenty[b] in the land of Egypt, and stored up food in the cities; he stored up in every city the food from the fields around it. [49]So Joseph stored up grain in such abundance—like the sand of the sea—that he stopped measuring it; it was beyond measure.

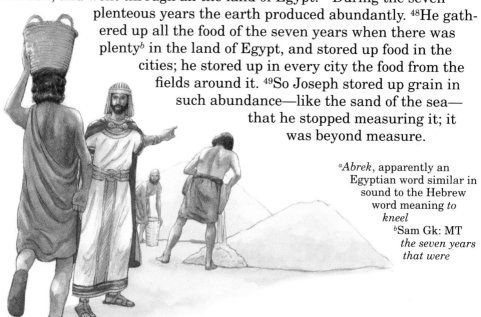

[a]*Abrek*, apparently an Egyptian word similar in sound to the Hebrew word meaning *to kneel*
[b]Sam Gk: MT *the seven years that were*

Prayer Starter: Make me wise, O Lord, that I might help other people like Joseph did.

Memory Verse: Do not repay anyone evil for evil . . . —*Romans 12.17*

Genesis 42.1–2, 6–8; 45.3–5

Joseph and His Brothers

When Jacob learned that there was grain in Egypt, he said to his sons, "Why do you keep looking at one another? 2I have heard," he said, "that there is grain in Egypt; go down and buy grain for us there, that we may live and not die."

6Now Joseph was governor over the land; it was he who sold to all the people of the land. And Joseph's brothers came and bowed themselves before him with their faces to the ground. 7When Joseph saw his brothers, he recognized them, but he treated them like strangers and spoke harshly to them. "Where do you come from?" he said. They said, "From the land of Canaan, to buy food." 8Although Joseph had recognized his brothers, they did not recognize him.

45 Joseph said to his brothers, "I am Joseph. Is my father still alive?" But his brothers could not answer him, so dismayed were they at his presence.

4Then Joseph said to his brothers, "Come closer to me." And they came closer. He said, "I am your brother, Joseph, whom you sold into Egypt. 5And now do not be distressed, or angry with yourselves, because you sold me here; for God sent me before you to preserve life."

Prayer Starter: Don't let me mistreat those who mistreat me. Help me do my best to live at peace with others.

Memory Verse: Do not repay anyone evil for evil, but take thought . . . —*Romans 12.17*

Joseph Sees Jacob Again

Pharaoh said to Joseph, "Say to your brothers, 'Do this: load your animals and go back to the land of Canaan. ¹⁸Take your father and your households and come to me, so that I may give you the best of the land of Egypt, and you may enjoy the fat of the land.'"

²¹The sons of Israel did so. Joseph gave them wagons according to the instruction of Pharaoh, and he gave them provisions for the journey. ²²To each one of them he gave a set of garments; but to Benjamin he gave three hundred pieces of silver and five sets of garments. ²³To his father he sent the following: ten donkeys loaded with the good things of Egypt, and ten female donkeys loaded with grain, bread, and provision for his father on the journey. ²⁴Then he sent his brothers on their way, and as they were leaving he said to them, "Do not quarrel*ᵃ* along the way."

²⁵So they went up out of Egypt and came to their father Jacob in the land of Canaan. ²⁶And they told him, "Joseph is still alive! He is even ruler over all the land of Egypt." He was stunned; he could not believe them. ²⁷But when they told him all the words of Joseph that he had said to them, and when he saw the wagons that Joseph had sent to carry him, the spirit of their father Jacob revived. ²⁸Israel said, "Enough! My son Joseph is still alive. I must go and see him before I die."

46When Israel set out on his journey with all that he had and came to Beer-sheba, he offered sacrifices to the God of his father Isaac. ²God spoke to Israel in visions of the night, and said, "Jacob, Jacob." And he said, "Here I am." ³Then he said, "I am God,*ᵇ* the God of your father; do not be afraid to go down to Egypt, for I will make of you a great nation there. ⁴I myself will go down with you to Egypt, and I will also bring you up again; and Joseph's own hand shall close your eyes."

⁵Then Jacob set out from Beer-sheba; and the sons of Israel carried their father Jacob, their little ones, and their wives, in the wagons that Pharaoh had sent to carry him. ⁶They also took their livestock and the goods that they had acquired in the land of Canaan, and they came into Egypt, Jacob and all his offspring with him, ⁷his sons, and his sons' sons with him, his daughters, and his sons' daughters; all his offspring he brought with him into Egypt.

ᵃOr be agitated
ᵇHeb the God

Prayer Starter: Bless my family, Lord, those I love. May we praise you together.

Memory Verse: Do not repay anyone evil for evil, but take thought for what is noble . . . —*Romans 12.17*

Baby on the Nile

Now a new king arose over Egypt, who did not know Joseph. ⁹He said to his people, "Look, the Israelite people are more numerous and more powerful than we. ¹⁰Come, let us deal shrewdly with them, or they will increase and, in the event of war, join our enemies and fight against us and escape from the land." ¹¹Therefore they set taskmasters over them to oppress them with forced labor. They built supply cities, Pithom and Rameses, for Pharaoh.

¹⁵The king of Egypt said to the Hebrew midwives, one of whom was named Shiphrah and the other Puah, ¹⁶"When you act as midwives to the Hebrew women, and see them on the birthstool, if it is a boy, kill him; but if it is a girl, she shall live." ¹⁷But the midwives feared God; they did not do as the king of Egypt commanded them, but they let the boys live.

2 Now a man from the house of Levi went and married a Levite woman. ²The woman conceived and bore a son; and when she saw that he was a fine baby, she hid him three months. ³When she could hide him no longer she got a papyrus basket for him, and plastered it with bitumen and pitch; she put the child in it and placed it among the reeds on the bank of the river. ⁴His sister stood at a distance, to see what would happen to him.

⁵The daughter of Pharaoh came down to bathe at the river, while her attendants walked beside the river. She saw the basket among the reeds and sent her maid to bring it. ⁶When she opened it, she saw the child. He was crying, and she took pity on him, "This must be one of the Hebrews' children," she said. ⁷Then his sister said to Pharaoh's daughter, "Shall I go and get you a nurse from the Hebrew women to nurse the child for you?" ⁸Pharaoh's daughter said to her, "Yes." So the girl went and called the child' s mother. ⁹Pharaoh's daughter said to her, "Take this child and nurse it for me, and I will give you your wages." So the woman took the child and nursed it. ¹⁰When the child grew up, she brought him to Pharaoh's daughter, and she took him as her son. She named him Moses,ᵃ "because," she said, "I drew him outᵇ of the water."

ᵃHeb *Mosheh*
ᵇHeb *mashah*

Prayer Starter: Lord, watch over me each night as I'm asleep and keep me from all harm. May your angels keep me safe.

Memory Verse: Do not repay anyone evil for evil, but take thought for what is noble in the sight of all.　　　　　—*Romans 12.17*

The Burning Bush

Moses was keeping the flock of his father-in-law Jethro, the priest of Midian; he led his flock beyond the wilderness, and came to Horeb, the mountain of God. ²There the angel of the Lord appeared to him in a flame of fire out of a bush; he looked, and the bush was blazing, yet it was not consumed. ³Then Moses said, "I must turn aside and look at this great sight, and see why the bush is not burned up." ⁴When the Lord saw that he had turned aside to see, God called to him out of the bush, "Moses, Moses!" And he said, "Here I am." ⁵Then he said, "Come no closer! Remove the sandals from your feet, for the place on which you are standing is holy ground." ⁶He said further, "I am the God of your father, the God of Abraham, the God of Isaac, and the God of Jacob." And Moses hid his face, for he was afraid to look at God.

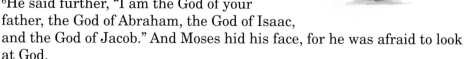

⁷Then the Lord said, "I have observed the misery of my people who are in Egypt; I have heard their cry on account of their taskmasters. Indeed, I know their sufferings, ⁸and I have come down to deliver them from the Egyptians, and to bring them up out of that land to a good and broad land, a land flowing with milk and honey, to the country of the Canaanites, the Hittites, the Amorites, the Perizzites, the Hivites, and the Jebusites. ⁹The cry of the Israelites has now come to me; I have also seen how the Egyptians oppress them. ¹⁰So come, I will send you to Pharaoh to bring my people, the Israelites, out of Egypt."

Prayer Starter: Dear Lord, you are the God worshiped by Abraham, Joseph, and Moses. Help us to honor and worship and praise you, too.

Memory Verse: Who is like you, O Lord . . .

—*Exodus 15.11*

What's That in Your Hand?

Then Moses answered, "But suppose they do not believe me or listen to me, but say, 'The LORD did not appear to you.'" [2]The LORD said to him, "What is that in your hand?" He said, "A staff." [3]And he said, "Throw it on the ground." So he threw the staff on the ground, and it became a snake; and Moses drew back

from it. [4]Then the LORD said to Moses, "Reach out your hand, and seize it by the tail" —so he reached out his hand and grasped it, and it became a staff in his hand— [5]"so that they may believe that the LORD, the God of their ancestors, the God of Abraham, the God of Isaac, and the God of Jacob, has appeared to you."

[6]Again, the LORD said to him, "Put your hand inside your cloak." He put his hand into his cloak; and when he took it out, his hand was leprous,[a] as white as snow. [7]Then God said, "Put your hand back into your cloak" —so he put his hand back into his cloak, and when he took it out, it was restored like the rest of his body— [8]"If they will not believe you or heed the first sign, they may believe the second sign. [9]If they will not believe even these two signs or heed you, you shall take some water from the Nile and pour it on the dry ground; and the water that you shall take from the Nile will become blood on the dry ground."

[10]But Moses said to the LORD, "O my Lord, I have never been eloquent, neither in the past nor even now that you have spoken to your servant; but I am slow of speech and slow of tongue." [11]Then the LORD said to him, "Who gives speech to mortals? Who makes them mute or deaf, seeing or blind? Is it not I, the LORD? [12]Now go, and I will be with your mouth and teach you what you are to speak." [13]But he said, "O my Lord, please send someone else." [14]Then the anger of the LORD was kindled against Moses and he said, "What of your brother Aaron, the Levite? I know that he can speak fluently; even now he is coming out to meet you, and when he sees you his heart will be glad. [15]You shall speak to him and put the words in his mouth; and I will be with your mouth and with his mouth, and will teach you what you shall do. [16]He indeed shall speak for you to the people; he shall serve as a mouth for you, and you shall serve

Prayer Starter: Lord, help me to speak up for you whenever I need to. Give me great courage and wise words. May I be your witness.

Memory Verse: Who is like you, O LORD, among the gods? . . .
—*Exodus 15.11*

as God for him. [17]Take in your hand this staff, with which you shall perform the signs."

[a]A term for several skin diseases; precise meaning uncertain

River of Blood

Then the LORD said to Moses, "Pharaoh's heart is hardened; he refuses to let the people go. ¹⁵Go to Pharaoh in the morning, as he is going out to the water; stand by at the river bank to meet him, and take in your hand the staff that was turned into a snake. ¹⁶Say to him, 'The LORD, the God of the Hebrews, sent me to you to say, "Let my people go, so that they may worship me in the wilderness." But until now you have not listened. ¹⁷Thus says the LORD, "By this you shall know that I am the LORD." See, with the staff that is in my hand I will strike the water that is in the Nile, and it shall be turned to blood. ¹⁸The fish in the river shall die, the river itself shall stink, and the Egyptians shall be unable to drink water from the Nile.' " ¹⁹The LORD said to Moses, "Say to Aaron, 'Take your staff and stretch out your hand over the waters of Egypt— over its rivers, its canals, and its ponds, and all its pools of water—so that they may become blood; and there shall be blood throughout the whole land of Egypt, even in vessels of wood and in vessels of stone.' "

²⁰Moses and Aaron did just as the LORD commanded. In the sight of Pharaoh and of his officials he lifted up the staff and struck the water in the river, and all the water in the river was turned into blood, ²¹and the fish in the river died. The river stank so that the Egyptians could not drink its water, and there was blood throughout the whole land of Egypt.

Prayer Starter: Thank you for being more powerful than anything or anyone else in all the universe, Lord. And thank you for your powerful love to me.

Memory Verse: Who is like you, O LORD, among the gods? Who is like you . . .
—*Exodus 15.11*

Leave Us Alone!

Then Moses called all the elders of Israel and said to them, "Go, select lambs for your families, and slaughter the passover lamb. ²²Take a bunch of hyssop, dip it in the blood that is in the basin, and touch the lintel and the two doorposts with the blood in the basin. None of you shall go outside the door of your house until morning. ²³For the LORD will pass through to strike down the Egyptians; when he sees the blood on the lintel and on the two doorposts, the LORD will pass over that door and will not allow the destroyer to enter your houses to strike you down. ²⁴You shall observe this rite as a perpetual ordinance for you and your children. ²⁵When you come to the land that the LORD will give you, as he has promised, you shall keep this observance. ²⁶And when your children ask you, 'What do you mean by this observance?' ²⁷you shall say, 'It is the passover sacrifice to the LORD, for he passed over the houses of the Israelites in Egypt, when he struck down the Egyptians but spared our houses.'" And the people bowed down and worshiped.

²⁸The Israelites went and did just as the LORD had commanded Moses and Aaron.

²⁹At midnight the LORD struck down all the firstborn in the land of Egypt, from the firstborn of Pharaoh who sat on his throne to the firstborn of the prisoner who was in the dungeon, and all the firstborn of the livestock. ³⁰Pharaoh arose in the night, he and all his officials and all the Egyptians; and there was a loud cry in Egypt, for there was not a house without someone dead. ³¹Then he summoned Moses and Aaron in the night, and said, "Rise up, go away from my people, both you and the Israelites! Go, worship the LORD, as you said. ³²Take your flocks and your herds, as you said, and be gone. And bring a blessing on me too!"

Prayer Starter: O Lord, no other gods compare with you. You are majestic and holy. I love you.

Memory Verse: Who is like you, O LORD, among the gods? Who is like you, majestic in holiness . . .   —*Exodus 15.11*

**Walls
of Water**

When the king of Egypt was told that the people had fled, the minds of Pharaoh and his officials were changed toward the people, and they said, "What have we done, letting Israel leave our service?" ⁶So he had his chariot made ready, and took his army with him; ⁷he took six hundred picked chariots and all the other chariots of Egypt with officers over all of them. ⁸The LORD hardened the heart of Pharaoh king of Egypt and he pursued the Israelites, who were going out boldly. ⁹The Egyptians pursued them, all Pharaoh's horses and chariots, his chariot drivers and his army; they overtook them camped by the sea, by Pi-hahiroth, in front of Baalzephon.

¹⁰As Pharaoh drew near, the Israelites looked back, and there were the Egyptians advancing on them. In great fear the Israelites cried out to the LORD. ¹³But Moses said to the people, "Do not be afraid, stand firm, and see the deliverance that the LORD will accomplish for you today; for the Egyptians whom you see today you shall never see again. ¹⁴The LORD will fight for you, and you have only to keep still."

¹⁵Then the LORD said to Moses, "Why do you cry out to me? Tell the Israelites to go forward. ¹⁶But you lift up your staff, and stretch out your hand over the sea and divide it, that the Israelites may go into the sea on dry ground. ¹⁷Then I will harden the hearts of the Egyptians so that they will go in after them; and so I will gain glory for myself over Pharaoh and all his army, his chariots, and his chariot drivers. ¹⁸And the Egyptians shall know that I am the LORD, when I have gained glory for myself over Pharaoh, his chariots, and his chariot drivers."

²¹Then Moses stretched out his hand over the sea. The LORD drove the sea back by a strong east wind all night, and turned the sea into dry land; and the waters were divided. ²²The Israelites went into the sea on dry ground, the waters forming a wall for them on their right and on their left.

Prayer Starter: Thank you, Lord, for the story of Moses and the children of Israel. Help me to trust you just as Moses did.

Memory Verse: Who is like you, O LORD, among the gods? Who is like you, majestic in holiness, awesome in splendor, doing wonders?
—*Exodus 15.11*

What Is It?

The whole congregation of the Israelites set out from Elim; and Israel came to the wilderness of Sin, which is between Elim and Sinai, on the fifteenth day of the second month after they had departed from the land of Egypt. ²The whole congregation of the Israelites complained against Moses and Aaron in the wilderness. ³The Israelites said to them, "If only we had died by the hand of the LORD in the land of Egypt, when we sat by the fleshpots and ate our fill of bread; for you have brought us out into this wilderness to kill this whole assembly with hunger."

⁴Then the LORD said to Moses, "I am going to rain bread from heaven for you, and each day the people shall go out and gather enough for that day. In that way I will test them, whether they will follow my instruction or not. ⁵On the sixth day, when they prepare what they bring in, it will be twice as much as they gather on other days." ⁶So Moses and Aaron said to all the Israelites, "In the evening you shall know that it was the LORD who brought you out of the land of Egypt, ⁷and in the morning you shall see the glory of the LORD, because he has heard your complaining against the LORD. For what are we, that you complain against us?"

¹³In the evening quails came up and covered the camp; and in the morning there was a layer of dew around the camp. ¹⁴When the layer of dew lifted, there on the surface of the wilderness was a fine flaky substance, as fine as frost on the ground. ¹⁵When the Israelites saw it, they said to one another, "What is it?"ᵃ For they did not know what it was. Moses said to them, "It is the bread that the LORD has given you to eat.

¹⁶This is what the LORD has commanded: 'Gather as much of it as each of you needs, an omer to a person according to the number of persons, all providing for those in their own tents.'" ¹⁷The Israelites did so, some gathering more, some less.

ᵃOr *"It is manna"* (Heb *man hu*)

Prayer Starter: Give us each day the food we need, Lord. Give me clothes and shelter and friends and family. Please provide for all my needs.

Memory Verse: Honor your father and your mother . . .

—*Exodus 20.12*

Water from a Rock

From the wilderness of Sin the whole congregation of the Israelites journeyed by stages, as the LORD commanded. They camped at Rephidim, but there was no water for the people to drink. ²The people quarreled with Moses, and said, "Give us water to drink." Moses said to them, "Why do you quarrel with me? Why do you test the LORD?" ³But the people thirsted there for water; and the people complained against Moses and said, "Why did you bring us out of Egypt, to kill us and our children and livestock with thirst?" ⁴So Moses cried out to the LORD, "What shall I do with this people? They are almost ready to stone me." ⁵The LORD said to Moses, "Go on ahead of the people, and take some of the elders of Israel with you; take in your hand the staff with which you struck the Nile, and go. ⁶I will be standing there in front of you on the rock at Horeb. Strike the rock, and water will come out of it, so that the people may drink."

Moses did so, in the sight of the elders of Israel.

Prayer Starter: Thank you, Lord, for making water. Thanks for giving us water for drinking, bathing, and swimming.

Memory Verse: Honor your father and your mother, so that your days . . .
—*Exodus 20.12*

God's Commands

On the morning of the third day there was thunder and lightning, as well as a thick cloud on the mountain, and a blast of a trumpet so loud that all the people who were in the camp trembled. ¹⁷Moses brought the people out of the camp to meet God. They took their stand at the foot of the mountain. ¹⁸Now Mount Sinai was wrapped in smoke, because the Lord had descended upon it in fire; the smoke went up like the smoke of a kiln, while the whole mountain shook violently. ¹⁹As the blast of the trumpet grew louder and louder, Moses would speak and God would answer him in thunder.

20 Then God spoke all these words: ²I am the Lord your God, who brought you out of the land of Egypt, out of the house of slavery; ³you shall have no other gods before*ᵃ* me.

⁴You shall not make for yourself an idol, whether in the form of anything that is in heaven above, or that is on the earth beneath, or that is in the water under the earth.

⁷You shall not make wrongful use of the name of the Lord your God, for the Lord will not acquit anyone who misuses his name.

⁸Remember the sabbath day, and keep it holy.

¹²Honor your father and your mother, so that your days may be long in the land that the Lord your God is giving you.

¹³You shall not murder.*ᵇ*

¹⁴You shall not commit adultery.

¹⁵You shall not steal.

¹⁶You shall not bear false witness against your neighbor.

¹⁷You shall not covet your neighbor's house; you shall not covet your neighbor's wife, or male or female slave, or ox, or donkey, or anything that belongs to your neighbor.

ᵃOr besides
ᵇOr kill

Prayer Starter: O Lord, you are the Lord my God. May I never worship anyone except you.

Memory Verse: Honor your father and your mother, so that your days may be long . . .
—*Exodus 20.12*

The Broken Law

When the people saw that Moses delayed to come down from the mountain, the people gathered around Aaron, and said to him, "Come, make gods for us, who shall go before us; as for this Moses, the man who brought us up out of the land of Egypt, we do not know what has become of him." ²Aaron said to them, "Take off the gold rings that are on the ears of your wives, your sons, and your daughters, and bring them to me." ³So all the people took off the gold rings from their ears, and brought them to Aaron. ⁴He took the gold from them, formed it in a mold,*ª* and cast an image of a calf; and they said, "These are your gods, O Israel, who brought you up out of the land of Egypt!" ⁵When Aaron saw this, he built an altar before it; and Aaron made proclamation and said, "Tomorrow shall be a festival to the LORD." ⁶They rose early the next day, and offered burnt offerings and brought sacrifices of well-being; and the people sat down to eat and drink, and rose up to revel.

⁷The LORD said to Moses, "Go down at once! Your people, whom you brought up out of the land of Egypt, have acted perversely."

¹⁵Then Moses turned and went down from the mountain, carrying the two tablets of the covenant*ᵇ* in his hands, tablets that were written on both sides, written on the front and on the back. ¹⁶The tablets were the work of God, and the writing was the writing of God, engraved upon the tablets.

¹⁹As soon as he came near the camp and saw the calf and the dancing, Moses' anger burned hot, and he threw the tablets from his hands and broke them at the foot of the mountain.

ªOr fashioned it with a graving tool; Meaning of Heb uncertain
ᵇOr treaty, or *testimony*; Heb *eduth*

Prayer Starter: Dear Lord, I know that many people act badly in this world. Keep me from following their example.

Memory Verse: Honor your father and your mother, so that your days may be long in the land . . . —*Exodus 20.12*

His Face Was Shining

The LORD said to Moses, "Cut two tablets of stone like the former ones, and I will write on the tablets the words that were on the former tablets, which you broke. ²Be ready in the morning, and come up in the morning to Mount Sinai and present yourself there to me, on the top of the mountain."

⁵The LORD descended in the cloud and stood with him there, and proclaimed the name, "The LORD."*ᵃ*

²⁸He was there with the LORD forty days and forty nights; he neither ate bread nor drank water. And he wrote on the tablets the words of the covenant, the ten commandments.*ᵇ*

²⁹Moses came down from Mount Sinai. As he came down from the mountain with the two tablets of the covenant*ᶜ* in his hand, Moses did not know that the skin of his face shone because he had been talking with God. ³⁰When Aaron and all the Israelites saw Moses, the skin of his face was shining, and they were afraid to come near him. ³¹But Moses called to them; and Aaron and all the leaders of the congregation returned to

him, and Moses spoke with them. ³²Afterward all the Israelites came near, and he gave them in commandment all that the LORD had spoken with him on Mount Sinai. ³³When Moses had finished speaking with them, he put a veil on his face; ³⁴but whenever Moses went in before the LORD to speak with him, he would take the veil off, until he came out; and when he came out, and told the Israelites what he had been commanded, ³⁵the Israelites would see the face of Moses, that the skin of his face was shining; and Moses would put the veil on his face again, until he went in to speak with him.

*ᵃ*Heb *YHWH*; The word "LORD" when spelled with capital letters stands for the divine name, *YHWH*, which is here connected with the verb *hayah*, "to be"
*ᵇ*Heb *words*
*ᶜ*Or *treaty*, or *testimony*; Heb *eduth*

Prayer Starter: Give me a cheerful face, dear Lord. Help me to smile easily. Give me eyes that express your love.

Memory Verse: Honor your father and your mother, so that your days may be long in the land that the LORD your God is giving you.
—*Exodus 20.12*

Two Goats

The LORD spoke to Moses after the death of the two sons of Aaron, when they drew near before the LORD and died. ²The LORD said to Moses:

Tell your brother Aaron not to come just at any time into the sanctuary inside the curtain before the mercy seat*ᵃ* that is upon the ark, or he will die; for I appear in the cloud upon the mercy seat.*ᵃ* ³Thus shall Aaron come into the holy place: with a young bull for a sin offering and a ram for a burnt offering. ⁴He shall put on the holy linen tunic, and shall have the linen undergarments next to his body, fasten the linen sash, and wear the linen turban; these are the holy vestments. He shall bathe his body in water, and then put them on. ⁵He shall take from the congregation of the people of Israel two male goats for a sin offering, and one ram for a burnt offering.

⁶Aaron shall offer the bull as a sin offering for himself, and shall make atonement for himself and for his house. ⁷He shall take the two goats and set them before the LORD at the entrance of the tent of meeting; ⁸and Aaron shall cast lots on the two goats, one lot for the LORD and the other lot for Azazel.*ᵇ* ⁹Aaron shall present the goat on which the lot fell for the LORD, and offer it as a sin offering; ¹⁰but the goat on which the lot fell for Azazel*ᵇ* shall be presented alive before the LORD to make atonement over it, that it may be sent away into the wilderness to Azazel.*ᵇ*

ᵃOr the cover
ᵇTraditionally rendered a scapegoat

Prayer Starter: O Lord, help me to understand more and more about what Christ has done for me.

Memory Verse: And just as Moses . . .   —*John 3.14*

Twelve Spies

So Moses sent them from the wilderness of Paran, according to the command of the LORD, all of them leading men among the Israelites. ¹⁷Moses sent them to spy out the land of Canaan, and said to them, "Go up there into the Negeb, and go up into the hill country, ¹⁸and see what the land is like, and whether the people who live in it are strong or weak, whether they are few or many, ¹⁹and whether the land they live in is good or bad, and whether the towns that they live in are unwalled or fortified, ²⁰and whether the land is rich or poor, and whether there are trees in it or not. Be bold, and bring some of the fruit of the land." Now it was the season of the first ripe grapes.

²¹So they went up and spied out the land from the wilderness of Zin to Rehob, near Lebo-hamath. ²²They went up into the Negeb, and came to Hebron; and Ahiman, Sheshai, and Talmai, the Anakites, were there. (Hebron was built seven years before Zoan in Egypt.) ²³And they came to the Wadi Eshcol, and cut down from there a branch with a single cluster of grapes, and they carried it on a pole between two of them. They also brought some pomegranates and figs. ²⁴That place was called the Wadi Eshcol,ᵃ because of the cluster that the Israelites cut down from there.

²⁵At the end of forty days they returned from spying out the land. ²⁶And they came to Moses and Aaron and to all the congregation of the Israelites in the wilderness of Paran, at Kadesh; they brought back word to them and to all the congregation, and showed them the fruit of the land. ²⁷And they told him, "We came to the land to which you sent us; it flows with milk and honey, and this is its fruit. ²⁸Yet the people who live in the land are strong, and the towns are fortified and very large; and besides, we saw the descendants of Anak there."

³⁰But Caleb quieted the people before Moses, and said, "Let us go up at once and occupy it, for we are well able to overcome it."

ᵃThat is *Cluster*

Prayer Starter: Give me more and more faith in you, O Lord. Help me to trust your word.

Memory Verse: And just as Moses lifted up the serpent . . .

—John 3.14

The Bronze Snake

From Mount Hor they set out by the way to the Red Sea,[a] to go around the land of Edom; but the people became impatient on the way. [5]The people spoke against God and against Moses, "Why have you brought us up out of Egypt to die in the wilderness? For there is no food and no water, and we detest this miserable food." [6]Then the LORD sent poisonous[b] serpents among the people, and they bit the people, so that many Israelites died. [7]The people came to Moses and said, "We have sinned by speaking against the LORD and against you; pray to the LORD to take away the serpents from us." So Moses prayed for the people. [8]And the LORD said to Moses, "Make a poisonous[c] serpent, and set it on a pole; and everyone who is bitten shall look at it and live." [9]So Moses made a serpent of bronze, and put it upon a pole; and whenever a serpent bit someone, that person would look at the serpent of bronze and live.

[10]The Israelites set out, and camped in Oboth. [11]They set out from Oboth, and camped at Iye-abarim, in the wilderness bordering Moab toward the sunrise. [12]From there they set out, and camped in the Wadi Zered. [13]From there they set out, and camped on the other side of the Arnon, in[d] the wilderness that extends from the boundary of the Amorites; for the Arnon is the boundary of Moab, between Moab and the Amorites. [14]Wherefore it is said in the Book of the Wars of the LORD,

"Waheb in Suphah and the wadis.
The Arnon ¹⁵and the slopes of the wadis
that extend to the seat of Ar,
and lie along the border of Moab."ᵉ

¹⁶From there they continued to Beer;ᶠ that is the well of which the LORD said to Moses, "Gather the people together, and I will give them water." ¹⁷Then Israel sang this song:

"Spring up, O well! —Sing to it!—
¹⁸   the well that the leaders sank,
that the nobles of the people dug,
with the scepter, with the staff."

From the wilderness to Mattanah, ¹⁹from Mattanah to Nahaliel, from Nahaliel to Bamoth, ²⁰and from Bamoth to the valley lying in the region of Moab by the top of Pisgah that overlooks the wasteland.ᵍ

ᵃOr *Sea of Reeds*
ᵇOr *fiery;* Heb *seraphim*
ᶜOr *fiery*; Heb *seraph*
ᵈGk: Heb *which is in*
ᵉMeaning of Heb uncertain
ᶠThat is *Well*
ᵍOr *Jeshimon*

Prayer Starter: Forgive me, Lord, when I complain and grumble and make others unhappy. Give me a happy spirit.

Memory Verse: And just as Moses lifted up the serpent in the wilderness . . .
—*John 3.14*

Balaam's Donkey

God's anger was kindled because [Balaam] was going, and the angel of the LORD took his stand in the road as his adversary. Now he was riding on the donkey, and his two servants were with him. ²³The donkey saw the angel of the LORD standing in the road, with a drawn sword in his hand; so the donkey turned off the road, and went into the field; and Balaam struck the donkey, to turn it back onto the road. ²⁴Then the angel of the LORD stood in a narrow path between the vineyards, with a wall on either side. ²⁵When the donkey saw the angel of the LORD, it scraped against the wall, and scraped Balaam's foot against the wall; so he struck it again. ²⁶Then the angel of the LORD went ahead, and stood in a narrow place, where there was no way to turn either to the right or to the left. ²⁷When the donkey saw the angel of the LORD, it lay down under Balaam; and Balaam's anger was kindled, and he struck the donkey with his staff. ²⁸Then the LORD opened the mouth of the donkey, and it said to Balaam, "What have I done to you, that you have struck me these three times?" ²⁹Balaam said to the donkey, "Because you have made a fool of me! I wish I had a sword in my hand! I would kill you right now!" ³⁰But the donkey said to Balaam, "Am I not your donkey, which you have ridden all your life to this day? Have I been in the habit of treating you this way?" And he said, "No."

³¹Then the LORD opened the eyes of Balaam, and he saw the angel of the

LORD standing in the road, with his drawn sword in his hand; and he bowed down, falling on his face. ³²The angel of the LORD said to him, "Why have you struck your donkey these three times? I have come out as an adversary, because your way is perverse*ᵃ* before me. ³³The donkey saw me, and turned away from me these three times. If it had not turned away from me, surely just now I would have killed you and let it live." ³⁴Then Balaam said to the angel of the LORD, "I have sinned, for I did not know that you were standing in the road to oppose me. Now therefore, if it is displeasing to you, I will return home."

ᵃMeaning of Heb uncertain

Prayer Starter: How wonderful you are, dear Lord. How wise and powerful!

Memory Verse: And just as Moses lifted up the serpent in the wilderness, so must the Son of Man . . .   —*John 3.14*

The Death of Moses

Then Moses went up from the plains of Moab to Mount Nebo, to the top of Pisgah, which is opposite Jericho, and the LORD showed him the whole land: Gilead as far as Dan, ²all Naphtali, the land of Ephraim and Manasseh, all the land of Judah as far as the Western Sea, ³the Negeb, and the Plain—that is, the valley of Jericho, the city of palm trees—as far as Zoar. ⁴The LORD said to him, "This is the land of which I swore to Abraham, to Isaac, and to Jacob, saying, 'I will give it to your descendants'; I have let you see it with your eyes, but you shall not cross over there." ⁵Then Moses, the servant of the LORD, died there in the land of Moab, at the LORD's command. ⁶He was buried in a valley in the land of Moab, opposite Beth-peor, but no one knows his burial place to this day. ⁷Moses was one hundred twenty years old when he died; his sight was unimpaired and his vigor had not abated. ⁸The Israelites wept for Moses in the plains of Moab thirty days; then the period of mourning for Moses was ended.

⁹Joshua son of Nun was full of the spirit of wisdom, because Moses had laid his hands on him; and the Israelites obeyed him, doing as the LORD had commanded Moses.

Prayer Starter: I love your promises in the Bible, dear Lord. Thank you for each one.

Memory Verse: And just as Moses lifted up the serpent in the wilderness, so must the Son of Man be lifted up.   —*John 3.14*

Rahab

Then Joshua son of Nun sent two men secretly from Shittim as spies, saying, "Go, view the land, especially Jericho." So they went, and entered the house of a prostitute whose name was Rahab, and spent the night there. ²The king of Jericho was told, "Some Israelites have come here tonight to search out the land." ³Then the king of Jericho sent orders to Rahab, "Bring out the men who have come to you, who entered your house, for they have come only to search out the whole land." ⁴But the woman took the two men and hid them. Then she said, "True, the men came to me, but I did not know where they came from. ⁵And when it was time to close the gate at dark, the men went out. Where the men went I do not know. Pursue them quickly, for you can overtake them." ⁶She had, however, brought them up to the roof and hidden them with the stalks of flax that she had laid out on the roof. ⁷So the men pursued them on the way to the Jordan as far as the fords. As soon as the pursuers had gone out, the gate was shut.

⁸Before they went to sleep, she came up to them on the roof ⁹and said to the men: "I know that the LORD has given you the land, and that dread of you has fallen on us, and that all the inhabitants of the land melt in fear before you. ¹²Now then, since I have dealt kindly with you, swear to me by the LORD that you in turn will deal kindly with my family. Give me a sign of good faith ¹³that you will spare my father and mother, my brothers and sisters, and all who belong to them, and deliver our lives from death." ¹⁴The men said to her, "Our life for yours! If you do not tell this business of ours, then we will deal kindly and faithfully with you when the LORD gives us the land."

Prayer Starter: Keep me safe each day, O Lord, and protect me throughout every night.

Memory Verse: I hereby command you . . .   —*Joshua 1.9*

Amazing Things

Then Joshua said to the people, "Sanctify yourselves; for tomorrow the LORD will do wonders among you." [6]To the priests Joshua said, "Take up the ark of the covenant, and pass on in front of the people." So they took up the ark of the covenant and went in front of the people.

[7]The LORD said to Joshua, "This day I will begin to exalt you in the sight of all Israel, so that they may know that I will be with you as I was with Moses. [8]You are the one who shall command the priests who bear the ark of the covenant, 'When you come to the edge of the waters of the Jordan, you shall stand still in the Jordan.'"

[14]When the people set out from their tents to cross over the Jordan, the priests bearing the ark of the covenant were in front of the people. [15]Now the Jordan overflows all its banks throughout the time of harvest. So when those who bore the ark had come to the Jordan, and the feet of the priests bearing the ark were dipped in the edge of the water, [16]the waters flowing from above stood still, rising up in a single heap far off at Adam, the city that is beside Zarethan, while those flowing toward the sea of the Arabah, the Dead Sea,[a] were wholly cut off. Then the people crossed over opposite Jericho. [17]While all Israel were crossing over on dry ground, the priests who bore the ark of the covenant of the LORD stood on dry ground in the middle of the Jordan, until the entire nation finished crossing over the Jordan.

[a]Heb *Salt Sea*

Prayer Starter: Lord, help me to worship you as I should, because you are going to do amazing things for me.

Memory Verse: I hereby command you: Be strong and courageous . . .
—*Joshua 1.9*

The Walls of Jericho

S o Joshua son of Nun summoned the priests and said to them, "Take up the ark of the covenant, and have seven priests carry seven trumpets of rams' horns in front of the ark of the LORD." ⁷To the people he said, "Go forward and march around the city; have the armed men pass on before the ark of the LORD."

⁸As Joshua had commanded the people, the seven priests carrying the seven trumpets of rams' horns before the LORD went

forward, blowing the trumpets, with the ark of the covenant of the LORD following them. ⁹And the armed men went before the priests who blew the trumpets; the rear guard came after the ark, while the trumpets blew continually. ¹⁰To the people Joshua gave this command: "You shall not shout or let your voice be heard, nor shall you utter a word, until the day I tell you to shout. Then you shall shout." ¹¹So the ark of the LORD went around the city, circling it once; and they came into the camp, and spent the night in the camp.

¹²Then Joshua rose early in the morning, and the priests took up the ark of the LORD. ¹³The seven priests carrying the seven trumpets of rams' horns before the ark of the LORD passed on, blowing the trumpets continually. The armed men went before them, and the rear guard came after the ark of the LORD, while the trumpets blew continually. ¹⁴On the second day they marched around the city once and then returned to the camp. They did this for six days.

¹⁵On the seventh day they rose early, at dawn, and marched around the city in the same manner seven times. It was only on that day that they marched around the city seven times. ¹⁶And at the seventh time, when the priests had blown the trumpets, Joshua said to the people, "Shout! For the LORD has given you the city."

²⁰So the people shouted, and the trumpets were blown. As soon as the people heard the sound of the trumpets, they raised a great shout, and the wall fell down flat; so the people charged straight ahead into the city and captured it.

Prayer Starter: You are a God who does miracles, Lord. I praise and worship you.

Memory Verse: I hereby command you: Be strong and courageous; do not be frightened or dismayed . . .   —*Joshua 1.9*

The Longest Day

$\mathbb{S}$o Joshua came upon them suddenly, having marched up all night from Gilgal. ¹⁰And the LORD threw them into a panic before Israel, who inflicted a great slaughter on them at Gibeon, chased them by the way of the ascent of Beth-horon, and struck them down as far as Azekah and Makkedah. ¹¹As they fled before Israel, while they were going down the slope of Beth-horon, the LORD threw down huge stones from heaven on them as far as Azekah, and they died; there were more who died because of the hailstones than the Israelites killed with the sword.

¹²On the day when the LORD gave the Amorites over to the Israelites, Joshua spoke to the LORD; and he said in the sight of Israel,
> "Sun, stand still at Gibeon,
> and Moon, in the valley of Aijalon."
¹³ And the sun stood still, and the moon stopped,
> until the nation took vengeance on their enemies.
Is this not written in the Book of Jashar? The sun stopped in midheaven, and did not hurry to set for about a whole day. ¹⁴There has been no day like it before or since, when the LORD heeded a human voice; for the LORD fought for Israel.

Prayer Starter: Thank you, Father, for the sun and moon. And thank you for the day they stood still.

Memory Verse: I hereby command you: Be strong and courageous; do not be frightened or dismayed, for the LORD your God . . .   —*Joshua 1.9*

Choose Right Now

Then Joshua gathered all the tribes of Israel to Shechem, and summoned the elders, the heads, the judges, and the officers of Israel; and they presented themselves before God. ²And Joshua said to all the people, "Thus says the LORD, the God of Israel: Long ago your ancestors—Terah and his sons Abraham and Nahor—lived beyond the Euphrates and served other gods. ³Then I took your father Abraham from beyond the River and led him through all the land of Canaan and made his offspring many. I gave him Isaac; ⁴and to Isaac I gave Jacob and Esau. I gave Esau the hill country of Seir to possess, but Jacob and his children went down to Egypt. ⁵Then I sent Moses and Aaron, and I plagued Egypt with what I did in its midst; and afterwards I brought you out. ⁶When I brought your ancestors out of Egypt, you came to the sea; and the Egyptians pursued your ancestors with chariots and horsemen to the Red Sea.ᵃ ⁷When they cried out to the LORD, he put darkness between you and the Egyptians, and made the sea come upon them and cover them; and your eyes saw what I did to Egypt. Afterwards you lived in the wilderness a long time. ⁸Then I brought you to the land of the Amorites, who lived on the other side of the Jordan; they fought with you, and I handed them over to you, and you took possession of their land, and I destroyed them before you. ⁹Then King Balak son of Zippor of Moab, set out to fight against Israel. He sent and invited Balaam son of Beor to curse you, ¹⁰but I would not

listen to Balaam; therefore he blessed you;
so I rescued you out of his hand.
[11]When you went over the Jordan
and came to Jericho, the citizens
of Jericho fought against you,
and also the Amorites, the
Perizzites, the Canaanites, the
Hittites, the Girgashites, the
Hivites, and the Jebusites; and
I handed them over to you. [12]I
sent the hornet[b] ahead of you,
which drove out before you the
two kings of the Amorites; it was
not by your sword or by your bow. [13]I
gave you a land on which you had not
labored, and towns that you had not built, and
you live in them; you eat the fruit of vineyards and oliveyards that you
did not plant.

[14]"Now therefore revere the LORD, and serve him in sincerity and in
faithfulness; put away the gods that your ancestors served beyond the
River and in Egypt, and serve the LORD. [15]Now if you are unwilling to
serve the LORD, choose this day whom you will serve, whether the gods
your ancestors served in the region beyond the River or the gods of the
Amorites in whose land you are living; but as for me and my household,
we will serve the LORD."

[a]Or *Sea of Reeds*
[b]Meaning of Heb uncertain

Prayer Starter: Father, may my family and I worship and obey you.

Memory Verse: I hereby command you: Be strong and courageous; do not be frightened or dismayed, for the LORD your God is with
you wherever you go.   —*Joshua 1.9*

Deborah and Barak

At that time Deborah, a prophetess, wife of Lappidoth, was judging Israel. ⁵She used to sit under the palm of Deborah between Ramah and Bethel in the hill country of Ephraim; and the Israelites came up to her for judgment. ⁶She sent and summoned Barak son of Abinoam from Kedesh in Naphtali, and said to him, "The LORD, the God of Israel, commands you, 'Go, take position at Mount Tabor, bringing ten thousand from the tribe of Naphtali and the tribe of Zebulun. ⁷I will draw out Sisera, the general of Jabin's army, to meet you by the Wadi Kishon with his chariots and his troops; and I will give him into your hand.'" ⁸Barak said to her, "If you will go with me, I will go; but if you will not go with me, I will not go." ⁹And she said, "I will surely go with you; nevertheless, the road on which you are going will not lead to your glory, for the LORD will sell Sisera into the hand of a woman." Then Deborah got up and went with Barak to Kedesh. ¹⁰Barak summoned Zebulun and Naphtali to Kedesh; and ten thousand warriors went up behind him; and Deborah went up with him.

Prayer Starter: Father, help my friends to live for you as they should. May they love and serve Jesus.

Memory Verse: I appeal to you therefore, brothers and sisters . . .
—*Romans 12.1*

We Praise You, Lord!

Then Deborah and Barak son of Abinoam sang on that day, saying:

2 "When locks are long in Israel,
when the people offer themselves willingly—
bless*ᵃ* the LORD!

3 "Hear, O kings; give ear, O princes;
to the LORD I will sing,
I will make melody to the LORD, the God of Israel.

4 "LORD, when you went out from Seir,
when you marched from the region of Edom,
the earth trembled,
and the heavens poured,
the clouds indeed poured water.
5 The mountains quaked before the LORD, the One of Sinai,
before the LORD, the God of Israel.

6 "In the days of Shamgar son of Anath,
in the days of Jael, caravans ceased
and travelers kept to the byways.
7 The peasantry prospered in Israel,
they grew fat on plunder,
because you arose, Deborah,
arose as a mother in Israel.
8 When new gods were chosen,
then war was in the gates.
Was shield or spear to be seen
among forty thousand in Israel?
9 My heart goes out to the commanders of Israel
who offered themselves willingly among the people.
Bless the LORD.

10 "Tell of it, you who ride on white donkeys,
you who sit on rich carpets*ᵇ*
and you who walk by the way.
11 To the sound of musicians*ᵇ* at the watering places,
there they repeat the triumphs of the LORD,
the triumphs of his peasantry in Israel."

ᵃOr You who offer yourselves willingly among the people, bless
ᵇMeaning of Heb uncertain

Prayer Starter: We praise you, O Lord, for giving us each day what we need. Thank you for loving us so much.

Memory Verse: I appeal to you therefore, brothers and sisters, by the mercies of God . . .
—*Romans 12.1*

Gideon

Now the angel of the LORD came and sat under the oak at Ophrah, which belonged to Joash the Abiezrite, as his son Gideon was beating out wheat in the wine press, to hide it from the Midianites. ¹²The angel of the LORD appeared to him and said to him, "The LORD is with you, you mighty warrior." ¹³Gideon answered him, "But sir, if the LORD is with us, why then has all this happened to us? And where are all his wonderful deeds that our ancestors recounted to us, saying, 'Did not the LORD bring us up from Egypt?' But now the LORD has cast us off, and given us into the hand of Midian." ¹⁴Then the LORD turned to him and said, "Go in this might of yours and deliver Israel from the hand of Midian; I hereby commission you." ¹⁵He responded, "But sir, how can I deliver Israel? My clan is the weakest in Manasseh, and I am the least in my family." ¹⁶The LORD said to him, "But I will be with you, and you shall strike down the Midianites, every one of them."

Prayer Starter: When I'm tempted to doubt your promises, Lord, strengthen my faith. Help me trust you as I should.

Memory Verse: I appeal to you therefore, brothers and sisters, by the mercies of God, to present your bodies as a living sacrifice . . . —*Romans 12.1*

Samson and Delilah

After this [Samson] fell in love with a woman in the valley of Sorek, whose name was Delilah. ⁵The lords of the Philistines came to her and said to her, "Coax him, and find out what makes his strength so great, and how we may overpower him, so that we may bind him in order to subdue him; and we will each give you eleven hundred pieces of silver."

¹⁵Then she said to him, "How can you say, 'I love you,' when your heart is not with me? You have mocked me three times now and have not told me what makes your strength so great." ¹⁶Finally, after she had nagged him with her words day after day, and pestered him, he was tired to death. ¹⁷So he told her his whole secret, and said to her, "A razor has never come upon my head; for I have been a nazirite*ᵃ* to God from my mother's womb. If my head were shaved, then my strength would leave me; I would become weak, and be like anyone else."

¹⁸When Delilah realized that he had told her his whole secret, she sent and called the lords of the Philistines, saying, "This time come up,

for he has told his whole secret to me." Then the lords of the Philistines came up to her, and brought the money in their hands. ¹⁹She let him fall asleep on her lap; and she called a man, and had him shave off the seven locks of his head. He began to weaken,*ᵇ* and his strength left him. ²⁰Then she said, "The Philistines are upon you, Samson!" When he awoke from his sleep, he thought, "I will go out as at other times, and shake myself free." But he did not know that the LORD had left him. ²¹So the Philistines seized him and gouged out his eyes. They brought him down to Gaza and bound him with bronze shackles; and he ground at the mill in the prison. ²²But the hair of his head began to grow again after it had been shaved.

ᵃThat is one separated or one consecrated
ᵇGk: Heb She began to torment him

Prayer Starter: Keep me from sin, Lord, and keep me from making foolish mistakes.

Memory Verse: I appeal to you therefore, brothers and sisters, by the mercies of God, to present your bodies as a living sacrifice, holy and acceptable to God . . .
—*Romans 12.1*

> ### One Last Time

Now the lords of the Philistines gathered to offer a great sacrifice to their god Dagon, and to rejoice; for they said, "Our god has given Samson our enemy into our hand." 24When the people saw him, they praised their god; for they said, "Our god has given our enemy into our hand, the ravager of our country, who has killed many of us." 25And when their hearts were merry, they said, "Call Samson, and let him entertain us." So they called Samson out of the prison, and he performed for them. They made him stand between the pillars;

28Then Samson called to the LORD and said, "Lord GOD, remember me and strengthen me only this once, O God, so that with this one act of revenge I may pay back the Philistines for my two eyes."[a] 29And Samson grasped the two middle pillars on which the house rested, and he leaned his weight against them, his right hand on the one and his left hand on the other. 30Then Samson said, "Let me die with the Philistines." He strained with all his might; and the house fell on the lords and all the people who were in it. So those he killed at his death were more than those he had killed during his life.

[a]Or *so that I may be avenged upon the Philistines for one of my two eyes*

Prayer Starter: Help those in prison, dear Lord. May they learn to love and serve you.

Memory Verse: I appeal to you therefore, brothers and sisters, by the mercies of God, to present your bodies as a living sacrifice, holy and acceptable to God, which is your spiritual worship.   —*Romans 12.1*

Ruth and Naomi

In the days when the judges ruled, there was a famine in the land, and a certain man of Bethlehem in Judah went to live in the country of Moab, he and his wife and two sons. ²The name of the man was Elimelech and the name of his wife Naomi, and the names of his two sons were Mahlon and Chilion; they were Ephrathites from Bethlehem in Judah. They went into the country of Moab and remained there. ³But Elimelech, the husband of Naomi, died, and she was left with her two sons. ⁴These took Moabite wives; the name of the one was Orpah and the name of the other Ruth. When they had lived there about ten years, ⁵both Mahlon and Chilion also died, so that the woman was left without her two sons and her husband.

⁶Then she started to return with her daughters-in-law from the country of Moab, for she had heard in the country of Moab that the LORD had considered his people and given them food. ⁷So she set out from the place where she had been living, she and her two daughters-in-law, and they went on their way to go back to the land of Judah. ⁸But Naomi said to her two daughters-in-law, "Go back each of you to your mother's house. May the LORD deal kindly with you, as you have dealt with the dead and with me. ⁹The LORD grant that you may find security, each of you in the house of your husband." Then she kissed them, and they wept aloud. ¹⁰They said to her, "No, we will return with you to your people." ¹¹But Naomi said, "Turn back, my daughters, why will you go with me? Do I still have sons in my womb that they may become your husbands? ¹²Turn back, my daughters,

go your way, for I am too old to have a husband. Even if I thought there was hope for me, even if I should have a husband tonight and bear sons, ¹³would you then wait until they were grown? Would you then refrain from marrying? No, my daughters, it has been far more bitter for me than for you, because the hand of the LORD has turned against me." ¹⁴Then they wept aloud again. Orpah kissed her mother-in-law, but Ruth clung to her.

¹⁵So she said, "See, your sister-in-law has gone back to her people and to her gods; return after your sister-in-law." ¹⁶But Ruth said,

"Do not press me to leave you
    or to turn back from following you!
Where you go, I will go;
    Where you lodge, I will lodge;
your people shall be my people,
    and your God my God.
¹⁷ Where you die, I will die—
    there will I be buried.
May the LORD do thus and so to me,
    and more as well,
if even death parts me from you!"

¹⁸When Naomi saw that she was determined to go with her, she said no more to her.

¹⁹So the two of them went on until they came to Bethlehem. When they came to Bethlehem, the whole town was stirred because of them; and the women said, "Is this Naomi?"

Prayer Starter: Thanks for giving us families, Lord. Bless my family today.

Memory Verse: But whenever you pray . . .   *—Matthew 6.6*

Boaz

Now Naomi had a kinsman on her husband's side, a prominent rich man, of the family of Elimelech, whose name was Boaz. [2]And Ruth the Moabite said to Naomi, "Let me go to the field and glean among the ears of grain, behind someone in whose sight I may find favor." She said to her, "Go, my daughter." [3]So she went. She came and gleaned in the field behind the reapers. As it happened, she came to the part of the field belonging to Boaz, who was of the family of Elimelech. [4]Just then Boaz came from Bethlehem. He said to the reapers, "The LORD be with you." They answered, "The LORD bless you." [5]Then Boaz said to his servant who was in charge of the reapers, "To whom does this young woman belong?" [6]The servant who was in charge of the reapers answered, "She is the Moabite who came back with Naomi from the country of Moab. [7]She said, 'Please, let me glean and gather among the sheaves behind the reapers.' So she came, and she has been on her feet from early this morning until now, without resting even for a moment."[a]

[8]Then Boaz said to Ruth, "Now listen, my daughter, do not go to glean in another field or leave this one, but keep close to my young women. [9]Keep your eyes on the field that is being reaped, and follow behind them. I have ordered the young men not to bother you. If you get thirsty, go to the vessels and drink from what the young men have drawn." [10]Then she fell prostrate, with her face to the ground, and said to him, "Why have I found favor in your sight, that you should take notice of me, when I am a foreigner?" [11]But Boaz answered her, "All that you have done for your mother-in-law since the death of your husband has been fully told me, and how you left your father and mother and your native land and came to a people that you did not know before. [12]May the LORD reward you for your deeds, and may you have a full reward from the LORD, the God of Israel, under whose wings you have come for refuge!"

4 So Boaz took Ruth and she became his wife. When they came together, the LORD made her conceive, and she bore a son. [16]Then Naomi took the child and laid him in her bosom, and became his nurse. [17]The women of the neighborhood gave him a name, saying, "A son has been born to Naomi." They named him Obed; he became the father of Jesse, the father of David.

[a]Compare Gk Vg: Meaning of Heb uncertain

Prayer Starter: Lead me each day, dear Father. Guide me to the people you want me to meet, and to the work you want me to do.

Memory Verse: But whenever you pray, go into your room and shut the door . . .   *—Matthew 6.6*

Hannah Prayed Silently

After they had eaten and drunk at Shiloh, Hannah rose and presented herself before the LORD.[a] Now Eli the priest was sitting on the seat beside the doorpost of the temple of the LORD. [10]She was deeply distressed and prayed to the LORD, and wept bitterly. [11]She made this vow: "O LORD of hosts, if only you will look on the misery of your servant, and remember me, and not forget your servant, but will give to your servant a male child, then I will set him before you as a nazirite[b] until the day of his death. He shall drink neither wine nor intoxicants,[c] and no razor shall touch his head."

[12]As she continued praying before the LORD, Eli observed her mouth. [13]Hannah was praying silently; only her lips moved, but her voice was not heard; therefore Eli thought she was drunk. [14]So Eli said to her, "How long will you make a drunken spectacle of yourself? Put away your wine." [15]But Hannah answered, "No, my lord, I am a woman deeply troubled; I have drunk neither wine nor strong drink, but I have been pouring out my soul before the LORD. [16]Do not regard your servant as a worthless woman, for I have been speaking out of my great anxiety and vexation all this time." [17]Then Eli answered, "Go in peace; the God of Israel grant the petition you have made to him."

[a]Gk: Heb lacks *and presented herself before the Lord*
[b]That is *one separated* or *one consecrated*
[c]Cn Compare Gk Q Ms 1.22: MT *then I will give him to the Lord all the days of his life*

Prayer Starter: Lord, I am sure you answer prayer. Please help me pray to you each day.

Memory Verse: But whenever you pray, go into your room and shut the door and pray to your Father who is in secret . . .   *—Matthew 6.6*

The Little Boy

They rose early in the morning and worshiped before the LORD; then they went back to their house at Ramah. Elkanah knew his wife Hannah, and the LORD remembered her. [20]In due time Hannah conceived and bore a son. She named him Samuel, for she said, "I have asked him of the LORD."

[21]The man Elkanah and all his household went up to offer to the LORD the yearly sacrifice, and to pay his vow. [22]But Hannah did not go up, for she said to her husband, "As soon as the child is weaned, I will bring him, that he may appear in the presence of the LORD, and remain there forever; I will offer him as a nazirite[a] for all time."[b] [23]Her husband Elkanah said to her, "Do what seems best to you, wait until you have weaned him; only—may the LORD establish his word."[c] So the woman remained and nursed her son, until she weaned him. [24]When she had weaned him, she took him up with her, along with a three-year-old bull,[d] an ephah of flour, and a skin of wine. She brought him to the house of the LORD at Shiloh; and the child was young. [25]Then they slaughtered the bull, and they brought the child to Eli. [26]And she said, "Oh, my lord! As you live, my lord, I am the woman who was standing here in your presence, praying to the LORD. [27]For this child I prayed; and the LORD has granted me the petition that I made to him. [28]Therefore I have lent him to the LORD; as long as he lives, he is given to the LORD."

She left him there for[e] the LORD.

[a]That is *one separated* or *one consecrated*
[b]Cn Compare Q Ms: MT lacks *I will offer him as a nazirite for all time*
[c]MT: Q Ms Gk Compare Syr *that which goes out of your mouth*
[d]Q Ms Gk Syr: MT *three bulls*
[e]Gk (Compare Q Ms) and Gk at 2.11: MT *And he* (that is, Elkanah) *worshiped there before*

Prayer Starter: I want to be your servant as long as I live, dear Lord.

Memory Verse: But whenever you pray, go into your room and shut the door and pray to your Father who is in secret; and your Father who sees in secret . . .
—*Matthew 6.6*

I'm Listening, Lord

Now the boy Samuel was ministering to the LORD under Eli. The word of the LORD was rare in those days; visions were not widespread. ²At that time Eli, whose eyesight had begun to grow dim so that he could not see, was lying down in his room; ³the lamp of God had not yet gone out, and Samuel was lying down in the temple of the LORD, where the ark of God was. ⁴Then the LORD called, "Samuel! Samuel!"ᵃ and he said, "Here I am!" ⁵and ran to Eli, and said, "Here I am, for you called me." But he said, "I did not call; lie down again." So he went and lay down. ⁶The LORD called again, "Samuel!" Samuel got up and went to Eli, and said, "Here I am, for you called me." But he said, "I did not call, my son; lie down again." ⁷Now Samuel did not yet know the LORD, and the word of the LORD had not yet been revealed to him. ⁸The LORD called Samuel again, a third time. And he got up and went to Eli, and said, "Here I am, for you called me." Then Eli perceived that the LORD was calling the boy. ⁹Therefore Eli said to Samuel, "Go, lie down; and if he calls you, you shall say, 'Speak, LORD, for your servant is listening.'" So Samuel went and lay down in his place.

¹⁰Now the LORD came and stood there, calling as before, "Samuel! Samuel!" And Samuel said, "Speak, for your servant is listening." ¹¹Then the LORD said to Samuel, "See, I am about to do something in Israel that will make both ears of anyone who hears of it tingle. ¹²On that day I will fulfill against Eli all that I have spoken concerning his house, from beginning to end. ¹³For I have told him that I am about to punish his house forever, for the iniquity that he knew, because his sons were blaspheming God,ᵇ and he did not restrain them. ¹⁴Therefore I swear to the house of Eli that the iniquity of Eli's house shall not be expiated by sacrifice or offering forever."

ᵃQ Ms Gk See 3.10: Mt *the Lord called Samuel*
ᵇAnother reading is *for themselves*

Prayer Starter: I'm listening to your word each day, dear Lord. Help me to do what you want me to do.

Memory Verse: But whenever you pray, go into your room and shut the door and pray to your Father who is in secret; and your Father who sees in secret will reward you. —*Matthew 6.6*

Saul Anointed King

Samuel took a vial of oil and poured it on his head, and kissed him; he said, "The LORD has anointed you ruler over his people Israel. You shall reign over the people of the LORD and you will save them from the hand of their enemies all around. Now this shall be the sign to you that the LORD has anointed you ruler[a] over his heritage: [2]When you depart from me today you will meet two men by Rachel's tomb in the territory of Benjamin at Zelzah; they will say to you, 'The donkeys that you went to seek are found, and now your father has stopped worrying about them and is worrying about you, saying: What shall I do about my son?' [3]Then you shall go on from there further and come to the oak of Tabor; three men going up to God at Bethel will meet you there, one carrying three kids, another carrying three loaves of bread, and another carrying a skin of wine. [4]They will greet you and give you two loaves of bread, which you shall accept from them. [5]After that you shall come to Gibeath-elohim,[b] at the place where the Philistine

garrison is; there, as you come to the town, you will meet a band of prophets coming down from the shrine with harp, tambourine, flute, and lyre playing in front of them; they will be in a prophetic frenzy. [6]Then the spirit of the LORD will possess you, and you will be in a prophetic frenzy along with them and be turned into a different person. [7]Now when these signs meet you, do whatever you see fit to do, for God is with you."

[a]Gk: Heb lacks *over his people Israel. You shall . . . anointed you ruler*
[b]Or *the Hill of God*

Prayer Starter: Father, I know you have a plan for my life. Thanks for loving me so much.

Memory Verse: And Samuel said, "Has the LORD as great delight . . ."
—*1 Samuel 15.22*

He Wants You to Obey

The word of the LORD came to Samuel: [11]"I regret that I made Saul king, for he has turned back from following me, and has not carried out my commands." Samuel was angry; and he cried out to the LORD all night. [12]Samuel rose early in the morning to meet Saul, and Samuel was told, "Saul went to Carmel, where he set up a monument for himself, and on returning he passed on down to Gilgal." [13]When Samuel came to Saul, Saul said to him, "May you be blessed by the LORD; I have carried out the command of the LORD." [14]But Samuel said, "What then is this bleating of sheep in my ears, and the lowing of cattle that I hear?" [15]Saul said, "They have brought them from the Amalekites; for the people spared the best of the sheep and the cattle, to sacrifice to the LORD your God; but the rest we have utterly destroyed." [16]Then Samuel said to Saul, "Stop! I will tell you what the LORD said to me last night." He replied, "Speak."

[17]Samuel said, "Though you are little in your own eyes, are you not the head of the tribes of Israel? The LORD anointed you king over Israel. [18]And the LORD sent you on a mission, and said, 'Go, utterly destroy the sinners, the Amalekites, and fight against them until they are consumed.' [19]Why then did you not obey the voice of the LORD? Why did you swoop down on the spoil, and do what was evil in the sight of the LORD?"

Prayer Starter: I know you want me to obey you, Lord. Give me an obedient heart.

Memory Verse: And Samuel said, "Has the LORD as great delight in burnt offerings and sacrifices . . ."   —*1 Samuel 15.22*

David's Harp

Now the spirit of the LORD departed from Saul, and an evil spirit from the LORD tormented him. ¹⁵And Saul's servants said to him, "See now, an evil spirit from God is tormenting you. ¹⁶Let our lord now command the servants who attend you to look for someone who is skillful in playing the lyre; and when the evil spirit from God is upon you, he will play it, and you will feel better." ¹⁷So Saul said to his servants, "Provide for me someone who can play well, and bring him to me." ¹⁸One of the young men answered, "I have seen a son of Jesse the Bethlehemite who is skillful in playing, a man of valor, a warrior, prudent in speech, and a man of good presence; and the LORD is with him." ¹⁹So Saul sent messengers to Jesse, and said, "Send me your son David who is with the sheep." ²⁰Jesse took a donkey loaded with bread, a skin of wine, and a kid, and sent them by his son David to Saul. ²¹And David came to Saul, and entered his service. Saul loved him greatly, and he became his armor-bearer. ²²Saul sent to Jesse, saying, "Let David remain in my service, for he has found favor in my sight." ²³And whenever the evil spirit from God came upon Saul, David took the lyre and played it with his hand, and Saul would be relieved and feel better, and the evil spirit would depart from him.

Prayer Starter: So many people are sad, dear Lord. Give me a message to cheer them up.

Memory Verse: And Samuel said, "Has the LORD as great delight in burnt offerings and sacrifices, as in obeying the voice of the LORD? . . ."
—*1 Samuel 15.22*

David's Sling

Now the Philistines gathered their armies for battle; they were gathered at Socoh, which belongs to Judah, and encamped between Socoh and Azekah, in Ephes-dammim. ⁴And there came out from the camp of the Philistines a champion named Goliath, of Gath, whose height was six cubits and a span.

¹³The three eldest sons of Jesse had followed Saul to the battle; the names of his three sons who went to the battle were Eliab the firstborn, and next to him Abinadab, and the third Shammah. ¹⁴David was the youngest; the three eldest followed Saul, ¹⁵but David went back and forth from Saul to feed his father's sheep at Bethlehem.

¹⁷Jesse said to his son David, "Take for your brothers an ephah of this parched grain and these ten loaves, and carry them quickly to the camp to your brothers."

²⁴All the Israelites, when they saw the man [Goliath], fled from him and were very much afraid. ²⁶David said to the men who stood by him, "What shall be done for the man who kills this Philistine, and takes away the reproach from Israel? For who is this uncircumcised Philistine that he should defy the armies of the living God?"

³¹When the words that David spoke were heard, they repeated them before Saul; and he sent for him. ³²David said to Saul, "Let no one's heart fail because of him; your servant will go and fight with this Philistine."

⁴²When the Philistine looked and saw David, he disdained him, for he was only a youth, ruddy and handsome in appearance. ⁴³The Philistine said to David, "Am I a dog, that you come to me with sticks?" And the Philistine cursed David by his gods. ⁴⁵But David said to the Philistine, "You come to me with sword and spear and javelin; but I come to you in the name of the LORD of hosts, the God of the armies of Israel, whom you have defied. ⁴⁶This very day the LORD will deliver you into my hand, and I will strike you down and cut off your head; and I will give the dead bodies of the Philistine army this very day to the birds of the air and to the wild animals of the earth, so that all the earth may know that there is a God in Israel, ⁴⁷and that all this assembly may know that the LORD does not save by sword and spear; for the battle is the LORD's and he will give you into our hand."

⁴⁸When the Philistine drew nearer to meet David, David ran quickly toward the battle line to meet the Philistine. ⁴⁹David put his hand in his bag, took out a stone, slung it, and struck the Philistine on his forehead; the stone sank into his forehead, and he fell face down on the ground.

Prayer Starter: Keep me strong and safe against bullies, dear Lord, and against anyone who might harm me.

Memory Verse: And Samuel said, "Has the LORD as great delight in burnt offerings and sacrifices, as in obeying the voice of the LORD? Surely, to obey is better than sacrifice . . ."
—*1 Samuel 15.22*

Saul Grows Angry

David went out and was successful wherever Saul sent him; as a result, Saul set him over the army. And all the people, even the servants of Saul, approved.

⁶As they were coming home, when David returned from killing the Philistine, the women came out of all the towns of Israel, singing and dancing, to meet King Saul, with tambourines, with songs of joy, and with musical instruments.ᵃ ⁷And the women sang to one another as they made merry,

"Saul has killed his thousands,
and David his ten thousands."

⁸Saul was very angry, for this saying displeased him. He said, "They have ascribed to David ten thousands, and to me they have ascribed thousands; what more can he have but the kingdom?" ⁹So Saul eyed David from that day on.

¹⁰The next day an evil spirit from God rushed upon Saul, and he raved within his house, while David was playing the lyre, as he did day by day. Saul had his spear in his hand; ¹¹and Saul threw the spear, for he thought, "I will pin David to the wall." But David eluded him twice.

¹²Saul was afraid of David, because the LORD was with him but had departed from Saul. ¹³So Saul removed him from his presence, and made him a commander of a thousand; and David marched out and came in, leading the army. ¹⁴David had success in all his undertakings; for the LORD was with him. ¹⁵When Saul saw that he had great success, he stood in awe of him. ¹⁶But all Israel and Judah loved David; for it was he who marched out and came in leading them.

³⁰Then the commanders of the Philistines came out to battle; and as often as they came out, David had more success than all the servants of Saul, so that his fame became very great.

ªOr *triangles*, or *three-stringed instruments*

Prayer Starter: Father, don't let me become jealous toward others. May I be happy when others are successful.

Memory Verse: And Samuel said, "Has the LORD as great delight in burnt offerings and sacrifices, as in obeying the voice of the LORD? Surely, to obey is better than sacrifice, and to heed than the fat of rams."

—*1 Samuel 15.22*

Good Friends Part

Then Jonathan answered his father Saul, "Why should he be put to death? What has he done?" [33]But Saul threw his spear at him to strike him; so Jonathan knew that it was the decision of his father to put David to death. [34]Jonathan rose from the table in fierce anger and ate no food on the second day of the month, for he was grieved for David, and because his father had disgraced him.

[35]In the morning Jonathan went out into the field to the appointment with David, and with him was a little boy. [36]He said to the boy, "Run and find the arrows that I shoot." As the boy ran, he shot an arrow beyond him. [37]When the boy came to the place where Jonathan's arrow had fallen, Jonathan called after the boy and said, "Is the arrow not beyond you?" [38]Jonathan called after the boy, "Hurry, be quick, do not linger." So Jonathan's boy gathered up the arrows and came to his master.

[40]Jonathan gave his weapons to the boy and said to him, "Go and carry them to the city." [41]As soon as the boy had gone, David rose from beside the stone heap[a] and prostrated himself with his face to the ground. He bowed three times, and they kissed each other, and wept with each other; David wept the more.[b] [42]Then Jonathan said to David, "Go in peace, since both of us have sworn in the name of the LORD, saying, 'The LORD shall be between me and you, and between my descendants and your descendants, forever.'" He got up and left; and Jonathan went into the city.[c]

[a]Gk: Heb *from beside the south*
[b]Vg: Meaning of Heb uncertain
[c]This sentence is 21.1 in Heb

Prayer Starter: Thank you for good friends. Please take care of them.

Memory Verse: I will both lie down . . .   *—Psalm 4.8*

The Spear and the Water Jar

Then the Ziphites came to Saul at Gibeah, saying, "David is in hiding on the hill of Hachilah, which is opposite Jeshimon."[a] ²So Saul rose and went down to the Wilderness of Ziph, with three thousand chosen men of Israel, to seek David in the Wilderness of Ziph. ³Saul encamped on the hill of Hachilah, which is opposite Jeshimon beside the road. But David remained in the wilderness. When he learned that Saul came after him into the wilderness, ⁴David sent out spies, and learned that Saul had indeed arrived. ⁵Then David set out and came to the place where Saul had encamped; and David saw the place where Saul lay, with Abner son of Ner, the commander of his army. Saul was lying within the encampment, while the army was encamped around him.

⁶Then David said to Ahimelech the Hittite, and to Joab's brother Abishai son of Zeruiah, "Who will go down with me into the camp to Saul?" Abishai said, "I will go down with you." ⁷So David and Abishai went to the army by night; there Saul lay sleeping within the encampment, with his spear stuck in the ground at his head; and Abner and the army lay around him. ⁸Abishai said to David, "God has given your enemy into your hand today; now therefore let me pin him to the ground with one stroke of the spear; I will not strike him twice." ⁹But David said to Abishai, "Do not destroy him; for who can raise his hand against the LORD's anointed, and be guiltless?" ¹⁰David said, "As the LORD lives, the LORD will strike him down; or his day will come to die; or he will go down into battle and perish. ¹¹The LORD forbid that I should raise my hand against the LORD's anointed; but now take the spear that is at his head, and the water jar, and let us go." ¹²So David took the spear that was at Saul's head and the water jar, and they went away. No one saw it, or knew it, nor did anyone awake; for they were all asleep, because a deep sleep from the LORD had fallen upon them.

[a]Or *opposite the wasteland*

Prayer Starter: Lord, you make the day and night, the light and the darkness. Bless me by day and keep me safe by night.

Memory Verse: I will both lie down and sleep in peace . . .—*Psalm 4.8*

The Ghost of Samuel

In those days the Philistines gathered their forces for war, to fight against Israel. Achish said to David, "You know, of course, that you and your men are to go out with me in the army." ²David said to Achish, "Very well, then you shall know what your servant can do." Achish said to David, "Very well, I will make you my bodyguard for life."

³Now Samuel had died, and all Israel had mourned for him and buried him in Ramah, his own city. Saul had expelled the mediums and the wizards from the land.

⁵When Saul saw the army of the Philistines, he was afraid, and his heart trembled greatly. ⁶When Saul inquired of the LORD, the LORD did not answer him, not by dreams, or by Urim, or by prophets. ⁷Then Saul said to his servants, "Seek out for me a woman who is a medium, so that I may go to her and inquire of her." His servants said to him, "There is a medium at Endor."

⁸So Saul disguised himself and put on other clothes and went there, he and two men with him. They came to the woman by night. And he said, "Consult a spirit for me, and bring up for me the one whom I name to you." ⁹The woman said to him, "Surely you know what Saul has done, how he has cut off the mediums and the wizards from the land. Why then are you laying a snare for my life to bring about my death?" ¹⁰But Saul swore to her by the LORD, "As the LORD lives, no punishment shall come upon you for this thing." ¹¹Then the woman said, "Whom shall I bring up for you?" He answered, "Bring up Samuel for me." ¹²When the woman saw Samuel, she cried out with a loud voice; and the woman said to Saul, "Why have you deceived me? You are Saul!" ¹³The king said to her, "Have no fear; what do you see?" The woman said to Saul, "I see a divine being[a] coming up out of the ground." ¹⁴He said to her, "What is his appearance?" She said, "An old man is coming up; he is wrapped in a robe." So Saul knew that it was Samuel, and he bowed with his face to the ground, and did obeisance.

¹⁵Then Samuel said to Saul, "Why have you disturbed me by bringing me up?" Saul answered, "I am in great distress, for the Philistines are warring against me, and God has turned away from me and answers me no more, either by prophets or by dreams; so I have summoned you to tell me what I should do." ¹⁶Samuel said, "Why then do you ask me, since the LORD has turned from you and become your enemy? ¹⁷The LORD has done to you just as he spoke by me; for the LORD has torn the kingdom out of your hand, and given it to your neighbor, David."

[a]Or a *god*; or *gods*

Prayer Starter: Keep us safe from the devil, Father. Protect us from the evil one.

Memory Verse: I will both lie down and sleep in peace; for you alone . . .
          —Psalm 4.8

Saul and His Sons Die

Now the Philistines fought against Israel; and the men of Israel fled before the Philistines, and many fell[a] on Mount Gilboa. ²The Philistines overtook Saul and his sons; and the Philistines killed Jonathan and Abinadab and Malchishua, the sons of Saul. ³The battle pressed hard upon Saul; the archers found him, and he was badly wounded by them. ⁴Then Saul said to his armor-bearer, "Draw your sword and thrust me through with it, so that these uncircumcised may not come and thrust me through, and make sport of me." But his armor-bearer was unwilling; for he was terrified. So Saul took his own sword and fell upon it. ⁵When his armor-bearer saw that Saul was dead, he also fell upon his sword and died with him. ⁶So Saul and his three sons and his armor-bearer and all his men died together on the same day. ⁷When the men of Israel who were on the other side of the valley and those beyond the Jordan saw that the men of Israel had fled and that Saul and his sons were dead, they forsook their towns and fled; and the Philistines came and occupied them.

[a]Heb *and they fell slain*

Prayer Starter: Dear Father, so many people are sad and afraid. Help me point them to Jesus.

Memory Verse: I will both lie down and sleep in peace; for you alone, O LORD, make me . . .

—*Psalm 4.8*

David and
the Sacred
Chest

David again gathered all the chosen men of Israel, thirty thousand. ²David and all the people with him set out and went from Baale-judah, to bring up from there the ark of God, which is called by the name of the LORD of hosts who is enthroned on the cherubim. ³They carried the ark of God on a new cart, and brought it out of the house of Abinadab, which was on the hill. Uzzah and Ahio,ᵃ the sons of Abinadab, were driving the new cart ⁴with the ark of God;ᵇ and Ahioᵃ went in front of the ark. ⁵David and all the house of Israel were dancing before the LORD with all their might, with songsᶜ and lyres and harps and tambourines and castanets and cymbals.

⁶When they came to the threshing floor of Nacon, Uzzah reached out his hand to the ark of God and took hold of it, for the oxen shook it. ⁷The anger of the LORD was kindled against Uzzah; and God struck him there because he reached out his hand to the ark;ᵈ and he died there beside the ark of God. ⁸David was angry because the LORD had burst forth with an outburst upon Uzzah; so that place is called Perez-uzzah,ᵉ to this day. ⁹David was afraid of the LORD that day; he said, "How can the ark of the

Lord come into my care?" ¹⁰So David was unwilling to take the ark of the Lord into his care in the city of David; instead David took it to the house of Obed-edom the Gittite. ¹¹The ark of the Lord remained in the house of Obed-edom the Gittite three months; and the Lord blessed Obed-edom and all his household.

¹²It was told King David, "The Lord has blessed the household of Obed-edom and all that belongs to him, because of the ark of God." So David went and brought up the ark of God from the house of Obed-edom to the city of David with rejoicing; ¹³and when those who bore the ark of the Lord had gone six paces, he sacrificed an ox and a fatling. ¹⁴David danced before the Lord with all his might; David was girded with a linen ephod. ¹⁵So David and all the house of Israel brought up the ark of the Lord with shouting, and with the sound of the trumpet.

¹⁶As the ark of the Lord came into the city of David, Michal daughter of Saul looked out of the window, and saw King David leaping and dancing before the Lord; and she despised him in her heart.

¹⁷They brought in the ark of the Lord, and set it in its place, inside the tent that David had pitched for it; and David offered burnt offerings and offerings of well-being before the Lord. ¹⁸When David had finished offering the burnt offerings and the offerings of well-being, he blessed the people in the name of the Lord of hosts, ¹⁹and distributed food among all the people, the whole multitude of Israel, both men and women, to each a cake of bread, a portion of meat,ᶠ and a cake of raisins. Then all the people went back to their homes.

ᵃOr *and his brother*
ᵇCompare Gk: Heb *and brought it out of the house of Abinadab, which was on the hill with the ark of God.*
ᶜQ Ms Gk 1 Chronicles 13.8: Heb *fir-trees*
ᵈ1 Chronicles 13.10 Compare Q Ms: Meaning of Heb uncertain
ᵉThat is *Bursting Out Against Uzzah*
ᶠVg: Meaning of Heb uncertain.

Prayer Starter: Sometimes I don't do the right thing, Lord, but please continue to show me how to follow you.

Memory Verse: I will both lie down and sleep in peace; for you alone, O Lord, make me lie down in safety.   —*Psalm 4.8*

Mephibosheth

Davi asked, "Is there still anyone left of the house of Saul to whom I may show kindness for Jonathan's sake?" [2]Now there was a servant of the house of Saul whose name was Ziba, and he was summoned to David. The king said to him, "Are you Ziba?" And he said, "At your service!" [3]The king said, "Is there anyone remaining of the house of Saul to whom I may show the kindness of God?" Ziba said to the king, "There remains a son of Jonathan; he is crippled in his feet." [4]The king said to him, "Where is he?" Ziba said to the king, "He is in the house of Machir son of Ammiel, at Lo-debar." [5]Then King David sent and brought him from the house of Machir son of Ammiel, at Lo-debar. [6]Mephibosheth[a] son of Jonathan son of Saul came to David, and fell on his face and did obeisance. David said, "Mephibosheth!"[a] He answered, "I am your servant." [7]David said to him, "Do not be afraid, for I will show you kindness for the sake of your father Jonathan; I will restore to you all the land of your grandfather Saul, and you yourself shall eat at my table always." [8]He did obeisance and said, "What is your servant, that you should look upon a dead dog such as I?"

[9]Then the king summoned Saul's servant Ziba, and said to him, "All that belonged to Saul and to all his house I have given to your master's grandson."

[11]Then Ziba said to the king, "According to all that my lord the king commands his servant, so your servant will do." Mephibosheth[a] ate at David's[b] table, like one of the king's sons. [12]Mephibosheth[a] had a young son whose name was Mica. And all who lived in Ziba's house became Mephibosheth's[c] servants. [13]Mephibosheth[a] lived in Jerusalem, for he always ate at the king's table. Now he was lame in both his feet.

[a]Or *Meribbaal*
[b]Gk: Heb *my*
[c]Or *Meribbaal's*

Prayer Starter: Give us kind hearts toward one another, Lord, for you are kind toward us.

Memory Verse: Pray for one another . . .   —*James 5.16b*

David Speaks to His Son

When David's time to die drew near, he charged his son Solomon, saying: ²"I am about to go the way of all the earth. Be strong, be courageous, ³and keep the charge of the LORD your God, walking in his ways and keeping his statutes, his commandments, his ordinances, and his testimonies, as it is written in the law of Moses, so that you may prosper in all that you do and wherever you turn. ⁴Then the LORD will establish his word that he spoke concerning me: 'If your heirs take heed to their way, to walk before me in faithfulness with all their heart and with all their soul, there shall not fail you a successor on the throne of Israel.'"

¹⁰Then David slept with his ancestors, and was buried in the city of David. ¹¹The time that David reigned over Israel was forty years; he reigned seven years in Hebron, and thirty-three years in Jerusalem.

3 At Gibeon the LORD appeared to Solomon in a dream by night; and God said, "Ask what I should give you." ⁶And Solomon said, "You have shown great and steadfast love to your servant my father David, because he walked before you in faithfulness, in righteousness, and in uprightness of heart toward you; and you have kept for him this great and steadfast love, and have given him a son to sit on his throne today. ⁷And now, O LORD my God, you have made your servant king in place of my father David, although I am only a little child; I do not know how to go out or come in. ⁸And your servant is in the midst of the people whom you have chosen, a great people, so numerous they cannot be numbered or counted. ⁹Give your servant therefore an understanding mind to govern your people, able to discern between good and evil; for who can govern this your great people?"

¹⁰It pleased the Lord that Solomon had asked this. ¹¹God said to him, "Because you have asked this, and have not asked for yourself long life or riches, or for the life of your enemies, but have asked for yourself understanding to discern what is right, ¹²I now do according to your word. Indeed I give you a wise and discerning mind; no one like you has been before you and no one like you shall arise after you."

Prayer Starter: Give me wisdom, dear Lord, and help me to think clearly.

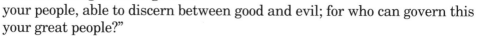

Memory Verse: Pray for one another, so that you may be healed. . . .

—*James 5.16b*

The Two Mothers

Later, two women who were prostitutes came to the king and stood before him. ¹⁷The one woman said, "Please, my lord, this woman and I live in the same house; and I gave birth while she was in the house. ¹⁸Then on the third day after I gave birth, this woman also gave birth. We were together; there was no one else with us in the house, only the two of us were in the house. ¹⁹Then this woman's son died in the night, because she lay on him. ²⁰She got up in the middle of the night and took my son from beside me while your servant slept. She laid him at her breast, and laid her dead son at my breast. ²¹When I rose in the morning to nurse my son, I saw that he was dead; but when I looked at him closely in the morning, clearly it was not the son I had borne." ²²But the other woman said, "No, the living son is mine, and the dead son is yours." The first said, "No, the dead son is yours, and the living son is mine." So they argued before the king.

²³Then the king said, "The one says, 'This is my son that is alive, and your son is dead'; while the other says, 'Not so! Your son is dead, and my son is the living one.'" ²⁴So the king said, "Bring me a sword," and they brought a sword before the king. ²⁵The king said, "Divide the living boy in two; then give half to the one, and half to the other." ²⁶But the woman whose son was alive said to the king—because compassion for her son burned within her—"Please, my lord, give her the living boy; certainly do not kill him!" The other said, "It shall be neither mine nor yours; divide it." ²⁷Then the king responded: "Give the first woman the living boy; do not kill him. She is his mother." ²⁸All Israel heard of the judgment that the king had rendered; and they stood in awe of the king, because they perceived that the wisdom of God was in him, to execute justice.

Prayer Starter: Use me, dear Lord, to help others solve their problems. Make me wise.

Memory Verse: Pray for one another, so that you may be healed. The prayer of the righteous . . .
—*James 5.16b*

The Queen of Sheba

When the queen of Sheba heard of the fame of Solomon, (fame due to[a] the name of the LORD), she came to test him with hard questions. [2]She came to Jerusalem with a very great retinue, with camels bearing spices, and very much gold, and precious stones; and when she came to Solomon, she told him all that was on her mind. [3]Solomon answered all her questions; there was nothing hidden from the king that he could not explain to her. [4]When the queen of Sheba had observed all the wisdom of Solomon, the house that he had built, [5]the food of his table, the seating of his officials, and the attendance of his servants, their clothing, his valets, and his burnt offerings that he offered at the house of the LORD, there was no more spirit in her.

[6]So she said to the king, "The report was true that I heard in my own land of your accomplishments and of your wisdom, [7]but I did not believe the reports until I came and my own eyes had seen it. Not even half had been told me; your wisdom and prosperity far surpass the report that I had heard. [8]Happy are your wives![b] Happy are these your servants, who continually attend you and hear your wisdom! [9]Blessed be the LORD your God, who has delighted in you and set you on the throne of Israel! Because the LORD loved Israel forever, he has made you king to execute justice and righteousness." [10]Then she gave the king one hundred twenty talents of gold, a great quantity of spices, and precious stones; never again did spices come in such quantity as that which the queen of Sheba gave to King Solomon.

[13]Meanwhile King Solomon gave to the queen of Sheba every desire that she expressed, as well as what he gave her out of Solomon's royal bounty. Then she returned to her own land, with her servants.

[a]Meaning of Heb uncertain
[b]Gk Syr: Heb *men*

Prayer Starter: Thank you for all you give us, dear Lord. Thanks for my home, my bed, my clothes, my food.

Memory Verse: Pray for one another, so that you may be healed. The prayer of the righteous is powerful . . .   —*James 5.16b*

Fed by Ravens

In the thirty-eighth year of King Asa of Judah, Ahab son of Omri began to reign over Israel; Ahab son of Omri reigned over Israel in Samaria twenty-two years. ³⁰Ahab son of Omri did evil in the sight of the LORD more than all who were before him.

³¹And as if it had been a light thing for him to walk in the sins of Jeroboam son of Nebat, he took as his wife Jezebel daughter of King Ethbaal of the Sidonians, and went and served Baal, and worshiped him. ³²He erected an altar for Baal in the house of Baal, which he built in Samaria. ³³Ahab also made a sacred pole.ᵃ Ahab did more to provoke the anger of the LORD, the God of Israel, than had all the kings of Israel who were before him. ³⁴In his days Hiel of Bethel built Jericho; he laid its foundation at the cost of Abiram his first-born, and set up its gates at the cost of his youngest son Segub, according to the word of the LORD, which he spoke by Joshua son of Nun.

17Now Elijah the Tishbite, of Tishbeᵇ in Gilead, said to Ahab, "As the LORD the God of Israel lives, before whom I stand, there shall be neither dew nor rain these years, except by my word." ²The word of the LORD came to him, saying, ³"Go from here and turn eastward, and hide yourself by the Wadi Cherith, which is east of the Jordan. ⁴You shall drink from the wadi, and I have commanded the ravens to feed you there." ⁵So he went and did according to the word of the LORD; he went and lived by the Wadi Cherith, which is east of the Jordan.

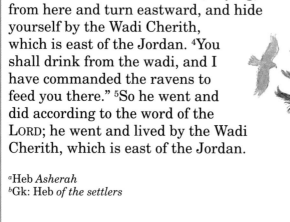

ᵃHeb *Asherah*
ᵇGk: Heb *of the settlers*

Prayer Starter: Thank you for the stories in the Bible, Father. Help me to pray like Elijah.

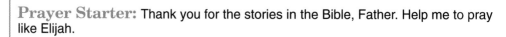

Memory Verse: Pray for one another, so that you may be healed. The prayer of the righteous is powerful and effective.   —*James 5.16b*

**A Handful
of Flour**

hen the word of the LORD came to him, saying, ⁹"Go now to Zarephath, which belongs to Sidon, and live there; for I have commanded a widow there to feed you." ¹⁰So he set out and went to Zarephath. When he came to the gate of the town, a widow was there gathering sticks; he called to her and said, "Bring me a little water in a vessel, so that I may drink." ¹¹As she was going to bring it, he called to her and said, "Bring me a morsel of bread in your hand." ¹²But she said, "As the LORD your God lives, I have nothing baked, only a handful of meal in a jar, and a little oil in a jug; I am now gathering a couple of sticks, so that I may go home and prepare it for myself and my son, that we may eat it, and die" ¹³Elijah said to her, "Do not be afraid; go and do as you have said; but first make me a little cake of it and bring it to me, and afterwards make something for yourself and your son. ¹⁴For thus says the LORD the God of Israel: The jar of meal will not be emptied and the jug of oil will not fail until the day that the LORD sends rain on the earth." ¹⁵She went and did as Elijah said, so that she as well as he and her household ate for many days. ¹⁶The jar of meal was not emptied, neither did the jug of oil fail, according to the word of the LORD that he spoke by Elijah.

¹⁷After this the son of the woman, the mistress of the house, became ill; his illness was so severe that there was no breath left in him. ¹⁸She then said to Elijah, "What have you against me, O man of God? You have come to me to bring my sin to remembrance, and to cause the death of my

son!" [19]But he said to her, "Give me your son." He took him from her bosom, carried him up into the upper chamber where he was lodging, and laid him on his own bed. [20]He cried out to the LORD, "O LORD my God, have you brought calamity even upon the widow with whom I am staying, by killing her son?" [21]Then he stretched himself upon the child three times, and cried out to the LORD, "O LORD my God, let this child's life come into him again." [22]The LORD listened to the voice of Elijah; the life of the child came into him again, and he revived.
[23]Elijah took the child, brought him down from the upper chamber into the house, and gave him to his mother; then Elijah said, "See, your son is alive." [24]So the woman said to Elijah, "Now I know that you are a man of God, and that the word of the LORD in your mouth is truth."

Prayer Starter: Give me a generous heart, O Lord, and make me willing to share.

Memory Verse: Keep the charge of the LORD your God . . .

—1 Kings 2.3a

The Lord Is God

Then Elijah said to the prophets of Baal, "Choose for yourselves one bull and prepare it first, for you are many; then call on the name of your god, but put no fire to it." ²⁶So they took the bull that was given them, prepared it, and called on the name of Baal from morning until noon, crying, "O Baal, answer us!" But there was no voice, and no answer. They limped about the altar that they had made. ²⁷At noon Elijah mocked them, saying, "Cry aloud! Surely he is a god; either he is meditating, or he has wandered away, or he is on a journey, or perhaps he is asleep and must be awakened." ²⁸Then they cried aloud and, as was their custom, they cut themselves with swords and lances until the blood gushed out over them. ²⁹As midday passed, they raved on until the time of the offering of the oblation, but there was no voice, no answer, and no response.

³⁰Then Elijah said to all the people, "Come closer to me"; and all the people came closer to him. First he repaired the altar of the Lord that had been thrown down; ³¹Elijah took twelve stones, according to the number of the tribes of the sons of Jacob, to whom the word of the Lord came, saying, "Israel shall be your name"; ³²with the stones he built an altar in the name of the Lord. Then he made a trench around the altar, large enough to contain two measures of seed. ³³Next he put the wood in order, cut the bull in pieces, and laid it on the wood. He said, "Fill four jars with water and pour it on the burnt offering and on the wood." ³⁴Then he said, "Do it a second time"; and they did it a second time. Again he said, "Do it a third time"; and they did it a third time, ³⁵so that the water ran all around the altar, and filled the trench also with water.

³⁶At the time of the offering of the oblation, the prophet Elijah came near and said, "O Lord, God of Abraham, Isaac, and Israel, let it be known this day that you are God in Israel, that I am your servant, and that I have done all these things at your bidding. ³⁷Answer me, O Lord, answer me, so that this people may know that you, O Lord, are God, and that you have turned their hearts back." ³⁸Then the fire of the Lord fell and consumed the burnt offering, the wood, the stones, and the dust, and even licked up the water that was in the trench. ³⁹When all the people saw it, they fell on their faces and said, "The Lord indeed is God; the Lord indeed is God."

Prayer Starter: I want to be true to you, Lord, even if I'm the only Christian in my group. Keep me faithful.

Memory Verse: Keep the charge of the LORD your God, walking in his ways . . .

—*1 Kings 2.3a*

Chariot of Fire

Elijah said to him, "Elisha, stay here; for the LORD has sent me to Jericho." But he said, "As the LORD lives, and as you yourself live, I will not leave you." So they came to Jericho. ⁵The company of prophets*ᵃ* who were at Jericho drew near to Elisha, and said to him, "Do you know that today the LORD will take your master away from you?" And he answered, "Yes, I know; be silent."

⁶Then Elijah said to him, "Stay here; for the LORD has sent me to the Jordan." But he said, "As the LORD lives, and as you yourself live, I will not leave you." So the two of them went on. ⁷Fifty men of the company of prophets also went, and stood at some distance from them, as they both were standing by the Jordan. ⁸Then Elijah took his mantle and rolled it up, and struck the water; the water was parted to the one side and to the other, until the two of them crossed on dry ground.

⁹When they had crossed, Elijah said to Elisha, "Tell me what I may do for you, before I am taken from you." Elisha said, "Please let me inherit a double share of your spirit." ¹⁰He responded, "You have asked a hard thing; yet, if you see me as I am being taken from you, it will be granted you; if not, it will not." ¹¹As they continued walking and talking, a chariot of fire and horses of fire separated the two of them, and Elijah ascended in a whirlwind into heaven. ¹²Elisha kept watching and crying out, "Father, father! The chariots of Israel and its horsemen!" But when he could no longer see him, he grasped his own clothes and tore them in two pieces.

ᵃHeb sons of the prophets

Prayer Starter: I praise you, Lord, for eternal life. Thank you for all the Bible says about heaven.

Memory Verse: Keep the charge of the LORD your God, walking in his ways and keeping his statutes . . .   —*1 Kings 2.3a*

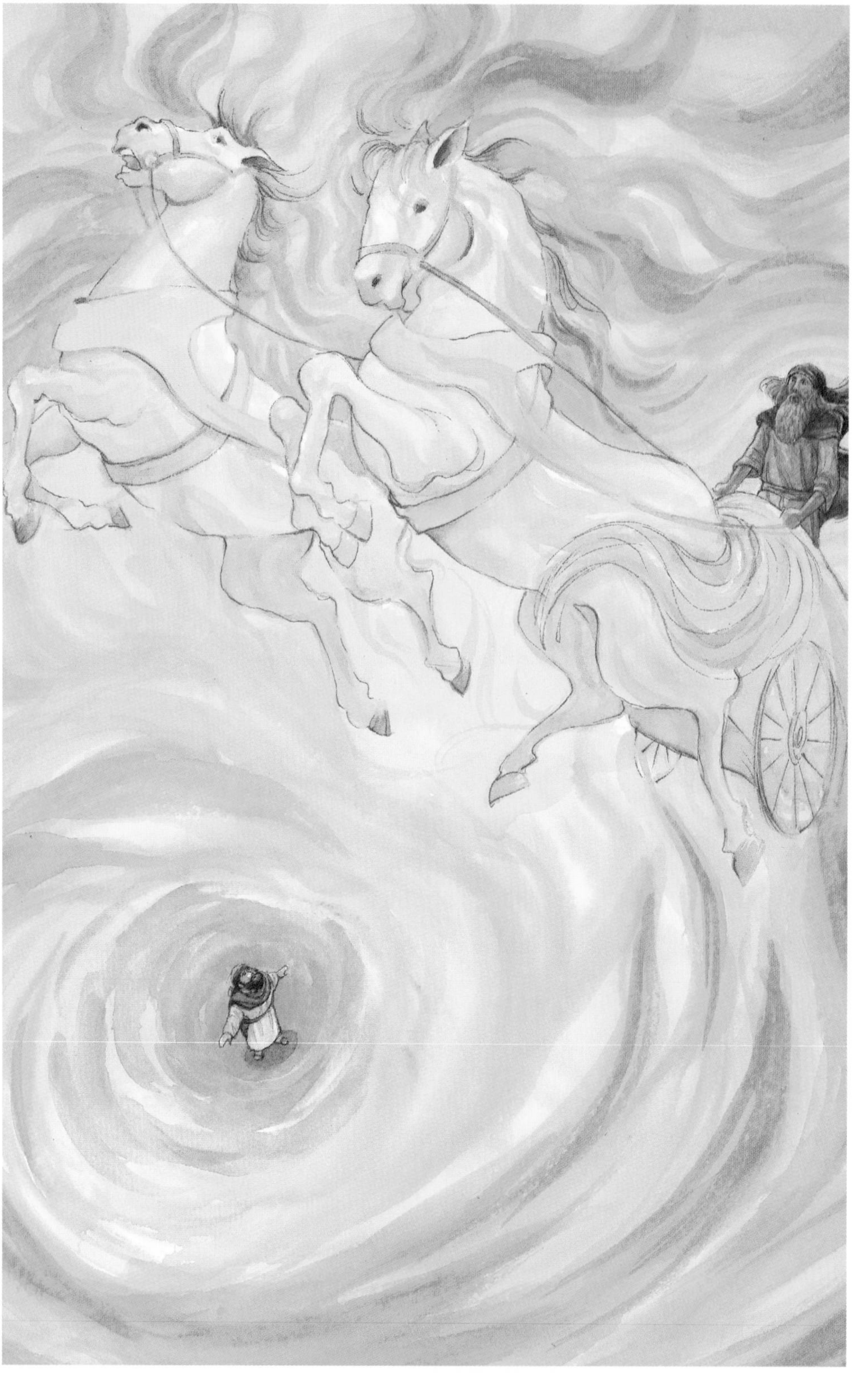

**Naaman's
Leprosy**

Naaman, commander of the army of the king of Aram, was a great man and in high favor with his master, because by him the LORD had given victory to Aram. The man, though a mighty warrior, suffered from leprosy.[a] ²Now the Arameans on one of their raids had taken a young girl captive from the land of Israel, and she served Naaman's wife. ³She said to her mistress, "If only my lord were with the prophet who is in Samaria! He would cure him of his leprosy."[a] ⁴So Naaman[b] went in and told his lord just what the girl from the land of Israel had said. ⁵And the king of Aram said, "Go then, and I will send along a letter to the king of Israel."

He went, taking with him ten talents of silver, six thousand shekels of gold, and ten sets of garments. ⁶He brought the letter to the king of Israel, which read, "When this letter reaches you, know that I have sent to you my servant Naaman, that you may cure him of his leprosy."[a] ⁷When the king of Israel read the letter, he tore his clothes and said, "Am I God, to give death or life, that this man sends word to me to cure a man of his leprosy?[a] Just look and see how he is trying to pick a quarrel with me."

⁸But when Elisha the man of God heard that the king of Israel had torn his clothes, he sent a message to the king, "Why have you torn your clothes? Let him come to me, that he may learn that there is a prophet in Israel." ⁹So Naaman came with his horses and chariots, and halted at the entrance of Elisha's house. ¹⁰Elisha sent a messenger to him, saying, "Go, wash in the Jordan seven times, and your flesh shall be restored and you shall be clean." ¹¹But Naaman became angry and went away, saying, "I thought that for me he would surely come out, and stand and call on the name of the LORD his God, and would wave his hand over the spot, and cure the leprosy![a] ¹²Are not Abana and Pharpar, the rivers of Damascus, better than all the waters of Israel? Could I not wash in them, and be clean?" He turned and went away in a rage. ¹³But his servants approached and said to him, "Father, if the prophet had commanded you to do something difficult, would you not have done it? How much more, when all he said to you was, 'Wash, and be clean'?" ¹⁴So he went down and immersed himsélf seven times in the Jordan, according to the word of the man of God; his flesh was restored like the flesh of a young boy, and he was clean.

¹⁵Then he returned to the man of God, he and all his company; he came and stood before him and said, "Now I know that there is no God in all the earth except in Israel; please accept a present from your servant."

[a]A term for several skin diseases; precise meaning uncertain
[b]Heb *he*

Prayer Starter: Make me clean on the inside, dear God. May my mind and spirit be holy.

Memory Verse: Keep the charge of the LORD your God, walking in his ways and keeping his statutes, his commandments, his ordinances . . .

—*1 Kings 2.3a*

Fiery Horses, Flaming Chariots

Once when the king of Aram was at war with Israel, he took counsel with his officers. He said, "At such and such a place shall be my camp." ⁹But the man of God sent word to the king of Israel, "Take care not to pass this place, because the Arameans are going down there." ¹⁰The king of Israel sent word to the place of which the man of God spoke. More than once or twice he warned such a place*ᵃ* so that it was on the alert.

¹¹The mind of the king of Aram was greatly perturbed because of this; he called his officers and said to them, "Now tell me who among us sides with the king of Israel?" ¹²Then one of his officers said, "No one, my lord king. It is Elisha, the prophet in Israel, who tells the king of Israel the words that you speak in your bedchamber." ¹³He said, "Go and find where he is; I will send and seize him." He was told, "He is in Dothan." ¹⁴So he sent horses and chariots there and a great army; they came by night, and surrounded the city.

¹⁵When an attendant of the man of God rose early in the morning and went out, an army with horses and chariots was all around the city. His servant said, "Alas, master! What shall we do?" ¹⁶He replied, "Do not be afraid, for there are more with us than there are with them." ¹⁷Then Elisha prayed: "O LORD, please open his eyes that he may see." So the LORD opened the eyes of the servant, and he saw; the mountain was full of horses and chariots of fire all around Elisha. ¹⁸When the Arameans*ᵇ* came down against him, Elisha prayed to the LORD, and said, "Strike this people, please, with blindness." So he struck them with blindness as Elisha had asked. ¹⁹Elisha said to them, "This is not the way, and this is not the city; follow me, and I will bring you to the man whom you seek." And he led them to Samaria.

²⁰As soon as they entered Samaria, Elisha said, "O LORD, open the eyes of these men so that they may see." The LORD opened their eyes, and they saw that they were inside Samaria. ²¹When the king of Israel saw them he said to Elisha, "Father, shall I kill them? Shall I kill them?" ²²He answered, "No! Did you capture with your sword and your bow those whom you want to kill? Set food and water before them so that they may eat and drink; and let them go to their master."

*ᵃ*Heb *warned it*
*ᵇ*Heb *they*

Prayer Starter: Keep your angels around us, heavenly Father. Keep us safe wherever we go.

Memory Verse: Keep the charge of the LORD your God, walking in his ways and keeping his statutes, his commandments, his ordinances, and his testimonies.

—*1 Kings 2.3a*

Jezebel

When Jehu came to Jezreel, Jezebel heard of it; she painted her eyes, and adorned her head, and looked out of the window. ³¹As Jehu entered the gate, she said, "Is it peace, Zimri, murderer of your master?" ³²He looked up to the window and said, "Who is on my side? Who?" Two or three eunuchs looked out at him. ³³He said, "Throw her down." So they threw her down; some of her blood spattered on the wall and on the horses, which trampled on her. ³⁴Then he went in and ate and drank; he said, "See to

that cursed woman and bury her; for she is a king's daughter." ³⁵But when they went to bury her, they found no more of her than the skull and the feet and the palms of her hands. ³⁶When they came back and told him, he said, "This is the word of the LORD, which he spoke by his servant Elijah the Tishbite, 'In the territory of Jezreel the dogs shall eat the flesh of Jezebel; ³⁷the corpse of Jezebel shall be like dung on the field in the territory of Jezreel, so that no one can say, This is Jezebel.'"

Prayer Starter: Some people are hard and cruel, dear Lord. Help me to leave them in your hands. Make me kind and strong.

Memory Verse: Be still . . .   *—Psalm 46.10*

Hezekiah Prays

When the king[a] heard concerning King Tirhakah of Ethiopia,[b] "See, he has set out to fight against you," he sent messengers again to Hezekiah, saying, [10]"Thus shall you speak to King Hezekiah of Judah: Do not let your God on whom you rely deceive you by promising that Jerusalem will not be given into the hand of the king of Assyria. [11]See, you have heard what the kings of Assyria have done to all lands, destroying them utterly. Shall you be delivered?"

[14]Hezekiah received the letter from the hand of the messengers and read it; then Hezekiah went up to the house of the LORD and spread it before the LORD. [15]And Hezekiah prayed before the LORD, and said: "O LORD the God of Israel, who are enthroned above the cherubim, you are God, you alone, of all the kingdoms of the earth; you have made heaven and earth. [16]Incline your ear, O LORD, and hear; open your eyes, O LORD, and see; hear the words of Sennacherib, which he has sent to mock the living God. [17]Truly, O LORD, the kings of Assyria have laid waste the nations and their lands, [18]and have hurled their gods into the fire, though they were no gods but the work of human hands—wood and stone—and so they were destroyed. [19]So now, O LORD our God, save us, I pray you, from his hand, so that all the kingdoms of the earth may know that you, O LORD, are God alone."

[35]That very night the angel of the LORD set out and struck down one hundred eighty-five thousand in the camp of the Assyrians; when morning dawned, they were all dead bodies. [36]Then King Sennacherib of Assyria left, went home, and lived at Nineveh.

[a]Heb *he*
[b]Or *Nubia*; Heb *Cush*

Prayer Starter: Protect our nation, dear Lord, and bless our country. Keep us safe from war.

Memory Verse: Be still, and know . . .   —*Psalm 46.10*

Hezekiah's Guests

In those days Hezekiah became sick and was at the point of death. The prophet Isaiah son of Amoz came to him, and said to him, "Thus says the LORD: Set your house in order, for you shall die; you shall not recover." ²Then Hezekiah turned his face to the wall and prayed to the LORD: ³"Remember now, O LORD, I implore you, how I have walked before you in faithfulness with a whole heart, and have done what is good in your sight." Hezekiah wept bitterly.

⁷Then Isaiah said, "Bring a lump of figs. Let them take it and apply it to the boil, so that he may recover."

⁸Hezekiah said to Isaiah, "What shall be the sign that the LORD will heal me, and that I shall go up to the house of the LORD on the third day?" ⁹Isaiah said, "This is the sign to you from the LORD, that the LORD will do the thing that he has promised: the shadow has now advanced ten intervals; shall it retreat ten intervals?" ¹⁰Hezekiah answered, "It is normal for the shadow to lengthen ten intervals; rather let the shadow retreat ten intervals." ¹¹The prophet Isaiah cried to the LORD; and he brought the shadow back the ten intervals, by which the sun[a] had declined on the dial of Ahaz.

¹²At that time King Merodach-baladan son of Baladan of Babylon sent envoys with letters and a present to Hezekiah, for he had heard that Hezekiah had been sick. ¹³Hezekiah welcomed them;[b] he showed them all his treasure house, the silver, the gold, the spices, the precious oil, his armory, all that was found in his storehouses; there was nothing in his house or in all his realm that Hezekiah did not show them. ¹⁴Then the prophet Isaiah came to King Hezekiah, and said to him, "What did these men say? From where did they come to you?" Hezekiah answered, "They have come from a far country, from Babylon." ¹⁵He said, "What have they seen in your house?" Hezekiah answered, "They have seen all that is in my house; there is nothing in my storehouses that I did not show them."

¹⁶Then Isaiah said to Hezekiah, "Hear the word of the LORD: ¹⁷Days are coming when all that is in your house, and that which your ancestors have stored up until this day, shall be carried to Babylon; nothing shall be left, says the LORD. ¹⁸Some of your own sons who are born to you shall be taken away; they shall be eunuchs in the palace of the king of Babylon." ¹⁹Then Hezekiah said to Isaiah, "The word of the LORD that you have spoken is good." For he thought, "Why not, if there will be peace and security in my days?"

[a]Syr See Isa 38.8 and Tg: Heb *it*
[b]Gk Vg Syr: Heb *When Hezekiah heard about them*

Prayer Starter: You know the future, Lord. Guide me day by day.

Memory Verse: Be still, and know that I am God! . . .   —*Psalm 46.10*

The Book of God's Law

Then the king directed that all the elders of Judah and Jerusalem should be gathered to him. [2]The king went up to the house of the LORD, and with him went all the people of Judah, all the inhabitants of Jerusalem, the priests, the prophets, and all the people, both small and great; he read in their hearing all the words of the book of the covenant that had been found in the house of the LORD. [3]The king stood by the pillar and made a covenant before the LORD, to follow the LORD, keeping his commandments, his decrees, and his statutes, with all his heart and all his soul, to perform the words of this covenant that were written in this book. All the people joined in the covenant.

[4]The king commanded the high priest Hilkiah, the priests of the second order, and the guardians of the threshold, to bring out of the temple of the LORD all the vessels made for Baal, for Asherah, and for all the host of heaven; he burned them outside Jerusalem in the fields of the Kidron, and carried their ashes to Bethel.

[24]Moreover Josiah put away the mediums, wizards, teraphim,[a] idols, and all the abominations that were seen in the land of Judah and in Jerusalem, so that he established the words of the law that were written in the book that the priest Hilkiah had found in the house of the LORD. [25]Before him there was no king like him, who turned to the LORD with all his heart, with all his soul, and with all his might, according to all the law of Moses; nor did any like him arise after him.

[a]Or *household gods*

Prayer Starter: Help me to try hard to obey your Word. And give me strength to live a holy life.

Memory Verse: Be still, and know that I am God! I am exalted among the nations . . .   *—Psalm 46.10*

The Three Warriors

David resided in the stronghold; therefore it was called the city of David. [8]He built the city all around, from the Millo in complete circuit; and Joab repaired the rest of the city. [9]And David became greater and greater, for the LORD of hosts was with him.

[10]Now these are the chiefs of David's warriors, who gave him strong support in his kingdom, together with all Israel, to make him king, according to the word of the LORD concerning Israel. [11]This is an account of David's mighty warriors: Jashobeam, son of Hachmoni,[a] was chief of the Three;[b] he wielded his spear against three hundred whom he killed at one time.

[12]And next to him among the three warriors was Eleazar son of Dodo, the Ahohite. [13]He was with David at Pas-dammim when the Philistines were gathered there for battle. There was a plot of ground full of barley. Now the people had fled from the Philistines, [14]but he and David took their stand in the middle of the plot, defended it, and killed the Philistines; and the LORD saved them by a great victory.

[15]Three of the thirty chiefs went down to the rock to David at the cave of Adullam, while the army of Philistines was encamped in the valley of Rephaim. [16]David was then in the stronghold; and the garrison of the Philistines was then at Bethlehem. [17]David said longingly, "O that someone would give me water to drink from the well of Bethlehem that is by the gate!" [18]Then the Three broke through the camp of the Philistines, and drew water from the well of Bethlehem that was by the gate, and they brought it to David. But David would not drink of it; he poured it out to the LORD.

[a]Or *a Hachmonite*
[b]Compare 2 Sam 23.8: *Thirty* or *captains*

Prayer Starter: You are so strong, dear Lord, that I can be brave when you are near me. I love you. I thank you.

Memory Verse: Be still, and know that I am God! I am exalted among the nations, I am exalted in the earth.   —*Psalm 46.10*

Solomon's Wealth

King Solomon made two hundred large shields of beaten gold; six hundred shekels of beaten gold went into each large shield.

[17]The king also made a great ivory throne, and overlaid it with pure gold. [18]The throne had six steps and a footstool of gold, which were attached to the throne, and on each side of the seat were arm rests and two lions standing beside the arm rests, [19]while twelve lions were standing, one on each end of a step on the six steps. The like of it was never made in any kingdom. [20]All King Solomon's drinking vessels were of gold, and all the vessels of the House of the Forest of Lebanon were of pure gold; silver was not considered as anything in the days of Solomon. [21]For the king's ships went to Tarshish with the servants of Huram; once every three years the ships of Tarshish used to come bringing gold, silver, ivory, apes, and peacocks.[a]

[22]Thus King Solomon excelled all the kings of the earth in riches and in wisdom.

[a]Or *baboons*

Prayer Starter: Keep me from loving money too much, Lord. Teach me to love your Word.

Memory Verse: For the eyes of the LORD . . .   *—2 Chronicles 16.9a*

Jehoshaphat's Ships

His [Asa's] son Jehoshaphat succeeded him, and strengthened himself against Israel. ²He placed forces in all the fortified cities of Judah, and set garrisons in the land of Judah, and in the cities of Ephraim that his father Asa had taken. ³The LORD was with Jehoshaphat, because he walked in the earlier ways of his father;*ᵃ* he did not seek the Baals, ⁴but sought the God of his father and walked in his commandments, and not according to the ways of Israel. ⁵Therefore the LORD established the kingdom in his hand. All Judah brought tribute to Jehoshaphat, and he had great riches and honor. ⁶His heart was courageous in the ways of the LORD; and furthermore he removed the high places and the sacred poles*ᵇ* from Judah.

20So Jehoshaphat reigned over Judah. He was thirty-five years old when he began to reign; he reigned twenty-five years in Jerusalem. His mother's name was Azubah daughter of Shilhi. ³²He walked in the way of his father Asa and did not turn aside from it, doing what was right in the sight of the LORD. ³³Yet the high places were not removed; the people had not yet set their hearts upon the God of their ancestors.

³⁴Now the rest of the acts of Jehoshaphat, from first to last, are written in the Annals of Jehu son of Hanani, which are recorded in the Book of the Kings of Israel.

*ᵃ*Another reading is *his father David*
*ᵇ*Heb *Asherim*

Prayer Starter: God, I know you are Lord of the winds and waves and storms. Thank you for your mighty power.

Memory Verse: For the eyes of the LORD range throughout . . .
                                                    —2 Chronicles 16.9a

Repairing the Temple

Joash was seven years old when he began to reign; he reigned forty years in Jerusalem; his mother's name was Zibiah of Beer-sheba. ²Joash did what was right in the sight of the LORD all the days of the priest Jehoiada. ³Jehoiada got two wives for him, and he became the father of sons and daughters.

⁴Some time afterward Joash decided to restore the house of the LORD. ⁵He assembled the priests and the Levites and said to them, "Go out to the cities of Judah and gather money from all Israel to repair the house of your God, year by year; and see that you act quickly." But the Levites did not act quickly. ⁶So the king summoned Jehoiada the chief, and said to him, "Why have you not required the Levites to bring in from Judah and Jerusalem the tax levied by Moses, the servant of the LORD, on*ᵃ* the congregation of Israel for the tent of the covenant?"*ᵇ* ⁷For the children of Athaliah, that wicked woman, had broken into the house of God, and had even used all the dedicated things of the house of the LORD for the Baals.

⁸So the king gave command, and they made a chest, and set it outside the gate of the house of the LORD. ⁹A proclamation was made throughout Judah and Jerusalem to bring in for the LORD the tax that Moses the ser-

vant of God laid on Israel in the wilderness. ¹⁰All the leaders and all the people rejoiced and brought their tax and dropped it into the chest until it was full. ¹¹Whenever the chest was brought to the king's officers by the Levites, when they saw that there was a large amount of money in it, the king's secretary and the officer of the chief priest would come and empty the chest and take it and return it to its place. So they did day after day, and collected money in abundance. ¹²The king and Jehoiada gave it to those who had charge of the work of the house of the LORD, and they hired masons and carpenters to restore the house of the LORD, and also workers in iron and bronze to repair the house of the LORD. ¹³So those who were engaged in the work labored, and the repairing went forward at their hands, and they restored the house of God to its proper condition and strengthened it. ¹⁴When they had finished, they brought the rest of the money to the king and Jehoiada, and with it were made utensils for the house of the LORD, utensils for the service and for the burnt offerings, and ladles, and vessels of gold and silver. They offered burnt offerings in the house of the LORD regularly all the days of Jehoiada.

¹⁵But Jehoiada grew old and full of days, and died; he was one hundred thirty years old at his death. ¹⁶And they buried him in the city of David among the kings, because he had done good in Israel, and for God and his house.

ᵃCompare Vg: Heb *and*
ᵇOr *treaty*, or *testimony*; Hed *eduth*

Prayer Starter: Thank you for our church, dear Lord. Please give wise and godly hearts to our church leaders.

Memory Verse: For the eyes of the LORD range throughout the entire earth . . .
—*2 Chronicles 16.9a*

Uzziah

Then all the people of Judah took Uzziah, who was sixteen years old, and made him king to succeed his father Amaziah. ²He rebuilt Eloth and restored it to Judah, after the king slept with his ancestors. ³Uzziah was sixteen years old when he began to reign, and he reigned fifty-two years in Jerusalem. His mother's name was Jecoliah of Jerusalem.

¹⁵And his fame spread far, for he was marvelously helped until he became strong.

¹⁶But when he had become strong he grew proud, to his destruction. For he was false to the LORD his God, and entered the temple of the LORD to make offering on the altar of incense. ¹⁷But the priest Azariah went in after him, with eighty priests of the LORD who were men of valor; ¹⁸they withstood King Uzziah, and said to him, "It is not for you, Uzziah, to make offering to the LORD, but for the priests the descendants of Aaron, who are consecrated to make offering. Go out of the sanctuary; for you have done wrong, and it will bring you no honor from the LORD God." ¹⁹Then Uzziah was angry. Now he had a censer in his hand to make offering, and when he became angry with the priests a leprous[a] disease broke out on his forehead, in the presence of the priests in the house of the LORD, by the altar of incense. ²⁰When the chief priest Azariah, and all the priests, looked at him, he was leprous[a] in his forehead. They hurried him out, and he himself hurried to get out, because the LORD had struck him.

[a]A term for several skin diseases; precise meaning uncertain

Prayer Starter: Keep me from becoming proud and thinking too highly of myself. May I always put you first.

Memory Verse: For the eyes of the LORD range throughout the entire earth, to strengthen those . . .   —2 Chronicles 16.9a

Ahaz Locks the Temple Doors

He [Ahaz] did not do what was right in the sight of the LORD, as his ancestor David had done, ²but he walked in the ways of the kings of Israel. He even made cast images for the Baals; ³and he made offerings in the valley of the son of Hinnom, and made his sons pass through fire, according to the abominable practices of the nations whom the LORD drove out before the people of Israel. ⁴He sacrificed and made offerings on the high places, on the hills, and under every green tree.

²²In the time of his distress he became yet more faithless to the LORD—this same King Ahaz. ²³For he sacrificed to the gods of Damascus, which had defeated him, and said, "Because the gods of the kings of Aram helped them, I will sacrifice to them so that they may help me." But they were the ruin of him, and of all Israel. ²⁴Ahaz gathered together the utensils of the house of God, and cut in pieces the utensils of the house of God. He shut up the doors of the house of the LORD and made himself altars in every corner of Jerusalem.

Prayer Starter: The doors of my heart are open to you, O Lord. Never let them close.

Memory Verse: For the eyes of the LORD range throughout the entire earth, to strengthen those whose heart is true to him .

—2 Chronicles 16.9a

**Nehemiah
Before
the King**

In the month of Nisan, in the twentieth year of King Artaxerxes, when wine was served him, I carried the wine and gave it to the king. Now, I had never been sad in his presence before. ²So the king said to me, "Why is your face sad, since you are not sick? This can only be sadness of the heart." Then I was very much afraid. ³I said to the king, "May the king live forever! Why should my face not be sad, when the city, the place of my ancestors' graves, lies waste, and its gates have been destroyed by fire?" ⁴Then the king said to me, "What do you request?" So I prayed to the God of heaven. ⁵Then I said to the king, "If it pleases the king, and if your servant has found favor with you, I ask that you send me to Judah, to the city of my ancestors' graves, so that I may rebuild it." ⁶The king said to me (the queen also was sitting beside him), "How long will you be gone, and when will you return?" So it pleased the king to send me, and I set him a date. ⁷Then I said to the king, "If it pleases the king, let letters be given me to the governors of the province Beyond the River, that they may grant me passage until I arrive in Judah; ⁸and a letter to Asaph, the keeper of the king's forest, directing him to give me timber to make beams for the gates of the temple fortress, and for the wall of the city, and for the house that I shall occupy." And the king granted me what I asked, for the gracious hand of my God was upon me.

Prayer Starter: Lord God of heaven, you are great, and you faithfully keep your promises.

Memory Verse: O LORD God of heaven . . .   *—Nehemiah 1.5*

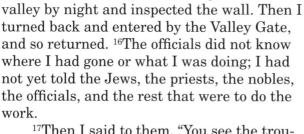

Rebuilding Jerusalem's Walls

So I came to Jerusalem and was there for three days. ¹²Then I got up during the night, I and a few men with me; I told no one what my God had put into my heart to do for Jerusalem. The only animal I took was the animal I rode. ¹³I went out by night by the Valley Gate past the Dragon's Spring and to the Dung Gate, and I inspected the walls of Jerusalem that had been broken down and its gates that had been destroyed by fire. ¹⁴Then I went on to the Fountain Gate and to the King's Pool; but there was no place for the animal I was riding to continue. ¹⁵So I went up by way of the valley by night and inspected the wall. Then I turned back and entered by the Valley Gate, and so returned. ¹⁶The officials did not know where I had gone or what I was doing; I had not yet told the Jews, the priests, the nobles, the officials, and the rest that were to do the work.

¹⁷Then I said to them, "You see the trouble we are in, how Jerusalem lies in ruins with its gates burned. Come, let us rebuild the wall of Jerusalem, so that we may no longer suffer disgrace." ¹⁸I told them that the hand of my God had been gracious upon me, and also the words that the king had spoken to me. Then they said, "Let us start building!" So they committed themselves to the common good.

Prayer Starter: Make me a hard worker, dear Lord.

Memory Verse: O Lord God of heaven, the great and awesome God . . .
—*Nehemiah 1.5*

Tobit Goes Blind

Then during the reign of Esar-haddon[a] I returned home, and my wife Anna and my son Tobias were restored to me. At our festival of Pentecost, which is the sacred festival of weeks, a good dinner was prepared for me and I reclined to eat. ²When the table was set for me and an abundance of food placed before me, I said to my son Tobias, "Go, my child, and bring whatever poor person you may find of our people among the exiles in Nineveh, who is wholeheartedly mindful of God,[b] and he shall eat together with me. I will wait for you, until you come back." ³So Tobias went to look for some poor person of our people. When he had returned he said, "Father!" And I replied, "Here I am, my child." Then he went on to say, "Look, father, one of our own people has been murdered and thrown into the market place, and now he lies there strangled." ⁴Then I sprang up, left the dinner before even tasting it, and removed the body[c] from the square[d] and laid it[c] in one of the rooms until sunset when I might bury it.[c] ⁵When I returned, I washed myself and ate my food in sorrow. ⁶Then I remembered the prophecy of Amos, how he said against Bethel,

> "Your festivals shall be turned into mourning,
> and all your songs into lamentation."

And I wept.

⁷When the sun had set, I went and dug a grave and buried him. ⁸And my neighbors laughed and said, "Is he still not afraid? He has already been hunted down to be put to death for doing this, and he ran away; yet here he is again burying the dead!" ⁹That same night I washed myself and went into my courtyard and slept by the wall of the courtyard; and my face was uncovered because of the heat. ¹⁰I did not know

Prayer Starter: Lord, please help me to be kind to all people.

Memory Verse: O Lord God of heaven, the great and awesome God who keeps covenant . . .   —*Nehemiah 1.5*

that there were sparrows on the wall; their fresh droppings fell into my eyes and produced white films. I went to physicians to be healed, but the more they treated me with ointments the more my vision was obscured by the white films, until I became completely blind. For four years I remained unable to see. All my kindred were sorry for me, and Ahikar took care of me for two years before he went to Elymais.

*a*Gk *Sacherdonos*
*b*Lat: Gk *wholeheartedly mindful*
*c*Gk *him*
*d*Other ancient authorities lack *from the square*

God Hears Tobit's Prayers

Then with much grief and anguish of heart I wept, and with groaning began to pray:
2 "You are righteous, O Lord,
    and all your deeds are just;
all your ways are mercy and truth;
    you judge the world.*a*
3 And now, O Lord, remember me
and look favorably upon me.
Do not punish me for my sins
    and for my unwitting offenses
    and those that my ancestors
        committed before you.
They sinned against you.

16At that very moment, the prayers of both of them were heard in the glorious presence of God. 17So Raphael was sent to heal both of them: Tobit, by removing the white films from his eyes, so that he might see God's light with his eyes; and Sarah, daughter of Raguel, by giving her in marriage to Tobias son of Tobit, and by setting her free from the wicked demon Asmodeus. For Tobias was entitled to have her before all others who had desired to marry her. At the same time that Tobit returned from the courtyard into his house, Sarah daughter of Raguel came down from her upper room.

*a*Other ancient authorities read *you render true and righteous judgment forever*

Prayer Starter: Thank you, God, for hearing prayer.

Memory Verse: O Lord God of heaven, the great and awesome God who keeps covenant and steadfast love with those . . .   —*Nehemiah 1.5*

Tobit Is Healed

When they came near to Kaserin, which is opposite Nineveh, Raphael said, [2]"You are aware of how we left your father. [3]Let us run ahead of your wife and prepare the house while they are still on the way." [4]As they went on together Raphael[a] said to him, "Have the gall ready." And the dog[b] went along behind them.

[5]Meanwhile Anna sat looking intently down the road by which her son would come. [6]When she caught sight of him coming, she said to his father, "Look, your son is coming, and the man who went with him!"

[7]Raphael said to Tobias, before he had approached his father, "I know that his eyes will be opened. [8]Smear the gall of the fish on his eyes; the medicine will make the white films shrink and peel off from his eyes, and your father will regain his sight and see the light."

[9]Then Anna ran up to her son and threw her arms around him, saying, "Now that I have seen you, my child, I am ready to die." And she wept. [10]Then Tobit got up and came stumbling out through the courtyard door. Tobias went up to him, [11]with the gall of the fish in his hand, and holding him firmly, he blew into his eyes, saying, "Take courage, father." With this he applied the medicine on his eyes, [12]and it made them smart.[c] [13]Next, with both his hands he peeled off the white films from the corners of his eyes. Then Tobit[a] saw his son and[d] threw his arms around him, [14]and he wept and said to him, "I see you, my son, the light of my eyes!" Then he said,

"Blessed be God,
    and blessed be his great name,
    and blessed be all his holy angels.
May his holy name be blessed[e]
    throughout all the ages."

[a]Gk *he*
[b]Codex Sinaiticus reads *And the Lord*
[c]Lat: Meaning of Gk uncertain
[d]Other ancient authorities lack *saw his son and*
[e]Codex Sinaiticus reads *May his great name be upon us and blessed be all the angels.*

Prayer Starter: Thank you, God, that you are the one who heals people.

Memory Verse: O Lord God of heaven, the great and awesome God who keeps covenant and steadfast love with those who love him and keep his commandments.
—*Nehemiah 1.5*

Judith Prays for Help

Then Judith prostrated herself, put ashes on her head, and uncovered the sackcloth she was wearing. At the very time when the evening incense was being offered in the house of God in Jerusalem, Judith cried out to the Lord with a loud voice, and said,

⁹"Look at their pride, and send your wrath upon their heads. Give to me, a widow, the strong hand to do what I plan. ¹⁰By the deceit of my lips strike down the slave with the prince and the prince with his servant; crush their arrogance by the hand of a woman.

¹¹"For your strength does not depend on numbers, nor your might on the powerful. But you are the God of the lowly, helper of the oppressed, upholder of the weak, protector of the forsaken, savior of those without hope. ¹²Please, please, God of my father, God of the heritage of Israel, Lord of heaven and earth, Creator of the waters, King of all your creation, hear my prayer! ¹³Make my deceitful words bring wound and bruise on those who have planned cruel things against your covenant, and against your sacred house, and against Mount Zion, and against the house your children possess. ¹⁴Let your whole nation and every tribe know and understand that you are God, the God of all power and might, and that there is no other who protects the people of Israel but you alone!"

Prayer Starter: Thank you, Lord, for being my all-powerful Protector.

Memory Verse: If you direct your heart rightly . . . —*Job 11.13–14a*

Judith's Song of Praise

And Judith said,
Begin a song to my God with tambourines,
    sing to my Lord with cymbals.
Raise to him a new psalm;[a]
    exalt him, and call upon his name.
2 For the Lord is a God who crushes wars;
    he sets up his camp among his people;
he delivered me from the hands of my pursuers.

5 But the Lord Almighty has foiled them
    by the hand of a woman.[b]

7 For she put away her widow's clothing
    to exalt the oppressed in Israel.
She anointed her face with perfume;
8   she fastened her hair with a tiara
    and put on a linen gown to beguile him.
9 Her sandal ravished his eyes,
    her beauty captivated his mind,
    and the sword severed his neck!

13 I will sing to my God a new song:
O Lord, you are great and glorious,
    wonderful in strength, invincible.
14 Let all your creatures serve you,
    for you spoke, and they were made.
You sent forth your spirit,[c] and it formed them;[d]
    there is none that can resist your voice.
15 For the mountains shall be shaken to their foundations
      with the waters;
    before your glance the rocks shall melt like wax.
But to those who fear you
    you show mercy.

[a]Other ancient authorities read *a psalm and praise*
[b]Other ancient authorities add *he has confounded them*
[c]Or *breath*
[d]Other ancient authorities read *they were created*

Prayer Starter: Dear God, help me to sing a new song of praise!

Memory Verse: If you direct your heart rightly, you will stretch out your hands toward him. . . .   *—Job 11.13–14a*

Mordecai[a] had brought up Hadassah, that is Esther, his cousin, for she had neither father nor mother; the girl was fair and beautiful, and when her father and her mother died, Mordecai adopted her as his own daughter. [8]So when the king's order and his edict were proclaimed, and when many young women were gathered in the citadel of Susa in custody of Hegai, Esther also was taken into the king's palace and put in custody of Hegai, who had charge of the women. [9]The girl pleased him and won his favor, and he quickly provided her with her cosmetic treatments and her portion of food, and with seven chosen maids from the king's palace, and advanced her and her maids to the best place in the harem. [10]Esther did not reveal her people or kindred, for Mordecai had charged her not to tell. [11]Every day Mordecai would walk around in front of the court of the harem, to learn how Esther was and how she fared.

[12]The turn came for each girl to go in to King Ahasuerus, after being twelve months under the regulations for the women, since this was the regular period of their cosmetic treatment, six months with oil of myrrh and six months with perfumes and cosmetics for women.

[15]When the turn came for Esther daughter of Abihail the uncle of Mordecai, who had adopted her as his own daughter, to go in to the king, she asked for nothing except what Hegai the king's eunuch, who had charge of the women, advised. Now Esther was admired by all who saw her. [16]When Esther was taken to King Ahasuerus in his royal palace in the tenth month, which is the month of Tebeth, in the seventh year of his reign, [17]the king loved Esther more than all the other women; of all the virgins she won his favor and devotion, so that he set the royal crown on her head and made her queen instead of Vashti. [18]Then the king gave a great banquet to all his officials and ministers—"Esther's banquet." He also granted a holiday[b] to the provinces, and gave gifts with royal liberality.

[a]Heb *He*
[b]Or *an amnesty*

Prayer Starter: Heavenly Father, I believe you guide world rulers even when they don't know it. Bless our nation and our leaders today.

Memory Verse: If you direct your heart rightly, you will stretch out your hands toward him. If iniquity . . .   —*Job 11.13–14a*

Mordecai and Esther Pray

After these things King Ahasuerus promoted Haman son of Hammedatha the Agagite, and advanced him and set his seat above all the officials who were with him.

⁸Then Haman said to King Ahasuerus, "There is a certain people scattered and separated among the peoples in all the provinces of your kingdom; their laws are different from those of every other people, and they do not keep the king's laws, so that it is not appropriate for the king to tolerate them. ⁹If it pleases the king, let a decree be issued for their destruction, and I will pay ten thousand talents of silver into the hands of those who have charge of the king's business, so that they may put it into the king's treasuries." ¹⁰So the king took his signet ring from his hand and gave it to Haman son of Hammedatha the Agagite, the enemy of the Jews. ¹¹The king said to Haman, "The money is given to you, and the people as well, to do with them as it seems good to you."

4When Mordecai learned all that had been done, Mordecai tore his clothes and put on sackcloth and ashes, and went through the city, wailing with a loud and bitter cry; ²he went up to the entrance of the king's gate clothed with sackcloth. ³In every province, wherever the king's command and his decree came, there was great mourning among the Jews, with fasting and weeping and lamenting, and most of them lay in sackcloth and ashes.

13Then Mordecai prayed to the Lord, calling to remembrance all the works of the Lord.

⁹He said, "O Lord, Lord, you rule as King over all things, for the universe is in your power and there is no one who can oppose you when it is your will to save Israel, ¹⁰for you have made heaven and earth and every wonderful thing under heaven. ¹¹You are Lord of all, and there is no one who can resist you, the Lord.

¹⁵"And now, O Lord God and King, God of Abraham, spare your people; for the eyes of our foes are upon us to annihilate us, and they desire to destroy the inheritance that has been yours from the beginning."

¹⁸And all Israel cried out mightily, for their death was before their eyes.

14Then Queen Esther, seized with deadly anxiety, fled to the Lord. ²She took off her splendid apparel and put on the garments of distress and mourning, and instead of costly perfumes she covered her head with ashes and dung, and she utterly humbled her body;

Prayer Starter: Thank you for thunder and lightning and wind and storms—signs of your power, dear Lord.

Memory Verse: If you direct your heart rightly, you will stretch out your hands toward him. If iniquity is in your hand . . .   —*Job 11.13–14a*

every part that she loved to adorn she covered with her tangled hair. ³She prayed to the Lord God of Israel, and said: "O my Lord, you only are our king; help me, who am alone and have no helper but you."

Save My People

On the third day, when she ended her prayer, she took off the garments in which she had worshiped, and arrayed herself in splendid attire. ⁵She was radiant with perfect beauty, and she looked happy, as if beloved, but her heart was frozen with fear. ⁶When she had gone through all the doors, she stood before the king. He was seated on his royal throne, clothed in the full array of his majesty, all covered with gold and precious stones. He was most terrifying.

¹¹Then he raised the golden scepter and touched her neck with it.

5The king said to her, "What is it, Queen Esther? What is your request? It shall be given you, even to the half of my kingdom." ⁴Then Esther said, "If it pleases the king, let the king and Haman come today to a banquet that I have prepared for the king."

7So the king and Haman went in to feast with Queen Esther. ²On the second day, as they were drinking wine, the king again said to Esther, "What is your petition, Queen Esther? It shall be granted you. And what is your request? Even to the half of my kingdom, it shall be fulfilled." ³Then Queen Esther answered, "If I have won your favor, O king, and if it pleases the king, let my life be given me—that is my petition—and the lives of my people—that is my request. ⁴For we have been sold, I and my people, to be destroyed, to be killed, and to be annihilated. If we had been sold merely as slaves, men and women, I would have held my peace; but no enemy can compensate for this damage to the king."ᵃ ⁵Then King Ahasuerus said to Queen Esther, "Who is he, and where is he, who has presumed to do this?" ⁶Esther said, "A foe and enemy, this wicked Haman!" Then Haman was terrified before the king and the queen. ⁷The king rose from the feast in wrath and went into the palace garden, but Haman stayed to beg his life from Queen Esther, for he saw that the king had determined to destroy him.

ᵃMeaning of Heb uncertain

Prayer Starter: Please help me to do the right thing always, especially during times when I am afraid.

Memory Verse: If you direct your heart rightly, you will stretch out your hands toward him. If iniquity is in your hand, put it far away.

—Job 11.13–14a

Mordecai's Dream Comes True

^aIn the second year of the reign of Ahasuerus the Great, on the first day of Nisan, Mordecai son of Jair son of Shimei^b son of Kish, of the tribe of Benjamin, had a dream. ³He was a Jew living in the city of Susa, a great man, serving in the court of the king. ⁴He was one of the captives whom King Nebuchadnezzar of Babylon had brought from Jerusalem with King Jeconiah of Judah. And this was his dream: ⁵Noises^c and confusion, thunders and earthquake, tumult on the earth! ⁶Then two great dragons came forward, both ready to fight, and they roared terribly. ⁷At their roaring every nation prepared for war, to fight against the righteous nation. ⁸It was a day of darkness and gloom, of tribulation and distress, affliction and great tumult on the earth! ⁹And the whole righteous nation was troubled; they feared the evils that threatened them,^d and were ready to perish. ¹⁰They they cried out to God; and at their outcry, as though from a tiny spring, there came a great river, with abundant water; ¹¹light came, and the sun rose, and the lowly were exalted and devoured those held in honor.

¹²Mordecai saw in this dream what God had determined to do, and after he awoke he had it on his mind, seeking all day to understand it in every detail.

10 ^eAnd Mordecai said, "These things have come from God; ⁵for I remember the dream that I had concerning these matters, and none of them has failed to be fulfilled. ⁶There was the little spring that became a river, and there was light and sun and abundant water—the river is Esther, whom the king married and made queen. ⁷The two dragons are Haman and myself. ⁸The nations are those that gathered to destroy the name of the Jews. ⁹And my nation, this is Israel, who cried out to God and were saved. The Lord has saved his people; the Lord has rescued us from all these evils; God has done great signs and wonders, wonders that have never happened among the nations. ¹⁰For this purpose he made two lots, one for the people of God and one for all the nations, ¹¹and these two lots came to the hour and moment and day of decision before God and among all the nations. ¹²And God remembered his people and vindicated his inheritance. ¹³So they will observe these days in the month of Adar, on the fourteenth and fifteenth^f of that month, with an assembly and joy and gladness before God, from generation to generation forever among his people Israel."

^aChapters 11.2—12.6 correspond to chapter A 1–17 in some translations.
^bGk *Semeios*
^cOr *Voices*
^dGk *their own evils*
^eChapters 10.4–13 and 11.1 correspond to chapter F 1–11 in some translations.
^fOther ancient authorities lack *and fifteenth*

Prayer Starter: Thank you, Lord, for choosing me.

Memory Verse: I will sing to my God a new song . . . *—Judith 16.13*

> **Judas Dedicates the Temple**

Then Judas and his brothers said, "See, our enemies are crushed; let us go up to cleanse the sanctuary and dedicate it." [37]So all the army assembled and went up to Mount Zion. [38]There they saw the sanctuary desolate, the altar profaned, and the gates burned. In the courts they saw bushes sprung up as in a thicket, or as on one of the mountains. They saw also the chambers of the priests in ruins. [39]Then they tore their clothes and mourned with great lamentation; they sprinkled themselves with ashes [40]and fell down on the ground. And when the signal was given with the trumpets, they cried out to Heaven.

[41]Then Judas detailed men to fight against those in the citadel until he had cleansed the sanctuary. [42]He chose blameless priests devoted to the law, [43]and they cleansed the sanctuary and removed the defiled stones to an unclean place. [44]They deliberated what to do about the altar of burnt offering which had been profaned. [45]And they thought it best to tear it down, so that it would not be a lasting shame to them that the Gentiles had defiled it. So they tore down the altar, [46]and stored the stones in a convenient place on the temple hill until a prophet should come to tell what to do with them. [47]Then they took unhewn[a] stones, as the law directs, and built a new altar like the former one. [48]They also rebuilt the sanctuary and the interior of the temple, and consecrated the courts. [49]They made new holy vessels, and brought the lampstand, the altar of incense, and the table into the temple. [50]Then they offered incense on the altar and lit the lamps on the lampstand, and these gave light in the temple. [51]They placed the bread on the table and hung up the curtains. Thus they finished all the work they had undertaken.

[52]Early in the morning on the twenty-fifth day of the ninth month, which is the month of Chislev in the one hundred forty-eighth year,[b] [53]they rose and offered sacrifice, as the law directs, on the new altar of burnt offering that they had built. [54]At the very season and on the very day that the Gentiles had profaned it, it was dedicated with songs and harps and lutes and cymbals. [55]All the people fell on their faces and worshiped and blessed Heaven, who had prospered them. [56]So they celebrated the dedication of the altar for eight days and joyfully offered burnt offerings; they offered a sacrifice of well-being and a thanksgiving offering. [57]They decorated the front of the temple with golden crowns and small shields; they restored the gates and the chambers for the priests, and fitted them with doors. [58]There was very great joy among the people, and the disgrace brought by the Gentiles was removed.

Prayer Starter: Help me, Lord, to worship you everywhere I go.

Memory Verse: I will sing to my God a new song: O Lord, you are great . . .
—Judith 16.13

⁵⁹Then Judas and his brothers and all the assembly of Israel determined that every year at that season the days of dedication of the altar should be observed with joy and gladness for eight days, beginning with the twenty-fifth day of the month of Chislev.

⁶⁰At that time they fortified Mount Zion with high walls and strong towers all around, to keep the Gentiles from coming and trampling them down as they had done before.

ᵃGk *whole*
ᵇ164 B.C.

Simon: A Good Leader

The land[a] had rest all the days of Simon.
    He sought the good of his nation;
his rule was pleasing to them,
    as was the honor shown him, all his days.
⁵ To crown all his honors he took Joppa for a
    harbor,
    and opened a way to the isles of the sea.

⁷ He gathered a host of captives;
    he ruled over Gazara and Beth-zur and the citadel,
and he removed its uncleanness from it:
    and there was none to oppose him.
⁸ They tilled their land in peace;
    the ground gave its increase,
    and the trees of the plains their fruit.
⁹ Old men sat in the streets;
    they all talked together of
        good things,
    and the youths put on splendid
        military attire.

¹⁰ He supplied the towns with food,
    and furnished them with the
        means of defense,
    until his renown spread to the
        ends of the earth.
¹¹ He established peace in the land,
    and Israel rejoiced with great
        joy.
¹² All the people sat under their own
        vines and fig trees,
    and there was none to make them afraid.

¹⁵ He made the sanctuary glorious,
    and added to the vessels of the sanctuary.

[a]Other ancient authorities add *of Judah*

Prayer Starter: Dear God, today I pray for the leaders of my country. Help them to do what is right in your sight.

Memory Verse: I will sing to my God a new song: O Lord, you are great and glorious . . .
—*Judith 16.13*

Heliodorus Tries to Rob the Temple

While they were calling upon the Almighty Lord that he would keep what had been entrusted safe and secure for those who had entrusted it, ²³Heliodorus went on with what had been decided. ²⁴But when he arrived at the treasury with his bodyguard, then and there the Sovereign of spirits and of all authority caused so great a manifestation that all who had been so bold as to accompany him were astounded by the power of God, and became faint with terror. ²⁵For there appeared to them a magnificently caparisoned horse, with a rider of frightening mien; it rushed furiously at Heliodorus and struck at him with its front hoofs. Its rider was seen to have armor and weapons of gold. ²⁶Two young men also appeared to him, remarkably strong, gloriously beautiful and splendidly dressed, who stood on either side of him and flogged him continuously, inflicting many blows on him. ²⁷When he suddenly fell to the ground and deep darkness came over him, his men took him up, put him on a stretcher, ²⁸and carried him away—this man who had just entered the aforesaid treasury with a great retinue and all his bodyguard but was now unable to help himself. They recognized clearly the sovereign power of God.

²⁹While he lay prostrate, speechless because of the divine interven-

tion and deprived of any hope of recovery, ³⁰they praised the Lord who had acted marvelously for his own place. And the temple, which a little while before was full of fear and disturbance, was filled with joy and gladness, now that the Almighty Lord had appeared.

³¹Some of Heliodorus's friends quickly begged Onias to call upon the Most High to grant life to one who was lying quite at his last breath. ³²So the high priest, fearing that the king might get the notion that some foul play had been perpetrated by the Jews with regard to Heliodorus, offered sacrifice for the man's recovery. ³³While the high priest was making an atonement, the same young men appeared again to Heliodorus dressed

in the same clothing, and they stood and said, "Be very grateful to the high priest Onias, since for his sake the Lord has granted you your life. [34]And see that you, who have been flogged by heaven, report to all people the majestic power of God." Having said this they vanished.

[35]Then Heliodorus offered sacrifice to the Lord and made very great vows to the Savior of his life, and having bidden Onias farewell, he marched off with his forces to the king. [36]He bore testimony to all concerning the deeds of the supreme God, which he had seen with his own eyes.

Prayer Starter: Dear Lord, please continue to protect everything that belongs to you.

Memory Verse: I will sing to my God a new song: O Lord, you are great and glorious, wonderful in strength . . .   —*Judith 16.13*

A Brave Mother

It happened also that seven brothers and their mother were arrested and were being compelled by the king, under torture with whips and thongs, to partake of unlawful swine's flesh.

²⁰The mother was especially admirable and worthy of honorable memory. Although she saw her seven sons perish within a single day, she bore it with good courage because of her hope in the Lord. ²¹She encouraged each of them in the language of their ancestors. Filled with a noble spirit, she reinforced her woman's reasoning with a man's courage.

²³Therefore the Creator of the world, who shaped the beginning of humankind and devised the origin of all things, will in his mercy give life and breath back to you again, since you now forget yourselves for the sake of his laws.

²⁴Antiochus felt that he was being treated with contempt, and he was suspicious of her reproachful tone. The youngest brother being still alive, Antiochus*^a* not only appealed to him in words, but promised with oaths that he would make him rich and enviable if he would turn from the ways of his ancestors, and that he would take him for his Friend and entrust him with public affairs. ²⁵Since the young man would not listen to him at all, the king called the mother to him and urged her to advise the youth to save himself. ²⁶After much urging on his part, she undertook to persuade her son. ²⁷But, leaning close to him, she spoke in their native language as follows, deriding the cruel tyrant: "My son, have pity on me. I carried you nine months in my womb, and nursed you for three years, and have reared you and brought you up to this point in your life, and taken care of you.*^b* ²⁸I beg you, my child, to look at the heaven and the earth and see everything that is in them, and recognize that God did not make them out of things that existed.*^c* And in the same way the human race came into being. ²⁹Do not fear this butcher, but prove worthy of your brothers. Accept death, so that in God's mercy I may get you back again along with your brothers."

*^a*Gk he
*^b*Or *have borne the burden of your education*
*^c*Or *God made them out of things that did not exist*

Prayer Starter: Thank you, God, for my parents. Help them to be brave.

Memory Verse: I will sing to my God a new song: O Lord, you are great and glorious, wonderful in strength, invincible.   —*Judith 16.13*

Job Loses Everything

There was once a man in the land of Uz whose name was Job. That man was blameless and upright, one who feared God and turned away from evil. ²There were born to him seven sons and three daughters. ³He had seven thousand sheep, three thousand camels, five hundred yoke of oxen, five hundred donkeys, and very many servants; so that this man was the greatest of all the people of the east.

2 One day the heavenly beings[a] came to present themselves before the LORD, and Satan[b] also came among them to present himself before the LORD. ²The LORD said to Satan,[b] "Where have you come from?" Satan[c] answered the LORD, "From going to and fro on the earth, and from walking up and down on it." ³The LORD said to Satan,[b] "Have you considered my servant Job? There is no one like him on the earth, a blameless and upright man who fears God and turns away from evil. He still persists in his integrity, although you incited me against him, to destroy him for no reason." ⁴Then Satan[b] answered the LORD, "Skin for skin! All that people have they will give to save their lives.[d] ⁵But stretch out your hand now and touch his bone and his flesh, and he will curse you to your face." ⁶The LORD said to Satan,[b] "Very well, he is in your power; only spare his life."

⁷So Satan[b] went out from the presence of the LORD, and inflicted loathsome sores on Job from the sole of his foot to the crown of his head. ⁸Job[e] took a potsherd with which to scrape himself, and sat among the ashes.

⁹Then his wife said to him, "Do you still persist in your integrity? Curse[f] God, and die." ¹⁰But he said to her, "You speak as any foolish woman would speak. Shall we receive the good at the hand of God, and not receive the bad?" In all this Job did not sin with his lips.

[a] Heb *sons of God*
[b] Or *the Accuser;* Heb *ha-satan*
[c] Or *The Accuser;* Heb *ha-satan*
[d] Or *All that the man has he will give for his life*
[e] Heb *He*

Prayer Starter: Keep me from being a complainer, Lord. Give me a good attitude in everything.

Memory Verse: The LORD is my shepherd . . .   —*Psalm 23.1–2*

My Shepherd

The LORD is my shepherd,
    I shall not want.
2   He makes me lie down in
        green pastures;
    he leads me beside still waters;*a*
3   he restores my soul.*b*
    He leads me in right paths*c*
    for his name's sake.

4 Even though I walk through the darkest valley,*d*
        I fear no evil;
    for you are with me;
        your rod and your staff—
        they comfort me.

5 You prepare a table before me
        in the presence of my enemies;
    you anoint my head with oil;
        my cup overflows.
6 Surely*e* goodness and mercy*f* shall follow me
        all the days of my life,
    and I shall dwell in the house of the LORD
        my whole life long.*g*

*a*Heb *waters of rest*
*b*Or *life*
*c*Or *paths of righteousness*
*d*Or *the valley of the shadow of death*
*e*Or *Only*
*f*Or *kindness*
*g*Heb *for length of days*

Prayer Starter: Thank you for being my shepherd, O Lord. May your kindness and love always be with me.

Memory Verse: The LORD is my shepherd, I shall not want. . . .
—*Psalm 23.1–2*

We Worship You, Lord

Happy are those whose
transgression is forgiven,
whose sin is covered.
2 Happy are those to whom the
LORD imputes no iniquity,
and in whose spirit there is no deceit.

3 While I kept silence, my body
wasted away
through my groaning all day long.
4 For day and night your hand
was heavy upon me;
my strength was dried up*a*
as by the heat of summer.
Selah

5 Then I acknowledged my sin to you,
and I did not hide my iniquity;
I said, "I will confess my transgressions
to the LORD,"
and you forgave the guilt of
my sin.   *Selah*

⁶ Therefore let all who are faithful
      offer prayer to you;
  at a time of distress,*ᵇ* the rush of mighty waters
      shall not reach them.
⁷ You are a hiding place for me;
      you preserve me from trouble;
      you surround me with glad
          cries of deliverance.   *Selah*

⁸ I will instruct you and teach you
      the way you should go;
      I will counsel you with my eye
      upon you.
⁹ Do not be like a horse or a mule,
      without understanding,
  whose temper must be curbed
      with bit and bridle,
  else it will not stay near you.

¹⁰ Many are the torments of the
      wicked,
  but steadfast love surrounds
      those who trust in the Lᴏʀᴅ.
¹¹ Be glad in the Lᴏʀᴅ and rejoice,
      O righteous,
  and shout for joy, all you
      upright in heart.

*ᵃ*Meaning of Heb uncertain
*ᵇ*Cn: Heb *at a time of finding only*

Prayer Starter: Forgive my sins today, O Lord, and wipe them away. Show me the road that I should follow.

Memory Verse: The Lᴏʀᴅ is my shepherd, I shall not want. He makes me lie down . . .
          —*Psalm 23.1–2*

Thirsty for God

A s a deer longs for flowing streams,
so my soul longs for you, O God.
² My soul thirsts for God,
for the living God.
When shall I come and behold
the face of God?
³ My tears have been my food
day and night,
while people say to me continually,
"Where is your God?"

⁴ These things I remember,
as I pour out my soul:
how I went with the throng,ᵃ
and led them in procession to
the house of God,
with glad shouts and songs of
thanksgiving,
a multitude keeping festival.
⁵ Why are you cast down, O my soul,
and why are you disquieted within me?
Hope in God; for I shall again praise him,
my help ⁶and my God.

My soul is cast down within me;
therefore I remember you
from the land of Jordan and of Hermon,
from Mount Mizar.
⁷ Deep calls to deep
at the thunder of your cataracts;
all your waves and your billows
have gone over me.
⁸ By day the LORD commands his
steadfast love,
and at night his song is with me,
a prayer to the God of my life.

ᵃMeaning of Heb uncertain

Prayer Starter: Make me thirsty for you, Lord, like a deer by streams of water.

Memory Verse: The LORD is my shepherd, I shall not want. He makes me lie down in green pastures . . .
—*Psalm 23.1–2*

You Water the Earth

Praise is due to you,
O God, in Zion;
and to you shall vows be performed,
² O you who answer prayer!
To you all flesh shall come.
³ When deeds of iniquity overwhelm us,
you forgive our transgressions.
⁴ Happy are those whom you choose and bring near
to live in your courts.
We shall be satisfied with the goodness of your house,
your holy temple.

⁵ By awesome deeds you answer us
with deliverance,
O God of our salvation;
you are the hope of all the ends
of the earth
and of the farthest seas.

⁶ By your*ᵃ* strength you established
the mountains;
you are girded with might.
⁷ You silence the roaring of the seas,
the roaring of their waves,
the tumult of the peoples.
⁸ Those who live at earth's farthest
bounds are awed by your signs;
you make the gateways of the morning and
the evening shout for joy.

⁹ You visit the earth and water it,
you greatly enrich it;
the river of God is full of water;
you provide the people with grain,
for so you have prepared it.
¹⁰ You water its furrows abundantly,
settling its ridges,
softening it with showers,
and blessing its growth.

*ᵃ*Gk Jerome: Heb *his*

Prayer Starter: I praise you, Father, for hearing and answering my prayers and meeting all my needs.

Memory Verse: The LORD is my shepherd, I shall not want. He makes me lie down in green pastures; he leads me beside still waters. —*Psalm 23.1–2*

> **Bless the Lord**

Bless the LORD, O my soul,
  and all that is within me,
    bless his holy name.
2 Bless the LORD, O my soul,
    and do not forget all his benefits—
3 who forgives all your iniquity,
    who heals all your diseases,
4 who redeems your life from the Pit,
    who crowns you with steadfast love and mercy,
5 who satisfies you with good as long as you live[a]
    so that your youth is renewed like the eagle's.

6 The LORD works vindication
    and justice for all who are oppressed.
7 He made known his ways to Moses,
    his acts to the people of Israel.

8 The LORD is merciful and gracious,
    slow to anger and abounding
      in steadfast love.
9 He will not always accuse,
    nor will he keep his anger forever.
10 He does not deal with us
      according to our sins,
    nor repay us according to our iniquities.
11 For as the heavens are high above the earth,
    so great is his steadfast love toward those who fear him;
12 as far as the east is from the west,
    so far he removes our transgressions from us.
13 As a father has compassion for his children,
    so the LORD has compassion for those who fear him.
14 For he knows how we were made;
    he remembers that we are dust.

[a]Meaning of Heb uncertain

Prayer Starter: With all my heart I praise you, Lord, and with my whole being I praise your holy name.

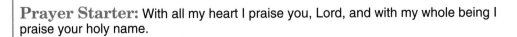

Memory Verse: Bless the LORD . . .   —*Psalm 103.1*

> **Teach Me
> Your Statutes**

Happy are those whose way is blameless,
  who walk in the law of the LORD.
2 Happy are those who keep his decrees,
    who seek him with their whole heart,
3 who also do no wrong,
    but walk in his ways.
4 You have commanded your precepts
  to be kept diligently.
5 O that my ways may be steadfast
  in keeping your statutes!
6 Then I shall not be put to shame,
    having my eyes fixed on
      all your commandments.
7 I will praise you with an upright heart,
    when I learn your righteous
      ordinances.
8 I will observe your statutes;
    do not utterly forsake me.

9 How can young people keep their way pure?
    By guarding it according to your word.
10 With my whole heart I seek you;
    do not let me stray from your commandments.
11 I treasure your word in my heart,
    so that I may not sin against you.
12 Blessed are you, O LORD;
    teach me your statutes.
13 With my lips I declare
    all the ordinances of your mouth.
14 I delight in the way of your decrees
    as much as in all riches.
15 I will meditate on your precepts,
    and fix my eyes on your ways.
16 I will delight in your statutes;
    I will not forget your word.

Prayer Starter: Lord, enable me to treasure your words above all else, so that I will not sin against you.

Memory Verse: Bless the LORD, O my soul . . .　　　　　　*—Psalm 103.1*

Come Praise the Lord

Praise the LORD!
Praise the LORD from the heavens;
   praise him in the heights!
2 Praise him, all his angels;
   praise him, all his host!

3 Praise him, sun and moon;
   praise him, all you shining stars!
4 Praise him, you highest heavens,
   and you waters above the heavens!

5 Let them praise the name of the LORD,
   for he commanded and they were created.
6 He established them forever and ever;
   he fixed their bounds, which
     cannot be passed.*a*

7 Praise the LORD from the earth,
　　you sea monsters and all deeps,
8 fire and hail, snow and frost,
　　stormy wind fulfilling his command!

9 Mountains and all hills,
　　fruit trees and all cedars!
10 Wild animals and all cattle,
　　creeping things and flying birds!
11 Kings of the earth and all peoples,
　　princes and all rulers of the earth!
12 Young men and women alike,
　　old and young together!

ªOr he set a law that cannot pass away

Prayer Starter: Thank you, Lord, that the sun, moon, and stars display your majesty and power.

Memory Verse: Bless the LORD, O my soul, and all that is within me . . .
　　　　　　　　　　　　　　　　　　　　—*Psalm 103.1*

Celebrate and Worship

Praise the LORD!
Sing to the LORD a new song,
    his praise in the assembly of the faithful.
2 Let Israel be glad in its Maker;
    let the children of Zion rejoice in their King.
3 Let them praise his name with dancing,
    making melody to him with tambourine and
    lyre.
4 For the LORD takes pleasure in his people;
    he adorns the humble with victory.
5 Let the faithful exult in glory;
    let them sing for joy on their couches.
6 Let the high praises of God be in their throats
    and two-edged swords in their hands,
7 to execute vengeance on the nations
    and punishment on the peoples,
8 to bind their kings with fetters
    and their nobles with chains of iron,
9 to execute on them the judgment decreed.
    This is glory for all his faithful ones.
Praise the LORD!

150 Praise the LORD!
Praise God in his sanctuary;
    praise him in his mighty firmament!*a*
2 Praise him for his mighty deeds;
    praise him according to his
      surpassing greatness!
3 Praise him with trumpet sound;
    praise him with lute and harp!
4 Praise him with tambourine and dance;
    praise him with strings and pipe!
5 Praise him with clanging cymbals;
    praise him with loud clashing cymbals!
6 Let everything that breathes
      praise the LORD!
Praise the LORD!

*a*Or *dome*

Prayer Starter: I praise you, God, for your deeds are wonderful, too marvelous to describe.

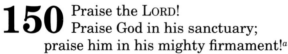

Memory Verse: Bless the LORD, O my soul, and all that is within me, bless . . .
    —Psalm 103.1

The proverbs of Solomon son of David,
king of Israel:

The Proverbs of Solomon

2 For learning about wisdom and instruction,
for understanding words of insight,
3 for gaining instruction in wise dealing,
righteousness, justice, and equity;
4 to teach shrewdness to the simple,
knowledge and prudence to the young—
5 Let the wise also hear and gain in learning,
and the discerning acquire skill,
6 to understand a proverb and a figure,
the words of the wise and their riddles.

7 The fear of the LORD is the beginning of knowledge;
fools despise wisdom and instruction.

8 Hear, my child, your father's instruction,
and do not reject your mother's teaching;
9 for they are a fair garland for your head,
and pendants for your neck.

¹⁰ My child, if sinners entice you,
     do not consent.
¹¹ If they say, "Come with us, let us lie in wait for blood;
     let us wantonly ambush the innocent;
¹² like Sheol let us swallow them alive
     and whole, like those who go down to the Pit.
¹³ We shall find all kinds of costly things;
     we shall fill our houses with booty.
¹⁴ Throw in your lot among us;
     we will all have one purse"—
¹⁵ my child, do not walk in their way,
     keep your foot from their paths;
¹⁶ for their feet run to evil,
     and they hurry to shed blood.
¹⁷ For in vain is the net baited
     while the bird is looking on;
¹⁸ yet they lie in wait—to kill themselves!
     and set an ambush—for their own lives!
¹⁹ Such is the end[a] of all who are greedy for gain;
     it takes away the life of its possessors.

3 My child, do not forget my teaching,
     but let your heart keep my commandments;
² for length of days and years of life
     and abundant welfare they will give you.

³ Do not let loyalty and faithfulness forsake you;
     bind them around your neck,
     write them on the tablet of your heart.
⁴ So you will find favor and good repute
     in the sight of God and of people.

⁵ Trust in the LORD with all your heart,
     and do not rely on your own insight.
⁶ In all your ways acknowledge him,
     and he will make straight your paths.

[a]Gk: Heb *ways*

Prayer Starter: Cause us to respect and obey you, Lord, that we may be wise.

Memory Verse: Bless the LORD, O my soul, and all that is within me, bless his holy name.   —*Psalm 103.1*

Proverbs 31.10–17, 20–22, 24–29

The Most Precious Treasure

A capable wife who can find?
  She is far more precious than jewels.
¹¹ The heart of her husband trusts in her,
  and he will have no lack of gain.
¹² She does him good, and not harm,
  all the days of her life.
¹³ She seeks wool and flax,
  and works with willing hands.
¹⁴ She is like the ships of the merchant,
  she brings her food from far away.
¹⁵ She rises while it is still night
  and provides food for her household
  and tasks for her servant-girls.
¹⁶ She considers a field and buys it;
  with the fruit of her hands she plants a vineyard.
¹⁷ She girds herself with strength,
  and makes her arms strong.

²⁰ She opens her hand to the poor,
  and reaches out her hands to the needy.
²¹ She is not afraid for her household when it snows,
  for all her household are clothed in crimson.
²² She makes herself coverings;
  her clothing is fine linen and purple.

²⁴ She makes linen garments and sells them;
  she supplies the merchant with sashes.
²⁵ Strength and dignity are her clothing,
  and she laughs at the time to come.
²⁶ She opens her mouth with wisdom,
  and the teaching of kindness is on
   her tongue.
²⁷ She looks well to the ways of her household,
  and does not eat the bread of idleness.
²⁸ Her children rise up and call her happy;
  her husband too, and he praises her:
²⁹ "Many women have done excellently,
  but you surpass them all."

Prayer Starter: Teach me, Lord, that loving you is more important than being beautiful.

Memory Verse: Charm is deceitful . . .   *—Proverbs 31.30*

Friends

He [God] has made everything suitable for its time; moreover he has put a sense of past and future into their minds, yet they cannot find out what God has done from the beginning to the end. [12]I know that there is nothing better for them than to be happy and enjoy themselves as long as they live; [13]moreover, it is God's gift that all should eat and drink and take pleasure in all their toil. [14]I know that whatever God does endures forever; nothing can be added to it, nor anything taken from it; God has done this, so that all should stand in awe before him. [15]That which is, already has been; that which is to be, already is; and God seeks out what has gone by.[a]

4 Two are better than one, because they have a good reward for their toil. [10]For if they fall, one will lift up the other; but woe to one who is alone and falls and does not have another to help. [11]Again, if two lie together, they keep warm; but how can one keep warm alone? [12]And though one might prevail against another, two will withstand one. A threefold cord is not quickly broken.

[13]Better is a poor but wise youth than an old but foolish king, who will no longer take advice. [14]One can indeed come out of prison to reign, even though born poor in the kingdom.

[a]Heb *what is pursued*

Prayer Starter: Thank you for being my best friend, dear Lord. Help me to be a good friend to others.

Memory Verse: Charm is deceitful, and beauty is vain . . .

—*Proverbs 31.30*

Solomon's Beautiful Song

The Song of Songs, which is Solomon's.
² Let him kiss me with the kisses of his mouth!
For your love is better than wine,
³   your anointing oils are fragrant,
    your name is perfume poured out;
        therefore the maidens love you.
⁴ Draw me after you, let us make haste.
    The king has brought me into his chambers.
We will exult and rejoice in you;
    we will extol your love more than wine;
    rightly do they love you.

⁵ I am black and beautiful,
    O daughters of Jerusalem,
like the tents of Kedar,
    like the curtains of Solomon.
⁶ Do not gaze at me because I am dark,
    because the sun has gazed on me.
My mother's sons were angry with me;
    they made me keeper of the vineyards,
    but my own vineyard I have not kept!
⁷ Tell me, you whom my soul loves,
    where you pasture your flock,
    where you make it lie down at noon;
for why should I be like one who is veiled
    beside the flocks of your companions?

¹⁵ Ah, you are beautiful, my love;
    ah, you are beautiful;
    your eyes are doves.
¹⁶ Ah, you are beautiful, my beloved,
    truly lovely.

Prayer Starter: Thank you for loving me, Lord. And for helping me to love others.

Memory Verse: Charm is deceitful, and beauty is vain, but a woman who fears . . .
—*Proverbs 31.30*

Solomon Prays for Wisdom

O God of my ancestors and Lord of mercy,
who have made all things by your word,
² and by your wisdom have formed humankind
to have dominion over the creatures you have made,
³ and rule the world in holiness and righteousness,
and pronounce judgment in uprightness of soul,
⁴ give me the wisdom that sits by your throne,
and do not reject me from among your servants.
⁵ For I am your servant[a] the son of your serving girl,
a man who is weak and short-lived,
with little understanding of judgment and laws;
⁶ for even one who is perfect among human beings
will be regarded as nothing without the wisdom
that comes from you.

[a]Gk *slave*

Prayer Starter: Please give me wisdom, Lord, as I grow.

Memory Verse: Charm is deceitful, and beauty is vain, but a woman who fears the LORD . . .
—*Proverbs 31.30*

Sirach 6.5–10, 14–17

Real Friendship

Pleasant speech multiplies friends,
and a gracious tongue multiplies courtesies.
6 Let those who are friendly with you be many,
but let your advisers be one in a thousand.
7 When you gain friends, gain them through testing,
and do not trust them hastily.
8 For there are friends who are such when it suits them,
but they will not stand by you in time of trouble.
9 And there are friends who change into enemies,
and tell of the quarrel to your disgrace.
10 And there are friends who sit at your table,
but they will not stand by you in time of trouble.

14 Faithful friends are a sturdy shelter;
whoever finds one has found a treasure.
15 Faithful friends are beyond price;
no amount can balance their worth.
16 Faithful friends are life-saving medicine;
and those who fear the Lord will find them.
17 Those who fear the Lord direct their friendship aright,
for as they are, so are their neighbors also.

Prayer Starter: Dear God, help me to be a good and loyal friend.

Memory Verse: Charm is deceitful, and beauty is vain, but a woman who fears the Lord is to be praised. —*Proverbs 31.30*

> ### Watch Your Mouth

L isten, my children, to instruction concerning the mouth;

the one who observes it will never be caught.

8 Sinners are overtaken through their lips;

by them the reviler and the arrogant are tripped up.

9 Do not accustom your mouth to oaths,

nor habitually utter the name of the Holy One;

13 Do not accustom your mouth to coarse, foul language,

for it involves sinful speech.

15 Those who are accustomed to using abusive language

will never become disciplined as long as they live.

28 If you blow on a spark, it will glow;

if you spit on it, it will be put out;

yet both come out of your mouth.

17 The blow of a whip raises a welt,

but a blow of the tongue crushes the bones.

18 Many have fallen by the edge of the sword,

but not as many as have fallen because of the tongue.

24 As you fence in your property with thorns,

so make a door and a bolt for your mouth.

25 As you lock up your silver and gold,

so make balances and scales for your words.

26 Take care not to err with your tongue,*

and fall victim to one lying in wait.

*Gk *with it*

Prayer Starter: Lord, help me to watch my mouth and to speak words that are good and kind.

Memory Verse: Come now, let us argue it out . . .   —Isaiah 1.18a

How to Act at the Table

A re you seated at the table of the great?[a]
　　Do not be greedy at it,
　　　and do not say, "How much food there is here!"
13 Remember that a greedy eye is a bad thing.
　　What has been created more greedy than
　　　the eye?
　　Therefore it sheds tears for any reason.
14 Do not reach out your hand for everything you see,
　　and do not crowd your neighbor[b] at the dish.

16 Eat what is set before you like a well brought-up person[c]
　　and do not chew greedily, or you will give offense.
17 Be the first to stop, as befits good manners,
　　and do not be insatiable, or you will give offense.
18 If you are seated among many persons,
　　do not help yourself[d] before they do.

22 Listen to me, my child, and do not disregard me,
　　and in the end you will appreciate my words,
　In everything you do, be moderate,[e]
　　and no sickness will overtake you.

[a]Heb Syr: Gk *at a great table*
[b]Gk *him*
[c]Heb: Gk *like a human being*
[d]Gk *reach out your hand*
[e]Heb Syr: Gk *industrious*

Prayer Starter: Help me, Lord, to use good manners everywhere I go.

Memory Verse: Come now, let us argue it out, says the LORD . . .
　　　　　　　　　　　　　　　　　　　—*Isaiah 1.18a*

God Hears Prayer

I give you thanks, O Lord and King,
    and praise you, O God my Savior.
    I give thanks to your name,
2   for you have been my protector and helper
    and have delivered me from destruction
        and from the trap laid by a slanderous tongue,
        from lips that fabricate lies.

In the face of my adversaries
    you have been my helper ³and delivered me,
    in the greatness of your mercy and of your name,
from grinding teeth about to devour me,
    from the hand of those seeking my life,
    from the many troubles I endured,
4 from choking fire on every side,
    and from the midst of fire that I had not kindled,
5 from the deep belly of Hades,
    from an unclean tongue and lying words—
6   the slander of an unrighteous tongue to the king.
My soul drew near to death,
    and my life was on the brink of Hades below.
7 They surrounded me on every side,
    and there was no one to help me;
I looked for human assistance,
    and there was none.
8 Then I remembered your mercy, O Lord,
    and your kindness*ᵃ* from of old,

for you rescue those who wait for you
>   and save them from the hand of their enemies.
9 And I sent up my prayer from the earth,
>   and begged for rescue from death.
10 I cried out, "Lord, you are my Father;[b]
>   do not forsake me in the days of trouble,
>   when there is no help against the proud.
11 I will praise your name continually,
>   and will sing hymns of thanksgiving."
My prayer was heard,
12   for you saved me from destruction
>   and rescued me in time of trouble.
For this reason I thank you and praise you,
>   and I bless the name of the Lord.

[a]Other ancient authorities read *work*
[b]Heb: Gk *the Father of my lord*

Prayer Starter: Thank you, God, that prayer works!

Memory Verse: Come now, let us argue it out, says the LORD;
though your sins . . .   —*Isaiah 1.18a*

Holy, Holy, Holy

In the year that King Uzziah died, I saw the Lord sitting on a throne, high and lofty; and the hem of his robe filled the temple. ²Seraphs were in attendance above him; each had six wings: with two they covered their faces, and with two they covered their feet, and with two they flew. ³And one called to another and said:

"Holy, holy, holy is the LORD of hosts;
the whole earth is full of his glory."

⁴The pivots*ᵃ* on the thresholds shook at the voices of those who called, and the house filled with smoke. ⁵And I said: "Woe is me! I am lost, for I am a man of unclean lips, and I live among a people of unclean lips; yet my eyes have seen the King, the LORD of hosts!"

⁶Then one of the seraphs flew to me, holding a live coal that had been taken from the altar with a pair of tongs. ⁷The seraph*ᵇ* touched my mouth with it and said: "Now that this has touched your lips, your guilt has departed and your sin is blotted out." ⁸Then I heard the voice of the Lord saying, "Whom shall I send, and who will go for us?" And I said, "Here am I; send me!" ⁹And he said, "Go and say to this people:

'Keep listening, but do not comprehend;
keep looking, but do not understand.'
10 Make the mind of this people dull,
and stop their ears,
and shut their eyes,
so that they may not look with their eyes,
and listen with their ears,
and comprehend with their minds,
and turn and be healed."
11 Then I said, "How long, O Lord?" And he said:
"Until cities lie waste
without inhabitant,
and houses without people,
and the land is utterly desolate;
12 until the LORD sends everyone far away,
and vast is the emptiness in the midst of the land.
13 Even if a tenth part remain in it,
it will be burned again,
like a terebinth or an oak
whose stump remains standing
when it is felled."*ᶜ*
The holy seed is its stump.

ᵃMeaning of Heb uncertain
ᵇHeb He
ᶜMeaning of Heb uncertain

Prayer Starter: You are holy, O Lord, and the whole earth is filled with your glory.

Memory Verse: Come now, let us argue it out, says the LORD: though your sins are like scarlet . . .
—Isaiah 1.18a

The Ruling Son

For a child has been born for us,
　　a son given to us;
　　authority rests upon his shoulders;
　　　and he is named
　　Wonderful Counselor, Mighty God,
　　　Everlasting Father, Prince of Peace.
⁷ His authority shall grow continually,
and there shall be endless peace
for the throne of David and his kingdom.
He will establish and uphold it
with justice and with righteousness
　　from this time onward and forevermore.
The zeal of the LORD of hosts will do this.
⁸ The Lord sent a word against Jacob,
　　and it fell on Israel;
⁹ and all the people knew it—
　　Ephraim and the inhabitants of Samaria—
　　but in pride and arrogance of heart they said:
¹⁰ "The bricks have fallen,
　　but we will build with dressed stones;
the sycamores have been cut down,
　　but we will put cedars in their place."
¹¹ So the LORD raised adversaries*a* against them,
　　and stirred up their enemies,
¹² the Arameans on the east and
　　　the Philistines on the west,
　　and they devoured Israel with open mouth.
For all this his anger has not turned away;
　　his hand is stretched out still.

*a*Cn: Heb *the adversaries of Rezin*

Prayer Starter: Dear heavenly Father, thank you for sending us your Son.

Memory Verse: Come now, let us argue it out, says the LORD: though your sins are like scarlet, they shall be like snow.   —*Isaiah 1.18a*

A Branch from David's Family

A shoot shall come out from the stump of Jesse,
and a branch shall grow out of his roots.
2 The spirit of the LORD shall rest on him,
the spirit of wisdom and understanding,
the spirit of counsel and might,
the spirit of knowledge and the fear of
the LORD.
3 His delight shall be in the fear of the LORD.

He shall not judge by what his eyes see,
or decide by what his ears hear;
4 but with righteousness he shall judge the poor,
and decide with equity for the meek of the earth;
he shall strike the earth with the rod of his mouth,
and with the breath of his lips he shall kill the wicked.
5 Righteousness shall be the belt around his waist,
and faithfulness the belt around his loins.

6 The wolf shall live with the lamb,
the leopard shall lie down with the kid,
the calf and the lion and the fatling together,
and a little child shall lead them.
7 The cow and the bear shall graze,
their young shall lie down together;
and the lion shall eat straw like the ox.
8 The nursing child shall play over the hole of the asp,
and the weaned child shall put its hand
on the adder's den.
9 They will not hurt or destroy
on all my holy mountain;
for the earth will be full of the knowledge of
the LORD
as the waters cover the sea.
10On that day the root of Jesse shall stand as a signal to the peoples;
the nations shall inquire of him, and his dwelling shall be glorious.

Prayer Starter: Thank you for giving us understanding, wisdom, and insight. Keep me reading your Word.

Memory Verse: The LORD of hosts has sworn . . .   *—Isaiah 14.24*

Egypt Punished	

An oracle concerning Egypt.

> See, the LORD is riding on a swift cloud
>   and comes to Egypt;
> the idols of Egypt will tremble at his presence,
>   and the heart of the Egyptians
>   will melt within them.

² I will stir up Egyptians against Egyptians,
>   and they will fight, one against the other,
>   neighbor against neighbor,
>   city against city, kingdom against kingdom;

³ the spirit of the Egyptians within them will be emptied out,
>   and I will confound their plans;
> they will consult the idols and the spirits of the dead
>   and the ghosts and the familiar spirits;

⁴ I will deliver the Egyptians
>   into the hand of a hard master;
> a fierce king will rule over them,
>   says the Sovereign, the LORD of hosts.

⁵ The waters of the Nile will be dried up,
>   and the river will be parched and dry;

⁶ its canals will become foul,
>   and the branches of Egypt's Nile will diminish and dry up,
>   reeds and rushes will rot away.

⁷ There will be bare places by the Nile,
>   on the brink of the Nile;
> and all that is sown by the Nile will dry up,
>   be driven away, and be no more.

⁸ Those who fish will mourn;
>   all who cast hooks in the Nile will lament,
>   and those who spread nets
>   on the water will languish.

⁹ The workers in flax will be in despair,
>   and the carders and those at
>   the loom will grow pale.

¹⁰ Its weavers will be dismayed,
>   and all who work for wages will be grieved.

Prayer Starter: Help me, Lord, to turn off television programs that you don't want me to watch.

Memory Verse: The LORD of hosts has sworn: As I have designed . . .
—*Isaiah 14.24*

The Glorious King

T hose who walk righteously and
          speak uprightly,
     who despise the gain of oppression,
   who wave away a bribe instead of
          accepting it,
     who stop their ears from hearing
          of bloodshed
     and shut their eyes from looking on evil,
16 they will live on the heights;
     their refuge will be the fortresses of rocks;
     their food will be supplied,
          their water assured.

17 Your eyes will see the king in his beauty;
     they will behold a land that stretches far away.
18 Your mind will muse on the terror:
     "Where is the one who counted?
     Where is the one who weighed the tribute?
     Where is the one who counted the towers?"
19 No longer will you see the insolent people,
   the people of an obscure speech
     that you cannot comprehend,
   stammering in a language that you
          cannot understand.
20 Look on Zion, the city of our appointed festivals!
     Your eyes will see Jerusalem,
     a quiet habitation, an immovable tent,
   whose stakes will never be pulled up,
     and none of whose ropes will be broken.
21 But there the LORD in majesty will be for us
     a place of broad rivers and streams,
   where no galley with oars can go,
     nor stately ship can pass.
22 For the LORD is our judge,
          the LORD is our ruler,
     the LORD is our king; he will save us.

Prayer Starter: Thank you, Lord, for the wonderful future you've promised those who love you.

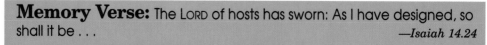

Memory Verse: The LORD of hosts has sworn: As I have designed, so shall it be . . .
                                                                —*Isaiah 14.24*

Hezekiah's Sickness

In those days Hezekiah became sick and was at the point of death. The prophet Isaiah son of Amoz came to him, and said to him, "Thus says the LORD: Set your house in order, for you shall die; you shall not recover." ²Then Hezekiah turned his face to the wall, and prayed to the LORD: ³"Remember now, O LORD, I implore you, how I have walked before you in faithfulness with a whole heart, and have done what is good in your sight." And Hezekiah wept bitterly.

⁴Then the word of the LORD came to Isaiah: ⁵"Go and say to Hezekiah, Thus says the LORD, the God of your ancestor David: I have heard your prayer, I have seen your tears; I will add fifteen years to your life. ⁶I will deliver you and this city out of the hand of the king of Assyria, and defend this city.

⁷"This is the sign to you from the LORD, that the LORD will do this thing that he has promised: ⁸See, I will make the shadow cast by the declining sun on the dial of Ahaz turn back ten steps." So the sun turned back on the dial the ten steps by which it had declined.ᵃ

⁹A writing of King Hezekiah of Judah, after he had been sick and had recovered from his sickness:

10 I said: In the noontide of my days
        I must depart;

I am consigned to the gates of Sheol
    for the rest of my years.
11 I said, I shall not see the LORD
        in the land of the living;
    I shall look upon mortals no more
        among the inhabitants of the world.
12 My dwelling is plucked up and removed from me
        like a shepherd's tent;
    like a weaver I have rolled up my life;
        he cuts me off from the loom;
    from day to night you bring me to an end;*a*

16 O Lord, by these things people live,
        and in all these is the life of my spirit.*a*
        Oh, restore me to health and make me live!
17 Surely it was for my welfare
        that I had great bitterness;
    but you have held back*b* my life
        from the pit of destruction,
    for you have cast all my sins
        behind your back.
18 For Sheol cannot thank you,
        death cannot praise you;
    those who go down to the Pit cannot hope
        for your faithfulness.
19 The living, the living, they thank you,
        as I do this day;
    fathers make known to children
        your faithfulness.

20 The LORD will save me,
        and we will sing to stringed instruments*c*
    all the days of our lives,
        at the house of the LORD.

*a*Meaning of Heb uncertain
*b*Cn Compare Gk Vg: Heb *loved*
*c*Heb *my stringed instruments*

Prayer Starter: May I praise you, heavenly Father, every day that I live.

Memory Verse: The LORD of hosts has sworn: As I have designed, so shall it be; and as I have planned . . .   —*Isaiah 14.24*

**God
Chooses
Jeremiah**

The words of Jeremiah son of Hilkiah, of the priests who were in Anathoth in the land of Benjamin, ²to whom the word of the LORD came in the days of King Josiah son of Amon of Judah, in the thirteenth year of his reign. ³It came also in the days of King Jehoiakim son of Josiah of Judah, and until the end of the eleventh year of King Zedekiah son of Josiah of Judah, until the captivity of Jerusalem in the fifth month.

⁴ Now the word of the LORD came to me saying,

⁵ "Before I formed you in the womb I knew you,
and before you were born I consecrated you;
I appointed you a prophet to the nations."

⁶Then I said, "Ah, Lord GOD! Truly I do not know how to speak, for I am only a boy." ⁷But the LORD said to me,

"Do not say, 'I am only a boy';
for you shall go to all to whom I send you,
and you shall speak whatever I command you.

⁸ Do not be afraid of them,
for I am with you to deliver you, says the LORD."

⁹ Then the LORD put out his hand and touched my mouth; and the LORD said to me,

"Now I have put my words in your mouth.

¹⁰ See, today I appoint you over nations and over kingdoms,
to pluck up and to pull down,
to destroy and to overthrow,
to build and to plant."

¹¹The word of the LORD came to me, saying, "Jeremiah, what do you see?" And I said, "I see a branch of an almond tree."[a] ¹²Then the LORD said to me, "You have seen well, for I am watching[b] over my word to perform it." ¹³The word of the LORD came to me a second time, saying, "What do you see?" And I said, "I see a boiling pot, tilted away from the north."

¹⁴Then the LORD said to me: Out of the north disaster shall break out on all the inhabitants of the land. ¹⁵For now I am calling all the tribes of the kingdoms of the north, says the LORD; and they shall come and all of them shall set their thrones at the entrance of the gates of Jerusalem, against all its surrounding walls and against all the cities of Judah.

[a]Heb *shaqed*
[b]Heb *shoqed*

Prayer Starter: You always rise early to keep your promises, Lord. Help me to trust every one of them.

Memory Verse: The LORD of hosts has sworn: As I have designed, so shall it be; and as I have planned, so shall it come to pass.   —*Isaiah 14.24*

Linen Shorts

Thus said the LORD to me, "Go and buy yourself a linen loincloth, and put it on your loins, but do not dip it in water." ²So I bought a loincloth according to the word of the LORD, and put it on my loins. ³And the word of the LORD came to me a second time, saying, ⁴"Take the loincloth that you bought and are wearing, and go now to the Euphrates,ᵃ and hide it there in a cleft of the rock." ⁵So I went, and hid it by the Euphrates,ᵇ as the LORD commanded me. ⁶And after many days the LORD said to me, "Go now to the Euphrates,ᵃ and take from there the loincloth that I commanded you to hide there." ⁷Then I went to the Euphrates,ᵃ and dug, and I took the loincloth from the place where I had hidden it. But now the loincloth was ruined; it was good for nothing.

⁸Then the word of the LORD came to me: ⁹Thus says the LORD: Just so I will ruin the pride of Judah and the great pride of Jerusalem. ¹⁰This evil people, who refuse to hear my words, who stubbornly follow their own will and have gone after other gods to serve them and worship them, shall be like this loincloth, which is good for nothing. ¹¹For as the loincloth clings to one's loins, so I made the whole house of Israel and the whole house of Judah cling to me, says the LORD, in order that they might be for me a people, a name, a praise, and a glory. But they would not listen.

> 15 Hear and give ear; do not be haughty,
>   for the LORD has spoken.
> 16 Give glory to the LORD your God
>   before he brings darkness,
>   and before your feet stumble
>   on the mountains at twilight.

ᵃOr *to Parah*; Heb *perath*
ᵇOr *by Parah;* Heb *perath*

Prayer Starter: Thank you for giving me a school to attend, Lord. Help me to study hard and do well. Bless my teachers.

Memory Verse: There is none . . .   *—Jeremiah 10.6*

Jeremiah Rescued

Now Shephatiah son of Mattan, Gedaliah son of Pashhur, Jucal son of Shelemiah, and Pashhur son of Malchiah heard the words that Jeremiah was saying to all the people, ²Thus says the LORD, Those who stay in this city shall die by the sword, by famine, and by pestilence; but those who go out to the Chaldeans shall live; they shall have their lives as a prize of war, and live. ³Thus says the LORD, This city shall surely be handed over to the army of the king of Babylon and be taken. ⁴Then the officials said to the king, "This man ought to be put to death, because he is discouraging the soldiers who are left in this city, and all the people, by speaking such words to them. For this man is not seeking the welfare of this people, but their harm." ⁵King Zedekiah said, "Here he is; he is in your hands; for the king is powerless against you." ⁶So they took Jeremiah and threw him into the cistern of Malchiah, the king's son, which was in the court of the guard, letting Jeremiah down by ropes. Now there was no water in the cistern, but only mud, and Jeremiah sank in the mud.

⁷Ebed-melech the Ethiopian*ᵃ*, a eunuch in the king's house, heard that they had put Jeremiah into the cistern. The king happened to be sitting at the Benjamin Gate, ⁸So Ebed-melech left the king's house and spoke to the king, ⁹"My lord king, these men have acted wickedly in all they did to the prophet Jeremiah by throwing him into the cistern to die there of hunger, for there is no bread left in the city." ¹⁰Then the king commanded Ebed-melech the Ethiopian,*ᵃ* "Take three men with you from here, and pull the prophet Jeremiah up from the cistern before he dies." ¹¹So Ebed-melech took the men with him and went to the house of the king, to a wardrobe of*ᵇ* the storehouse, and took from there old rags and worn-out clothes, which he let down to Jeremiah in the cistern by ropes. ¹²Then Ebed-melech the Ethiopian*ᵃ* said to Jeremiah, "Just put the rags and clothes between your armpits and the ropes." Jeremiah did so. ¹³Then they drew Jeremiah up by the ropes and pulled him out of the cistern. And Jeremiah remained in the court of the guard.

*ᵃ*Or *Nubian*; Heb *Cushite*
*ᵇ*Cn: Heb *to under*

Prayer Starter: Protect your people all over the world, dear Lord. Keep us safe from those who would like to hurt us because of our faith in you.

Memory Verse: There is none like you, O LORD . . .　　　*—Jeremiah 10.6*

Jerusalem Captured

A nd in the ninth year of his reign, in the tenth month, on the tenth day of the month, King Nebuchadrezzar of Babylon came with all his army against Jerusalem, and they laid siege to it; they built siegeworks against it all around. 5So the city was besieged until the eleventh year of King Zedekiah. 6On the ninth day of the fourth month the famine became so severe in the city that there was no food for the people of the land. 7Then a breach was made in the city wall;ᵃ and all the soldiers fled and went out from the city by night by the way of the gate between the two walls, by the king's garden, though the Chaldeans were all around the city. They went in the direction of the Arabah. 8But the army of the Chaldeans pursued the king, and overtook Zedekiah in the plains of Jericho; and all his army was scattered, deserting him. 9Then they captured the king, and brought him up to the king of Babylon at Riblah in the land of Hamath, and he passed sentence on him. 10The king of Babylon killed the sons of Zedekiah before his eyes, and also killed all the officers of Judah at Riblah. 11He put out the eyes of Zedekiah, and bound him in fetters, and the king of Babylon took him to Babylon, and put him in prison until the day of his death.

12In the fifth month, on the tenth day of the month—which was the nineteenth year of King Nebuchadrezzar, king of Babylon—Nebuzaradan the captain of the bodyguard who served the king of Babylon, entered Jerusalem. 13He burned the house of the LORD, the king's house, and all the houses of Jerusalem; every great house he burned down. 14All the army of the Chaldeans, who were with the captain of the guard, broke down all the walls around Jerusalem. 15Nebuzaradan the captain of the guard carried into exile some of the poorest of the people and the rest of the people who were left in the city and the deserters who had defected to

the king of Babylon, together with the rest of the artisans. [16]But Neb-uzaradan the captain of the guard left some of the poorest people of the land to be vinedressers and tillers of the soil.

[a]Heb lacks *wall*

Prayer Starter: It is so important to obey your commands, dear Lord. Help me and my friends to serve you.

Memory Verse: There is none like you, O LORD; you are great . . .
—*Jeremiah 10.6*

> **Where Wisdom Comes From**

Hear the commandments of life, O Israel;
   give ear, and learn wisdom!
10 Why is it, O Israel, why is it that
     you are in the land of your enemies,
      that you are growing old in a foreign country,
    that you are defiled with the dead,
11   that you are counted among those in Hades?
12 You have forsaken the fountain of wisdom.
13 If you had walked in the way of God,
   you would be living in peace forever.
14 Learn where there is wisdom,
   where there is strength,
   where there is understanding,
 so that you may at the same time discern
   where there is length of days, and life,
   where there is light for the eyes, and peace.
15 Who has found her place?
   And who has entered her storehouses?
16 Where are the rulers of the nations,
   and those who lorded it over the animals on earth;
17 those who made sport of the birds of the air,
   and who hoarded up silver and gold
 in which people trust,
   and there is no end to their getting;
18 those who schemed to get silver, and were anxious,
   but there is no trace of their works?
19 They have vanished and gone down to Hades,
   and others have arisen in their place.
20 Later generations have seen the light of day,
   and have lived upon the earth;
 but they have not learned the way to knowledge,
   nor understood her paths,
   nor laid hold of her.
21 Their descendants have strayed far from her[a] way.

32 But the one who knows all things knows her,
   he found her by his understanding,
 The one who prepared the earth for all time
   filled it with four-footed creatures;

Prayer Starter: Help me to tell others about you, dear Lord. May I never be ashamed of Jesus.

Memory Verse: There is none like you, O LORD; you are great, and your name . . .
     —Jeremiah 10.6

35 This is our God;
      no other can be compared to him.
36 He found the whole way to knowledge,
      and gave her to his servant Jacob
      and to Israel, whom he loved.
37 Afterward she appeared on earth
      and lived with humankind.

4 She is the book of the commandments of God,
      the law that endures forever.
All who hold her fast will live,
      and those who forsake her will die.

*a*Other ancient authorities read *their*

Idols Are Not Gods

Their tongues are smoothed by the carpenter, and they themselves are overlaid with gold and silver; but they are false and cannot speak. [9]People[a] take gold and make crowns for the heads of their gods, as they might for a girl who loves ornaments. [10]Sometimes the priests secretly take gold and silver from their gods and spend it on themselves, [11]or even give some of it to the prostitutes on the terrace. They deck their gods[b] out with garments like human beings—these gods of silver and gold and wood [12]that cannot save themselves from rust and corrosion. When they have been dressed in purple robes, [13]their faces are wiped because of the dust from the temple, which is thick upon them. [14]One of them holds a scepter, like a district judge, but is unable to destroy anyone who offends it. [15]Another has a dagger in its right hand, and an ax, but cannot defend itself from war and robbers. [16]From this it is evident that they are not gods; so do not fear them.

[17]For just as someone's dish is useless when it is broken, [18]so are their gods when they have been set up in the temples. Their eyes are full of the dust raised by the feet of those who enter. And just as the gates are shut on every side against anyone who has offended a king, as though under sentence of death, so the priests make their temples secure with doors and locks and bars, in order that they may not be plundered by robbers. [19]They light more lamps for them than they light for themselves, though their gods[c] can see none of them. [20]They are[d] just like a beam of the temple, but their hearts, it is said, are eaten away when crawling creatures from the earth devour them and their robes. They do not notice [21]when their faces have been blackened by the smoke of the temple. [22]Bats, swallows, and birds alight on their bodies and heads; and so do cats. [23]From this you will know that they are not gods; so do not fear them.

[26]Having no feet, they are carried on the shoulders of others, revealing to humankind their worthlessness. And those who serve them are put to shame.

[73]Better, therefore, is someone upright who has no idols; since such a person will be far above reproach.

[a]Gk *They*
[b]Gk *them*
[c]Gk *they*
[d]Gk *It is*

Prayer Starter: Thank you, Lord, that you are the only true God.

Memory Verse: There is none like you, O Lord; you are great, and your name is great in might.
—*Jeremiah 10.6*

Ezekiel Eats a Scroll

He said to me, O mortal, eat what is offered to you; eat this scroll, and go, speak to the house of Israel. ²So I opened my mouth, and he gave me the scroll to eat. ³He said to me, Mortal, eat this scroll that I give you and fill your stomach with it. Then I ate it; and in my mouth it was as sweet as honey.

⁴He said to me: Mortal, go to the house of Israel and speak my very words to them. ⁵For you are not sent to a people of obscure speech and difficult language, but to the house of Israel— ⁶not to many peoples of obscure speech and difficult language, whose words you cannot understand. Surely, if I sent you to them, they would listen to you. ⁷But the house of Israel will not listen to you, for they are not willing to listen to me; because all the house of Israel have a hard forehead and a stubborn heart. ⁸See, I have made your face hard against their faces, and your forehead hard against their foreheads. ⁹Like the hardest stone, harder than flint, I have made your forehead; do not fear them or be dismayed at their looks, for they are a rebellious house. ¹⁰He said to me: Mortal, all my words that I shall speak to you receive in your heart and hear with your ears; ¹¹then go to the exiles, to your people, and speak to them. Say to them, "Thus says the Lord GOD"; whether they hear or refuse to hear.

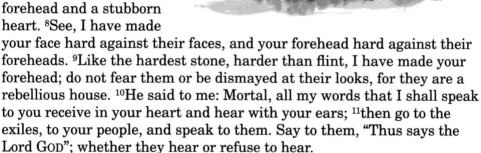

¹²Then the spirit lifted me up, and as the glory of the LORD rose*ᵃ* from its place, I heard behind me the sound of loud rumbling; ¹³it was the sound of the wings of the living creatures brushing against one another, and the sound of the wheels beside them, that sounded like a loud rumbling. ¹⁴The spirit lifted me up and bore me away.

ᵃCn: Heb and blessed be the glory of the LORD

Prayer Starter: Help me to tell others about you, dear Lord. May I never be ashamed of Jesus.

Memory Verse: Blessed be the name . . .   —*Daniel 2.20*

Dry Bones

The hand of the LORD came upon me, and he brought me out by the spirit of the LORD and set me down in the middle of a valley; it was full of bones. ²He led me all around them; there were very many lying in the valley, and they were very dry. ³He said to me, "Mortal, can these bones live?" I answered, "O Lord GOD, you know." ⁴Then he said to me, "Prophesy to these bones, and say to them: O dry bones, hear the word of the LORD. ⁵Thus says the Lord GOD to these bones: I will cause breath*a* to enter you, and you shall live. ⁶I will lay sinews on you, and will cause flesh to come upon you, and cover you with skin, and put breath*a* in you, and you shall live; and you shall know that I am the LORD."

⁷So I prophesied as I had been commanded; and as I prophesied, suddenly there was a noise, a rattling, and the bones came together, bone to its bone. ⁸I looked, and there were sinews on them, and flesh had come upon them, and skin had covered them; but there was no breath in them. ⁹Then he said to me, "Prophesy to the breath, prophesy, mortal, and say to the breath:*b* Thus says the Lord GOD: Come from the four winds, O breath,*b* and breathe upon these slain, that they may live." ¹⁰I prophesied as he commanded me, and the breath came into them, and they lived, and stood on their feet, a vast multitude.

¹¹Then he said to me, "Mortal, these bones are the whole house of Israel. They say, 'Our bones are dried up, and our hope is lost; we are cut off completely.' ¹²Therefore prophesy, and say to them, Thus says the Lord GOD: I am going to open your graves, and bring you up from your graves, O my people; and I will bring you back to the land of Israel. ¹³And you shall know that I am the LORD, when I open your graves, and bring you up from your graves, O my people. ¹⁴I will put my spirit within you, and you shall live, and I will place you on your own soil; then you shall know that I, the LORD, have spoken and will act," says the LORD.

¹⁵The word of the LORD came to me: ¹⁶Mortal, take a stick and write on it, "For Judah, and the Israelites associated with it"; then take another stick and write on it, "For Joseph (the stick of Ephraim) and all the house of Israel associated with it"; ¹⁷and join them together into one stick, so that they may become one in your hand. ¹⁸And when your people say to you, "Will you not show us what you mean by these?" ¹⁹say to them, Thus says the Lord GOD: I am about to take the stick of Joseph (which is in the hand of Ephraim) and the tribes of Israel associated with it; and I will put the stick of Judah upon it,*c* and make them one stick, in order that they may be one in my hand. ²⁰When the sticks on which you write are in your hand before their eyes, ²¹then say to them, Thus says

the Lord GOD: I will take the people of Israel from the nations among which they have gone, and will gather them from every quarter, and bring them to their own land. ²²I will make them one nation in the land, on the mountains of Israel; and one king shall be king over them all. Never again shall they be two nations, and never again shall they be divided into two kingdoms.

ᵃOr *spirit*
ᵇOr *wind* or *spirit*
ᶜHeb *I will put them upon it*

Prayer Starter: Keep me from saying the wrong thing today, Lord. Give me good words to speak.

Memory Verse: Blessed be the name of God . . .   —*Daniel 2.20*

Three Hebrews Saved in the Fire

Then Nebuchadnezzar was so filled with rage against Shadrach, Meshach, and Abednego that his face was distorted. He ordered the furnace heated up seven times more than was customary, ²⁰and ordered some of the strongest guards in his army to bind Shadrach, Meshach, and Abednego and to throw them into the furnace of blazing fire. ²¹So the men were bound, still wearing their tunics,ᵃ their trousers,ᵃ their hats, and their other garments, and they were thrown into the furnace of blazing fire. ²²Because the king's command was urgent and the furnace was so over-heated, the raging flames killed the men who lifted Shadrach, Meshach, and Abednego. ²³But the three men, Shadrach, Meshach, and Abednego, fell down, bound, into the furnace of blazing fire.

⁴⁶Now the king's servants who threw them in kept stoking the furnace with naphtha, pitch, tow, and brushwood. ⁴⁷And the flames poured out above the furnace forty-nine cubits, ⁴⁸and spread out and burned those Chaldeans who were caught near the furnace. ⁴⁹But the angel of the Lord came down into the furnace to be with Azariah and his companions, and drove the fiery flame out of the furnace, ⁵⁰and made the inside of the furnace as though a moist wind were whistling through it. The fire did not touch them at all and caused them no pain or distress.

⁵¹Then the three with one voice praised and glorified and blessed God in the furnace:

⁵² "Blessed are you, O Lord, God of our ancestors,
　　and to be praised and highly exalted forever;
　And blessed is your glorious, holy name,
　　and to be highly praised and highly exalted forever.

ᵃMeaning of Aram word uncertain

Prayer Starter: Thank you, God, that you are always kind and merciful.

Memory Verse: Blessed be the name of God from age to age . . .

—Daniel 2.20

Nebuchad-nezzar Eats Grass

All this came upon King Nebuchadnezzar. ²⁹At the end of twelve months he was walking on the roof of the royal palace of Babylon, ³⁰and the king said, "Is this not magnificent Babylon, which I have built as a royal capital by my mighty power and for my glorious majesty?" ³¹While the words were still in the king's mouth, a voice came from heaven: "O King Nebuchadnezzar, to you it is declared: The kingdom has departed from you! ³²You shall be driven away from human society, and your dwelling shall be with the animals of the field. You shall be made to eat grass like oxen, and seven times shall pass over you, until you have learned that the Most High has sovereignty over the kingdom of mortals and gives it to whom he will." ³³Immediately the sentence was fulfilled against Nebuchadnezzar. He was driven away from human society, ate grass like oxen, and his body was bathed with the dew of heaven, until his hair grew as long as eagles' feathers and his nails became like birds' claws.

³⁴When that period was over, I, Nebuchadnezzar, lifted my eyes to heaven, and my reason returned to me.

> I blessed the Most High,
> and praised and honored the one who lives forever.
> For his sovereignty is an everlasting sovereignty,
> and his kingdom endures from generation to generation.

Prayer Starter: Thank you for ruling over the nations, dear Lord. You are King of kings and Lord of lords. And I love you.

Memory Verse: Blessed be the name of God from age to age, for wisdom . . .
—*Daniel 2.20*

Writing on the Wall

King Belshazzar made a great festival for a thousand of his lords, and he was drinking wine in the presence of the thousand.

²Under the influence of the wine, Belshazzar commanded that they bring in the vessels of gold and silver that his father Nebuchadnezzar had taken out of the temple in Jerusalem, so that the king and his lords, his wives, and his concubines might drink from them.

⁴They drank the wine and praised the gods of gold and silver, bronze, iron, wood, and stone.

⁵Immediately the fingers of a human hand appeared and began writing on the plaster of the wall of the royal palace, next to the lampstand. The king was watching the hand as it wrote. ⁶Then the king's face turned pale, and his thoughts terrified him. His limbs gave way, and his knees knocked together. ⁷The king cried aloud to bring in the enchanters, the Chaldeans, and the diviners; and the king said to the wise men of Babylon, "Whoever can read this writing and tell me its interpretation shall be clothed in purple, have a chain of gold around his neck, and rank third in the kingdom." ⁸Then all the king's wise men came in, but they could not read the writing or tell the king the interpretation. ⁹Then King Belshazzar became greatly terrified and his face turned pale, and his lords were perplexed.

¹⁷Then Daniel answered in the presence of the king, "Let your gifts be for yourself, or give your rewards to someone else! Nevertheless I will read the writing to the king and let him know the interpretation.

²⁵And this is the writing that was inscribed: MENE, MENE, TEKEL, and PARSIN. ²⁶This is the interpretation of the matter: MENE, God has numbered the days of[a] your kingdom and brought it to an end; ²⁷TEKEL, you have been weighed on the scales and found wanting; ²⁸PERES,[b] your kingdom is divided and given to the Medes and Persians."

²⁹Then Belshazzar gave the command, and Daniel was clothed in purple, a chain of gold was put around his neck, and a proclamation was made concerning him that he should rank third in the kingdom.

[a]Aram lacks *the days of*
[b]The singular of *Parsin*

Prayer Starter: Help me to be respectful to my teachers, Father. May they know that I am one of your children.

Memory Verse: Blessed be the name of God from age to age, for wisdom and power are his.
—*Daniel 2.20*

The Lions' Den

Then they responded to the king, "Daniel, one of the exiles from Judah, pays no attention to you, O king, or to the interdict you have signed, but he is saying his prayers three times a day." ¹⁴When the king heard the charge, he was very much distressed. He was determined to save Daniel, and until the sun went down he made every effort to rescue him. ¹⁵Then the conspirators came to the king and said to him, "Know, O king, that it is a law of the Medes and Persians that no interdict or ordinance that the king establishes can be changed."

¹⁶Then the king gave the command, and Daniel was brought and thrown into the den of lions. The king said to Daniel, "May your God, whom you faithfully serve, deliver you!" ¹⁷A stone was brought and laid on the mouth of the den, and the king sealed it with his own signet and with the signet of his lords, so that nothing might be changed concerning Daniel. ¹⁸Then the king went to his palace and spent the night fasting; no food was brought to him, and sleep fled from him.

¹⁹Then, at break of day, the king got up and hurried to the den of lions. ²⁰When he came near the den where Daniel was, he cried out anxiously to Daniel, "O Daniel, servant of the living God, has your God whom you faithfully serve been able to deliver you from the lions?" ²¹Daniel then said to the king, "O king, live forever! ²²My God sent his angel and shut the lions' mouths so that they would not hurt me, because I was found blameless before him; and also before you, O king, I have done no wrong." ²³Then the king was exceedingly glad and commanded that Daniel be taken up out of the den. So Daniel was taken up out of the den, and no kind of harm was found on him, because he had trusted in his God.

Prayer Starter: May I be as faithful in praying each day as Daniel was, dear Lord.

Memory Verse: I make a decree . . .   —*Daniel 6.26a*

Daniel Kills the Dragon

Now in that place[a] there was a great dragon, which the Babylonians revered. [24]The king said to Daniel, "You cannot deny that this is a living god; so worship him." [25]Daniel said, "I worship the Lord my God, for he is the living God. [26]But give me permission, O king, and I will kill the dragon without sword or club." The king said, "I give you permission."

[27]Then Daniel took pitch, fat, and hair, and boiled them together and made cakes, which he fed to the dragon. The dragon ate them, and burst open. Then Daniel said, "See what you have been worshiping!"

[28]When the Babylonians heard about it, they were very indignant and conspired against the king, saying, "The king has become a Jew; he has destroyed Bel, and killed the dragon, and slaughtered the priests." [29]Going to the king, they said, "Hand Daniel over to us, or else we will kill you and your household." [30]The king saw that they were pressing him hard, and under compulsion he handed Daniel over to them.

[31]They threw Daniel into the lions' den, and he was there for six days. [32]There were seven lions in the den, and every day they had been given two human bodies and two sheep; but now they were given nothing, so that they would devour Daniel.

[40]On the seventh day the king came to mourn for Daniel. When he came to the den he looked in, and there sat Daniel! [41]The king shouted with a loud voice, "You are great, O Lord, the God of Daniel, and there is no other besides you!" [42]Then he pulled Daniel[b] out, and threw into the den those who had attempted his destruction, and they were instantly eaten before his eyes.

[a]Other ancient authorities lack *In that place*
[b]Gk *him*

Prayer Starter: Dear God, help me to be strong like Daniel.

Memory Verse: I make a decree, that in all my royal dominion . . .
—Daniel 6.26a

Hosea and Gomer

The word of the LORD that came to Hosea son of Beeri, in the days of Kings Uzziah, Jotham, Ahaz, and Hezekiah of Judah, and in the days of King Jeroboam son of Joash of Israel. ²When the LORD first spoke through Hosea, the LORD said to Hosea, "Go, take for yourself a wife of whoredom and have children of whoredom, for the land commits great whoredom by forsaking the LORD." ³So he went and took Gomer daughter of Diblaim, and she conceived and bore him a son.

⁴And the LORD said to him, "Name him Jezreel;ᵃ for in a little while I will punish the house of Jehu for the blood of Jezreel, and I will put an end to the kingdom of the house of Israel. ⁵On that day I will break the bow of Israel in the valley of Jezreel."

⁶She conceived again and bore a daughter. Then the LORD said to him, "Name her Lo-ruhamah,ᵇ for I will no longer have pity on the house of Israel or forgive them. ⁷But I will have pity on the house of Judah, and I will save them by the LORD their God; I will not save them by bow, or by sword, or by war, or by horses, or by horsemen."

⁸When she had weaned Lo-ruhamah, she conceived and bore a son. ⁹Then the LORD said, "Name him Lo-ammi,ᶜ for you are not my people and I am not your God."ᵈ

¹⁰ᵉYet the number of the people of Israel shall be like the sand of the sea, which can be neither measured nor numbered; and in the place where it was said to them, "You are not my people," it shall be said to them, "Children of the living God."

ᵃThat is *God sows*
ᵇThat is *Not pitied*
ᶜThat is *Not my people*
ᵈHeb *I am not yours*
ᵉCh 2.1 in Heb

Prayer Starter: Lord, so many people are homeless. Please have mercy on them, and show us who we can help.

Memory Verse: I make a decree, that in all my royal dominion people should tremble and fear . . . —*Daniel 6.26a*

Swarms of Locusts

The word of the LORD that came to Joel son of Pethuel:

2 Hear this, O elders,
     give ear, all inhabitants of the land!
Has such a thing happened in your days,
     or in the days of your ancestors?
3 Tell your children of it,
and let your children tell their children,
and their children another generation.

4 What the cutting locust left,
     the swarming locust has eaten.
What the swarming locust left,
     the hopping locust has eaten,
and what the hopping locust left,
     the destroying locust has eaten.

5 Wake up, you drunkards, and weep;
     and wail, all you wine-drinkers,
over the sweet wine,
     for it is cut off from your mouth.
6 For a nation has invaded my land,
     powerful and innumerable;
its teeth are lions' teeth,
     and it has the fangs of a lioness.

7 It has laid waste my vines,
     and splintered my fig trees;
it has stripped off their bark and thrown it down;
     their branches have turned white.

8 Lament like a virgin dressed in sackcloth
     for the husband of her youth.
9 The grain offering and the drink offering are cut off
     from the house of the LORD.
The priests mourn,
     the ministers of the LORD.
10 The fields are devastated,
     the ground mourns;
for the grain is destroyed,
     the wine dries up,
     the oil fails.

Prayer Starter: Thank you for insects, Lord. Especially for lightning bugs, lady bugs, and caterpillars.

Memory Verse: I make a decree, that in all my royal dominion people should tremble and fear before the God of Daniel. . . .—*Daniel 6.26a*

Women of Samaria

Hear this word, you cows of Bashan
    who are on Mount Samaria,
who oppress the poor, who crush the needy,
    who say to their husbands,
        "Bring something to drink!"
² The Lord GOD has sworn by his holiness:
    The time is surely coming upon you,
when they shall take you away with hooks,
    even the last of you with fishhooks.
³ Through breaches in the wall you shall leave,
    each one straight ahead;
    and you shall be flung out into Harmon,*ᵃ*
        says the LORD.

⁴ Come to Bethel—and transgress;
    to Gilgal—and multiply transgression;
bring your sacrifices every morning,
    your tithes every three days;
⁵ bring a thank-offering of leavened bread,
    and proclaim freewill offerings, publish them;

for so you love to do, O people of Israel!
> says the Lord G<small>OD</small>.

⁶ I gave you cleanness of teeth in all your cities,
> and lack of bread in all your places,
yet you did not return to me,
> > says the L<small>ORD</small>.

⁷ And I also withheld the rain from you
> when there were still three months to the harvest;
I would send rain on one city,
> and send no rain on another city;
one field would be rained upon,
> and the field on which it did not rain withered;
⁸ so two or three towns wandered to one town
> to drink water, and were not satisfied;
yet you did not return to me,
> > says the L<small>ORD</small>.

⁹ I struck you with blight and mildew;
> I laid waste*ᵇ* your gardens and your vineyards;
the locust devoured your fig trees
> and your olive trees;
yet you did not return to me,
> > says the L<small>ORD</small>.

*ᵃ*Meaning of Heb uncertain
*ᵇ*Cn: Heb *the muiltitude of*

Prayer Starter: Lord, help me to always be concerned for the poor and needy.

Memory Verse: I make a decree, that in all my royal dominion people should tremble and fear before the God of Daniel. For he is the living God.
> > > —*Daniel 6.26a*

Jonah and the Fish

Now the word of the LORD came to Jonah son of Amittai, saying, [2]"Go at once to Nineveh, that great city, and cry out against it; for their wickedness has come up before me." [3]But Jonah set out to flee to Tarshish from the presence of the LORD. He went down to Joppa and found a ship going to Tarshish; so he paid his fare and went on board, to go with them to Tarshish, away from the presence of the LORD.

[4]But the LORD hurled a great wind upon the sea, and such a mighty storm came upon the sea that the ship threatened to break up. [5]Then the mariners were afraid, and each cried to his god. They threw the cargo that was in the ship into the sea, to lighten it for them. Jonah, meanwhile, had gone down into the hold of the ship and had lain down, and was fast asleep. [6]The captain came and said to him, "What are you doing sound asleep? Get up, call on your god! Perhaps the god will spare us a thought so that we do not perish."

[7]The sailors[a] said to one another, "Come, let us cast lots, so that we may know on whose account this calamity has come upon us." So they cast lots, and the lot fell on Jonah.

[15]So they picked Jonah up and threw him into the sea; and the sea ceased from its raging. [16]Then the men feared the LORD even more, and they offered a sacrifice to the LORD and made vows.

[17b]But the LORD provided a large fish to swallow up Jonah; and Jonah was in the belly of the fish three days and three nights.

[a]Heb *They*
[b]Ch 2.1 in Heb

Prayer Starter: I want to serve you with my whole heart, dear Lord, and with my whole life.

Memory Verse: For all the peoples walk . . .

—*Micah 4.5*

In the Future

In days to come
     the mountain of the LORD's house
shall be established as the
          highest of the mountains,
     and shall be raised up above the hills.
Peoples shall stream to it,
2   and many nations shall come and say:
"Come, let us go up to the mountain of the LORD,
     to the house of the God of Jacob;
that he may teach us his ways
     and that we may walk in his paths."
For out of Zion shall go forth instruction,
     and the word of the LORD from Jerusalem.
3 He shall judge between many peoples,
     and shall arbitrate between strong nations far away;
they shall beat their swords into plowshares,
     and their spears into pruning hooks;
nation shall not lift up sword against nation,
     neither shall they learn war any more;
4 but they shall all sit under their own vines
          and under their own fig trees,
     and no one shall make them afraid;
     for the mouth of the LORD of hosts has spoken.

5 For all the peoples walk,
     each in the name of its god,
but we will walk in the name of the LORD our God
     forever and ever.
6 In that day, says the LORD,
     I will assemble the lame
and gather those who have been driven away,
     and those whom I have afflicted.
7 The lame I will make the remnant,
     and those who were cast off, a strong nation;
and the LORD will reign over them
          in Mount Zion
     now and forevermore.

Prayer Starter: Others may follow their gods, but we will always follow you, O Lord.

Memory Verse: For all the peoples walk, each in the name of its god . . .
—*Micah 4.5*

The Coming Shepherd

B ut you, O Bethlehem of Ephrathah,
 who are one of the little clans of Judah,
 from you shall come forth for me
 one who is to rule in Israel,
whose origin is from of old,
 from ancient days.
³ Therefore he shall give them up until the time
 when she who is in labor has brought forth;
then the rest of his kindred shall return
 to the people of Israel.
⁴ And he shall stand and feed his flock
 in the strength of the LORD,
in the majesty of the name of the LORD his God.
And they shall live secure, for now he shall be great
 to the ends of the earth;
⁵ and he shall be the one of peace.

6 "With what shall I come before the LORD,
 and bow myself before God on high?
Shall I come before him with burnt offerings,
 with calves a year old?
⁷ Will the LORD be pleased with thousands of rams,
 with ten thousands of rivers of oil?
Shall I give my firstborn for my transgression,
 the fruit of my body for the sin of my soul?"
⁸ He has told you, O mortal, what is good;
 and what does the Lord require of you
but to do justice, and to love kindness,
 and to walk humbly with your God?

7 Who is a God like you, pardoning iniquity
 and passing over the transgression
 of the remnant of your*ᵃ* possession?
He does not retain his anger forever,
 because he delights in showing clemency.
¹⁹ He will again have compassion upon us;
 he will tread our iniquities under foot.
You will cast all our*ᵇ* sins into the depths of the sea.

*ᵃ*Heb *his*
*ᵇ*Gk Syr Tg: Heb *their*

Prayer Starter: Thank you for being God. No one is like you!

Memory Verse: For all the peoples walk, each in the name of its god, but we will walk . . .   —*Micah 4.5*

The Prophet Nahum

An oracle concerning Nineveh. The book of the vision of Nahum of Elkosh.

² A jealous and avenging God is the LORD,
   the LORD is avenging and wrathful;
the LORD takes vengeance on his adversaries
   and rages against his enemies.
³ The LORD is slow to anger but great in power,
and the LORD will by no means clear the guilty.

His way is in whirlwind and storm,
   and the clouds are the dust of his feet.
⁴ He rebukes the sea and makes it dry,
   and he dries up all the rivers;
Bashan and Carmel wither,
   and the bloom of Lebanon fades.
⁵ The mountains quake before him,
   and the hills melt;
the earth heaves before him,
   the world and all who live in it.

⁶ Who can stand before his indignation?
   Who can endure the heat of his anger?
His wrath is poured out like fire,
   and by him the rocks are broken in pieces.
⁷ The LORD is good,
   a stronghold in a day of trouble;
he protects those who take refuge in him,
⁸   even in a rushing flood.

Prayer Starter: You are so good, dear Lord. Protect me in times of trouble.

Memory Verse: For all the peoples walk, each in the name of its god, but we will walk in the name of the LORD . . .   —*Micah 4.5*

Feet of a Deer

A prayer of the prophet Habakkuk according to Shigionoth.

2 O LORD, I have heard of your renown,
and I stand in awe, O LORD, of your work.
In our own time revive it;
in our own time make it known;
in wrath may you remember mercy.

3 God came from Teman,
the Holy One from Mount Paran. *Selah*
His glory covered the heavens,
and the earth was full of his praise.

4 The brightness was like the sun;
rays came forth from his hand,
where his power lay hidden.

9 You split the earth with rivers.
10 The mountains saw you, and writhed;
a torrent of water swept by;
the deep gave forth its voice.
The sun[a] raised high its hands;
11 the moon[b] stood still in its exalted place,
at the light of your arrows speeding by,
at the gleam of your flashing spear.

17 Though the fig tree does not blossom,
and no fruit is on the vines;
though the produce of the olive fails,
and the fields yield no food;
though the flock is cut off from the fold,
and there is no herd in the stalls,
18 yet I will rejoice in the LORD;
I will exult in the God of my salvation.
19 GOD, the Lord, is my strength;
he makes my feet like the feet of a deer,
and makes me tread upon the heights.[c]

[a]Heb *It*
[b]Heb *sun, moon*
[c]Heb *my heights*

Prayer Starter: Father, give me strength every day to do what is right.

Memory Verse: For all the peoples walk, each in the name of its god, but we will walk in the name of the LORD our God forever and ever.
—*Micah 4.5*

The Prophet Zechariah

In the eighth month, in the second year of Darius, the word of the Lord came to the prophet Zechariah son of Berechiah son of Iddo, saying:

2 [a]I looked up and saw a man with a measuring line in his hand. ²Then I asked, "Where are you going?" He answered me, "To measure Jerusalem, to see what is its width and what is its length." ³Then the angel who talked with me came forward, and another angel came forward to meet him, ⁴and said to him, "Run, say to that young man:
Jerusalem shall be inhabited like villages without walls, because of the multitude of people and animals in it. ⁵For I will be a wall of fire all around it, says the Lord, and I will be the glory within it."

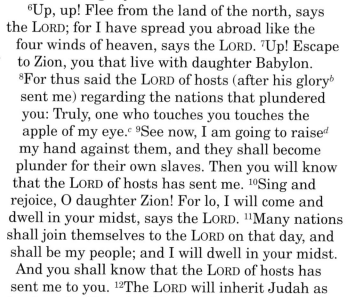

⁶Up, up! Flee from the land of the north, says the Lord; for I have spread you abroad like the four winds of heaven, says the Lord. ⁷Up! Escape to Zion, you that live with daughter Babylon. ⁸For thus said the Lord of hosts (after his glory[b] sent me) regarding the nations that plundered you: Truly, one who touches you touches the apple of my eye.[c] ⁹See now, I am going to raise[d] my hand against them, and they shall become plunder for their own slaves. Then you will know that the Lord of hosts has sent me. ¹⁰Sing and rejoice, O daughter Zion! For lo, I will come and dwell in your midst, says the Lord. ¹¹Many nations shall join themselves to the Lord on that day, and shall be my people; and I will dwell in your midst. And you shall know that the Lord of hosts has sent me to you. ¹²The Lord will inherit Judah as his portion in the holy land, and will again choose Jerusalem.

¹³Be silent, all people, before the Lord; for he has roused himself from his holy dwelling.

[a]Ch 2.5 in Heb
[b]Cn: Heb *after glory he*
[c]Heb *his eye*
[d]Or *wave*

Prayer Starter: Thank you for making this day. I celebrate your goodness.

Memory Verse: She will bear a son . . .   —*Matthew 1.21*

**Zechariah's
Four
Chariots**

And again I looked up and saw four chariots coming out from between two mountains— mountains of bronze. ²The first chariot had red horses, the second chariot black horses, ³the third chariot white horses, and the fourth chariot dappled gray*ᵃ* horses. ⁴Then I said to the angel who talked with me, "What are these, my lord?" ⁵The angel answered me, "These are the four winds*ᵇ* of heaven going out, after presenting themselves before the LORD of all the earth. ⁶The chariot with the black horses

goes toward the north country, the white ones go toward the west coun-try,[c] and the dappled ones go toward the south country." [7]When the steeds came out, they were impatient to get off and patrol the earth. And he said, "Go, patrol the earth." So they patrolled the earth. [8]Then he cried out to me, "Lo, those who go toward the north country have set my spirit at rest in the north country."

[9]The word of the LORD came to me: [10]Collect silver and gold[d] from the exiles—from Heldai, Tobijah, and Jedaiah—who have arrived from Baby-lon; and go the same day to the house of Josiah son of Zephaniah. [11]Take the silver and gold and make a crown', and set it on the head of the high priest Joshua son of Jehozadak; [12]say to him: Thus says the LORD of hosts: Here is a man whose name is Branch: for he shall branch out in his place, and he shall build the temple of the LORD. [13]It is he that shall build the temple of the LORD; he shall bear royal honor, and shall sit and rule on his throne. There shall be a priest by his throne, with peaceful understanding between the two of them. [14]And the crown[f] shall be in the care of Heldai,[g] Tobijah, Jedaiah, and Josiah[h] son of Zephaniah, as a memorial in the temple of the LORD.

[15]Those who are far off shall come and help to build the temple of the LORD; and you shall know that the LORD of hosts has sent me to you. This will happen if you diligently obey the voice of the LORD your God.

[a]Compare Gk: Meaning of Heb uncertain
[b]Or *spirits*
[c]Cn: Heb *go after them*
[d]Cn Compare verse 11: Heb lacks *silver and gold*
[e]Gk Mss Syr Tg: Heb *crowns*
[f]Gk Syr: Heb *crowns*
[g]Syr Compare verse 10: Heb *Helem*
[h]Syr Compare verse 10: Heb *Hen*

Prayer Starter: You watch over all the earth, Lord. Help the world be at peace.

Memory Verse: She will bear a son, and you are . . . —*Matthew 1.21*

**The Entire
Ten Percent**

For I the LORD do not change; therefore you, O children of Jacob, have not perished. [7]Ever since the days of your ancestors you have turned aside from my statutes and have not kept them. Return to me, and I will return to you, says the LORD of hosts. But you say, "How shall we return?"

[8]Will anyone rob God? Yet you are robbing me! But you say, "How are we robbing you?" In your tithes and offerings! [9]You are cursed with a curse, for you are robbing me—the whole nation of you! [10]Bring the full tithe into the storehouse, so that there may be food in my house, and thus put me to the test, says the LORD of hosts; see if I will not open the windows of heaven for you and pour down for you an overflowing blessing. [11]I will rebuke the locust[a] for you, so that it will not destroy the produce of your soil; and your vine in the field shall not be barren, says the LORD of hosts. [12]Then all nations will count you happy, for you will be a land of delight, says the LORD of hosts.

[16]Then those who revered the LORD spoke with one another. The LORD took note and listened, and a book of remembrance was written before him of those who revered the LORD and thought on his name. [17]They shall be mine, says the LORD of hosts, my special possession on the day when I act, and I will spare them as parents spare their children who serve them. [18]Then once more you shall see the difference between the righteous and the wicked, between one who serves God and one who does not serve him.

[a]Heb *devourer*

Prayer Starter: Make me generous, Lord, in giving my money to your work.

Memory Verse: She will bear a son, and you are to name him Jesus . . .
—*Matthew 1.21*

227

Wise Men from the East

In the time of King Herod, after Jesus was born in Bethlehem of Judea, wise men*a* from the East came to Jerusalem, ²asking, "Where is the child who has been born king of the Jews? For we observed his star at its rising,*b* and have come to pay him homage." ³When King Herod heard this, he was frightened, and all Jerusalem with him; ⁴and calling together all the chief priests and scribes of the people, he inquired of them where the Messiah*c* was to be born. ⁵They told him, "In Bethlehem of Judea; for so it has been written by the prophet."

⁷Then Herod secretly called for the wise men*a* and learned from them the exact time when the star had appeared. ⁸Then he sent them to Bethlehem, saying, "Go and search diligently for the child; and when you have found him, bring me word so that I may also go and pay him homage." ⁹When they had heard the king, they set out; and there, ahead of them, went the star that they had seen at its rising,*b* until it stopped over the place where the child was. ¹⁰When they saw that the star had stopped,*d* they were overwhelmed with joy. ¹¹On entering the house, they saw the child with Mary his mother; and they knelt down and paid him homage. Then, opening their treasure chests, they offered him gifts of gold, frankincense, and myrrh. ¹²And having been warned in a dream not to return to Herod, they left for their own country by another road.

*a*Or *astrologers*; Gk *magi*
*b*Or *in the East*
*c*Or *the Christ*
*d*Gk *saw the star*

Prayer Starter: Thank you for Jesus, born on Christmas Day.

Memory Verse: She will bear a son, and you are to name him Jesus, for he will save his people . . .
—*Matthew 1.21*

**Hiding
in Egypt**

Now after they had left, an angel of the Lord appeared to Joseph in a dream and said, "Get up, take the child and his mother, and flee to Egypt, and remain there until I tell you; for Herod is about to search for the child, to destroy him." ¹⁴Then Joseph[a] got up, took the child and his mother by night, and went to Egypt, ¹⁵and remained there until the death of Herod. This was to fulfill what had been spoken by the Lord through the prophet, "Out of Egypt I have called my son."

¹⁶When Herod saw that he had been tricked by the wise men,[b] he was infuriated, and he sent and killed all the children in and around Bethlehem who were two years old or under, according to the time that he had learned from the wise men.[b]

¹⁹When Herod died, an angel of the Lord suddenly appeared in a dream to Joseph in Egypt and said, ²⁰"Get up, take the child and his mother, and go to the land of Israel, for those who were seeking the

child's life are dead." ²¹Then Joseph*ᵃ* got up, took the child and his mother, and went to the land of Israel.

²²But when he heard that Archelaus was ruling over Judea in place of his father Herod, he was afraid to go there. And after being warned in a dream, he went away to the district of Galilee. ²³There he made his home in a town called Nazareth, so that what had been spoken through the prophets might be fulfilled, "He will be called a Nazorean."

*ᵃ*Gk *he*
*ᵇ*Or *astrologers;* Gk *magi*

Prayer Starter: Lord, help the people of Israel and Egypt and all the other nations to know and love Jesus Christ.

Memory Verse: She will bear a son, and you are to name him Jesus, for he will save his people from their sins. *—Matthew 1.21*

Jesus Is Tempted by Satan

Then Jesus was led up by the Spirit into the wilderness to be tempted by the devil. ²He fasted forty days and forty nights, and afterwards he was famished. ³The tempter came and said to him, "If you are the Son of God, command these stones to become loaves of bread." ⁴But he answered, "It is written,

'One does not live by bread alone,
   but by every word that comes from the mouth of God.'"

⁵Then the devil took him to the holy city and placed him on the pinnacle of the temple, ⁶saying to him, "If you are the Son of God, throw yourself down; for it is written,

'He will command his angels concerning you,'
   and 'On their hands they will bear you up,
so that you will not dash your foot against a stone.'"

⁷Jesus said to him, "Again it is written, 'Do not put the Lord your God to the test.'"

⁸Again, the devil took him to a very high mountain and showed him all the kingdoms of the world and their splendor; ⁹and he said to him, "All these I will give you, if you will fall down and worship me." ¹⁰Jesus said to him, "Away with you, Satan! for it is written,

'Worship the Lord your God,
   and serve only him.'"

¹¹Then the devil left him, and suddenly angels came and waited on him.

Prayer Starter: Keep us safe from the devil's traps, Lord. Deliver us from evil.

Memory Verse: But strive first . . . _—Matthew 6.33_

The Sermon
on the
Mount

And great crowds followed him from Galilee, the Decapolis, Jerusalem, Judea, and from beyond the Jordan.

5When Jesus[a] saw the crowds, he went up the mountain; and after he sat down, his disciples came to him. 2Then he began to speak, and taught them, saying:

3"Blessed are the poor in spirit, for theirs is the kingdom of heaven.

4"Blessed are those who mourn, for they will be comforted.

5"Blessed are the meek, for they will inherit the earth.

6"Blessed are those who hunger and thirst for righteousness, for they will be filled.

7"Blessed are the merciful, for they will receive mercy.

8"Blessed are the pure in heart, for they will see God.

9"Blessed are the peacemakers, for they will be called children of God.

10"Blessed are those who are persecuted for righteousness' sake, for theirs is the kingdom of heaven.

11"Blessed are you when people revile you and persecute you and utter all kinds of evil against you falsely on my account. 12Rejoice and be glad, for your reward is great in heaven, for in the same way they persecuted the prophets who were before you."

[a]Gk *he*

Prayer Starter: Lord, bless us. May we depend only on you.

Memory Verse: But strive first for the kingdom of God . . .

—*Matthew 6.33*

When You Pray

" And whenever you pray, do not be like the hypocrites; for they love to stand and pray in the synagogues and at the street corners, so that they may be seen by others. Truly I tell you, they have received their reward. ⁶But whenever you pray, go into your room and shut the door and pray to your Father who is in secret; and your Father who sees in secret will reward you.*

⁷"When you are praying, do not heap up empty phrases as the Gentiles do; for they think that they will be heard because of their many words. ⁸Do not be like them, for your Father knows what you need before you ask him.

⁹"Pray then in this way:
Our Father in heaven,
hallowed be your name.
¹⁰ Your kingdom come.
Your will be done, on earth as it is in heaven.
¹¹ Give us day our daily bread.*
¹² And forgive us our debts,
    as we also have forgiven our debtors.
¹³ And do not bring us to the time of trial,*
    but rescue us from the evil one.*

¹⁴For if you forgive others their trespasses, your heavenly Father will also forgive you; ¹⁵but if you do not forgive others, neither will your Father forgive your trespasses.

¹⁶"And whenever you fast, do not look dismal, like the hypocrites, for they disfigure their faces so as to show others that they are fasting. Truly I tell you, they have received their reward. ¹⁷But when you fast, put oil on your head and wash your face, ¹⁸so that your fasting may be seen not by others but by your Father

who is in secret; and your Father who sees in secret will reward you."*

*Other ancient authorities add *openly*
*Or *our bread for tomorrow*
*Or *us into temptation*
*Or *from evil.* Other ancient authorities add, in some form, *For the kingdom and the power and the glory are yours forever. Amen.*

Prayer Starter: Our father in heaven, help us to honor your name.

Memory Verse: But strive first for the kingdom of God and his righteousness . . .
—*Matthew 6.33*

Look at the Birds

"No one can serve two masters; for a slave will either hate the one and love the other, or be devoted to the one and despise the other. You cannot serve God and wealth.[a]

25"Therefore I tell you, do not worry about your life, what you will eat or what you will drink,[b] or about your body, what you will wear. Is not life more than food, and the body more than clothing? 26Look at the birds of the air; they neither sow nor reap nor gather into barns, and yet your heavenly Father feeds them. Are you not of more value than they? 27And can any of you by worrying add a single hour to your span of life?[c] 28And why do you worry about clothing? Consider the lilies of the field, how they grow; they neither toil nor spin, 29yet I tell you, even Solomon in all his glory was not clothed like one of these. 30But if God so clothes the grass of the field, which is alive today and tomorrow is thrown into the oven, will he not much more clothe you—you of little faith? 31Therefore do not worry, saying, 'What will we eat?' or 'What will we drink?' or 'What will we wear?' 32For it is the Gentiles who strive for all these things; and indeed your heavenly Father knows that you need all these things. 33But strive first for the kingdom of God[d] and his[e] righteousness, and all these things will be given to you as well."

[a]Gk *mammon*
[b]Other ancient authorities lack *or what you will drink*
[c]Or *add one cubit to your height*
[d]Other ancient authorities lack *of God*
[e]Or *its*

Prayer Starter: Keep me from worry, dear Lord, for I know you love and care for me.

Memory Verse: But strive first for the kingdom of God and his righteousness, and all these things . . .   —*Matthew 6.33*

Jesus Walks on Water

Immediately he made the disciples get into the boat and go on ahead to the other side, while he dismissed the crowds. ²³And after he had dismissed the crowds, he went up the mountain by himself to pray. When evening came, he was there alone, ²⁴but by this time the boat, battered by the waves, was far from the land,ᵃ for the wind was against them. ²⁵And early in the morning he came walking toward them on the sea. ²⁶But when the disciples saw him walking on the sea, they were terrified, saying, "It is a ghost!" And they cried out in fear. ²⁷But immediately Jesus spoke to them and said, "Take heart, it is I; do not be afraid."

²⁸Peter answered him, "Lord, if it is you, command me to come to you on the water." ²⁹He said, "Come." So Peter got out of the boat, started walking on the water, and came toward Jesus. ³⁰But when he noticed the strong wind,ᵇ he became frightened, and beginning to sink, he cried out, "Lord, save me!" ³¹Jesus immediately reached out his hand and caught him, saying to him, "You of little faith, why did you doubt?" ³²When they got into the boat, the wind ceased. ³³And those in the boat worshiped him, saying, "Truly you are the Son of God."

³⁴When they had crossed over, they came to land at Gennesaret. ³⁵After the people of that place recognized him, they sent word throughout the region and brought all who were sick to him, ³⁶and begged him that they might touch even the fringe of his cloak; and all who touched it were healed.

ᵃOther ancient authorities read *was out on the sea*
ᵇOther ancient authorities read *the wind*

Prayer Starter: Give me a stronger faith, dear Lord.

Memory Verse: But strive first for the kingdom of God and his righteousness, and all these things will be given to you as well. —*Matthew 6.33*

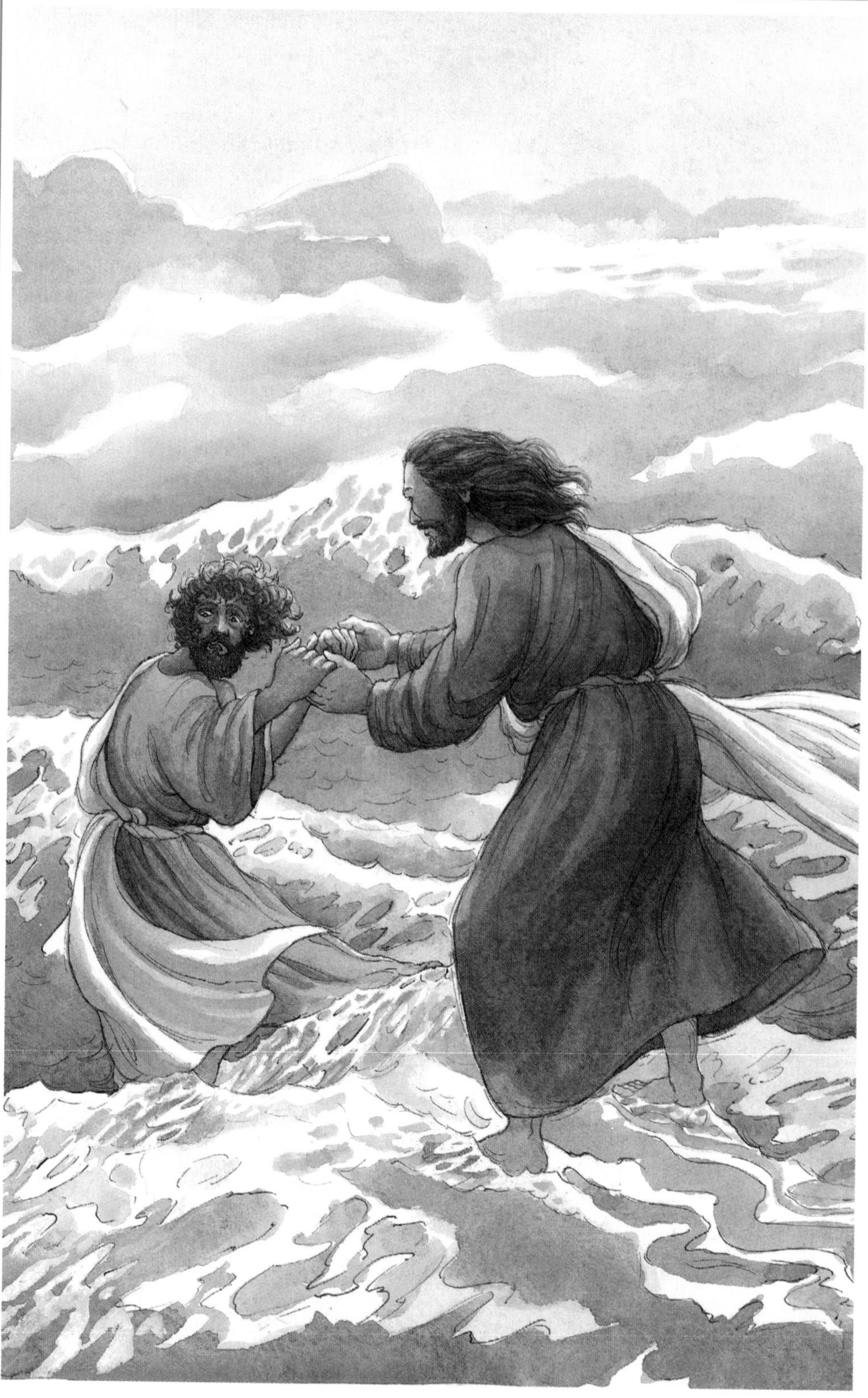

Who Is Jesus?

Now when Jesus came into the district of Caesarea Philippi, he asked his disciples, "Who do people say that the Son of Man is?" [14]And they said, "Some say John the Baptist, but others Elijah, and still others Jeremiah or one of the prophets." [15]He said to them, "But who do you say that I am?" [16]Simon Peter answered, "You are the Messiah,[a] the Son of the living God." [17]And Jesus answered him, "Blessed are you, Simon son of Jonah! For flesh and blood has not revealed this to you, but my Father in heaven. [18]And I tell you, you are Peter,[b] and on this rock[c] I will build my church, and the gates of Hades will not prevail against it. [19]I will give you the keys of the kingdom of heaven, and whatever you bind on earth will be bound in heaven, and whatever you loose on earth will be loosed in heaven." [20]Then he sternly ordered the disciples not to tell anyone that he was[d] the Messiah.[a]

[21]From that time on, Jesus began to show his disciples that he must go to Jerusalem and undergo great suffering at the hands of the elders and chief priests and scribes, and be killed, and on the third day be raised.

[24]Then Jesus told his disciples, "If any want to become my followers, let them deny themselves and take up their cross and follow me."

[a]Or *the Christ*
[b]Gk *Petros*
[c]Gk *petra*
[d]Other ancient authorities add *Jesus*

Prayer Starter: I praise you for Jesus, the Messiah, Son of the living God.

Memory Verse: The crowds that went ahead of him . . .
—*Matthew 21.9*

My Own Dear Son

Six days later, Jesus took with him Peter and James and his brother John and led them up a high mountain, by themselves. ²And he was transfigured before them, and his face shone like the sun, and his clothes became dazzling white. ³Suddenly there appeared to them Moses and Elijah, talking with him. ⁴Then Peter said to Jesus, "Lord, it is good for us to be here; if you wish, I[a] will make three dwellings[b] here, one for you, one for Moses, and one for Elijah." ⁵While he was still speaking, suddenly a bright cloud overshadowed them, and from the cloud a voice said, "This is my Son, the Beloved;[c] with him I am well pleased; listen to him!" ⁶When the disciples heard this, they fell to the ground and were overcome by fear. ⁷But Jesus came and touched them, saying, "Get up and do not be afraid." ⁸And when they looked up, they saw no one except Jesus himself alone.

⁹As they were coming down the mountain, Jesus ordered them, "Tell no one about the vision until after the Son of Man has been raised from the dead." ¹⁰And the disciples asked him, "Why, then, do the scribes say that Elijah must come first?" ¹¹He replied, "Elijah is indeed coming and will restore all things; ¹²but I tell you that Elijah has already come, and they did not recognize him, but they did to him whatever they pleased. So also the Son of Man is about to suffer at their hands." ¹³Then the disciples understood that he was speaking to them about John the Baptist.

[a]Other ancient authorities read *we*
[b]Or *tents*
[c]Or *my beloved Son*

Prayer Starter: I love your Word, Lord. Thank you for every verse in the Bible.

Memory Verse: The crowds that went ahead of him and that followed were shouting . . .
—*Matthew 21.9*

Jesus Enters Jerusalem

hen they had come near Jerusalem and had reached Bethphage, at the Mount of Olives, Jesus sent two disciples, [2]saying to them, "Go into the village ahead of you, and immediately you will find a donkey tied, and a colt with her; untie them and bring them to me. [3]If anyone says anything to you, just say this, 'The Lord needs them.' And he will send them immediately."[a] [4]This took place to fulfill what had been spoken through the prophet, saying,

5 "Tell the daughter of Zion,
   Look, your king is coming to you,
   humble, and mounted on a donkey,
       and on a colt, the foal of a donkey."
⁶The disciples went and did as Jesus had directed them; ⁷they brought the donkey and the colt, and put their cloaks on them, and he sat on them. ⁸A very large crowd*ᵇ* spread their cloaks on the road, and others cut branches from the trees and spread them on the road. ⁹The crowds that went ahead of him and that followed were shouting,

   "Hosanna to the Son of David!
       Blessed is the one who comes in the name of the Lord!
   Hosanna in the highest heaven!"

¹⁰When he entered Jerusalem, the whole city was in turmoil, asking, "Who is this?" ¹¹The crowds were saying, "This is the prophet Jesus from Nazareth in Galilee."

¹²Then Jesus entered the temple*ᶜ* and drove out all who were selling and buying in the temple, and he overturned the tables of the money changers and the seats of those who sold doves. ¹³He said to them, "It is written,

   'My house shall be called a house of prayer';
       but you are making it a den of robbers."

¹⁴The blind and the lame came to him in the temple, and he cured them.

ᵃOr *'The Lord needs them and will send them back immediately.'*
ᵇOr *Most of the crowd*
ᶜOther ancient authorities add *of God*

Prayer Starter: Dear Lord, help me always to welcome Jesus into my life.

Memory Verse: The crowds that went ahead of him and that followed were shouting, "Hosanna to the Son of David! . . . —*Matthew 21.9*

Peter Denies Jesus

Those who had arrested Jesus took him to Caiaphas the high priest, in whose house the scribes and the elders had gathered. [58]But Peter was following him at a distance, as far as the courtyard of the high priest; and going inside, he sat with the guards in order to see how this would end. [59]Now the chief priests and the whole council were looking for false testimony against Jesus so that they might put him to death.

[69]Now Peter was sitting outside in the courtyard. A servant-girl came to him and said, "You also were with Jesus the Galilean." [70]But he denied it before all of them, saying, "I do not know what you are talking about." [71]When he went out to the porch, another servant-girl saw him, and she said to the bystanders, "This man was with Jesus of Nazareth."[a]  [72]Again he denied it with an oath, "I do not know the man." [73]After a little while the bystanders came up and said to Peter, "Certainly you are also one of them, for your accent betrays you." [74]Then he began to curse, and he swore an oath, "I do not know the man!" At that moment the cock crowed. [75]Then Peter remembered what Jesus had said: "Before the cock crows, you will deny me three times." And he went out and wept bitterly.

[a]Gk *the Nazorean*

Prayer Starter: Dear God, keep me from ever being ashamed of being a Christian.

Memory Verse: The crowds that went ahead of him and that followed were shouting, "Hosanna to the Son of David! Blessed is the one who comes . . ."
—*Matthew 21.9*

The Crowd Decides

Now at the festival the governor was accustomed to release a prisoner for the crowd, anyone whom they wanted. [16]At that time they had a notorious prisoner, called Jesus[a] Barabbas. [17]So after they had gathered, Pilate said to them, "Whom do you want me to release for you, Jesus[a] Barabbas or Jesus who is called the Messiah?"[b] [18]For he realized that it was out of jealousy that they had handed him over. [19]While he was sitting on the judgment seat, his wife sent word to him, "Have nothing to do with that innocent man, for today I have suffered a great deal because of a dream about him." [20]Now the chief priests and the elders persuaded the crowds to ask for Barabbas and to have Jesus killed. [21]The governor again said to them, "Which of the two do you want me to release for you?" And they said, "Barabbas." [22]Pilate said to them, "Then what should I do with Jesus who is called the Messiah?"[b] All of them said, "Let him be crucified!" [23]Then he asked, "Why, what evil has he done?" But they shouted all the more, "Let him be crucified!"

[24]So when Pilate saw that he could do nothing, but rather that a riot was beginning, he took some water and washed his hands before the crowd, saying, "I am innocent of this man's blood;[c] see to it yourselves." [25]Then the people as a whole answered, "His blood be on us and on our children!" [26]So he released Barabbas for them; and after flogging Jesus, he handed him over to be crucified.

[a]Other ancient authorities lack *Jesus*
[b]Or *the Christ*
[c]Other ancient authorities read *this righteous blood,* or *this righteous man's blood*

Prayer Starter: How can I ever thank you enough for the Lord Jesus Christ?

Memory Verse: The crowds that went ahead of him and that followed were shouting, "Hosanna to the Son of David! Blessed is the one who comes in the name of the Lord!"   —*Matthew 21.9*

Jesus Heals the Sick

They were astounded at his teaching, for he [Jesus] taught them as one having authority, and not as the scribes. ²³Just then there was in their synagogue a man with an unclean spirit, ²⁴and he cried out, "What have you to do with us, Jesus of Nazareth? Have you come to destroy us? I know who you are, the Holy One of God." ²⁵But Jesus rebuked him, saying, "Be silent, and come out of him!" ²⁶And the unclean spirit, convulsing him and crying with a loud voice, came out of him. ²⁷They were all amazed, and they kept on asking one another, "What is this? A new teaching—with authority! He*a* commands even the unclean spirits, and they obey him." ²⁸At once his fame began to spread throughout the surrounding region of Galilee.

²⁹As soon as they*b* left the synagogue, they entered the house of Simon and Andrew, with James and John. ³⁰Now Simon's mother-in-law was in bed with a fever, and they told him about her at once. ³¹He came and took her by the hand and lifted her up. Then the fever left her, and she began to serve them.

³²That evening, at sundown, they brought to him all who were sick or possessed with demons. ³³And the whole city was gathered around the door. ³⁴And he cured many who were sick with various diseases, and cast out many demons; and he would not permit the demons to speak, because they knew him.

*a*Or *A new teaching! With authority he*
*b*Other ancient authorities read *he*

Prayer Starter: Help me to tell the good news about Jesus to someone this week.

Memory Verse: Let the little children come to me . . .   —*Mark 10.14*

Lots of Evil Spirits

They came to the other side of the sea, to the country of the Gerasenes.*a* 2And when he had stepped out of the boat, immediately a man out of the tombs with an unclean spirit met him. 3He lived among the tombs; and no one could restrain him any more, even with a chain; 4for he had often been restrained with shackles and chains, but the chains he wrenched apart, and the shackles he broke in pieces; and no one had the strength to subdue him. 5Night and day among the tombs and on the mountains he was always howling and bruising himself with stones. 6When he saw Jesus from a distance, he ran and bowed down before him; 7and he shouted at the top of his voice, "What have you to do with me, Jesus, Son of the Most High God? I adjure you by God, do not torment me." 8For he had said to him, "Come out of the man, you unclean spirit!" 9Then Jesus*b* asked him, "What is your name?" He replied, "My name is Legion; for we are many." 10He begged him earnestly not to send them out of the country. 11Now there on the hillside a great herd of swine was feeding; 12and the unclean spirits*c* begged him, "Send us into the swine; let us enter them." 13So he gave them permission. And the unclean spirits came out and entered the swine; and the herd, numbering about two thousand, rushed down the steep bank into the sea, and were drowned in the sea.

*a*Other ancient authorities read *Gergesenes*; others *Gadarenes*
*b*Gk *he*
*c*Gk *they*

Prayer Starter: You are stonger than the devil and all the demons, God. You are Lord over all the earth.

Memory Verse: Let the little children come to me; do not stop them . . .
—*Mark 10.14*

Jairus

When Jesus had crossed again in the boat[a] to the other side, a great crowd gathered around him; and he was by the sea. 22Then one of the leaders of the synagogue named Jairus came and, when he saw him, fell at his feet 23and begged him repeatedly, "My little daughter is at the point of death. Come and lay your hands on her, so that she may be made well, and live." 24So he went with him.

And a large crowd followed him and pressed in on him.

35While he was still speaking, some people came from the leader's house to say, "Your daughter is dead. Why trouble the teacher any further?" 36But overhearing[b] what they said, Jesus said to the leader of the synagogue, "Do not fear, only believe." 37He allowed no one to follow him

except Peter, James, and John, the brother of James. 38When they came to the house of the leader of the synagogue, he saw a commotion, people weeping and wailing loudly. 39When he had entered, he said to them, "Why do you make a commotion and weep? The child is not dead but sleeping." 40And they laughed at him. Then he put them all outside, and took the child's father and mother and those who were with him, and went in where the child was. 41He took her by the hand and said to her, "Talitha cum," which means, "Little girl, get up!" 42And immediately the girl got up and began to walk about (she was twelve years of age).

[a]Other ancient authorities lack *in the boat*
[b]Or *ignoring*; other ancient authorities read *hearing*

Prayer Starter: Keep me from worry. Give me faith instead of fear.

Memory Verse: Let the little children come to me; do not stop them; for it is to such as these . . .
—*Mark 10.14*

Jesus Feeds Five Thousand

The apostles gathered around Jesus, and told him all that they had done and taught. [31]He said to them, "Come away to a deserted place all by yourselves and rest a while." For many were coming and going, and they had no leisure even to eat. [32]And they went away in the boat to a deserted place by themselves. [33]Now many saw them going and recognized them, and they hurried there on foot from all the towns and arrived ahead of them. [34]As he went ashore, he saw a great crowd; and he had compassion for them, because they were like sheep without a shepherd; and he began to teach them many things. [35]When it grew late, his disciples came to him and said, "This is a deserted place, and the hour is now very late; [36]send them away so that they may go into the surrounding country and villages and buy something for themselves to eat." [37]But he answered them, "You give them something to eat." They said to him, "Are we to go and buy two hundred denarii[a] worth of bread, and give it to them to eat?" [38]And he said to them, "How many loaves have you? Go and see." When they had found out, they said, "Five, and two fish." [39]Then he ordered them to get all the people to sit down in groups on the green grass. [40]So they sat down in groups of hundreds and of fifties. [41]Taking the five loaves and the two fish, he looked up to heaven, and blessed and broke the loaves, and gave them to his disciples to set before the people; and he divided the two fish among them all. [42]And all ate and were filled; [43]and they took up twelve baskets full of broken pieces and of the fish. [44]Those who had eaten the loaves numbered five thousand men.

[a]The denarius was the usual day's wage for a laborer

Prayer Starter: Thank you, Lord, for fish and bread and pizzas and ice cream, and for all good things to eat.

Memory Verse: Let the little children come to me; do not stop them; for it is to such as these that the kingdom . . . —*Mark 10.14*

Jesus Blesses Children

Some Pharisees came, and to test him [Jesus] they asked, "Is it lawful for a man to divorce his wife?" ³He answered them, "What did Moses command you?" ⁴They said, "Moses allowed a man to write a certificate of dismissal and to divorce her." ⁵But Jesus said to them, "Because of your hardness of heart he wrote this commandment for you. ⁶But from the beginning of creation, 'God made them male and female.' ⁷For this reason a man shall leave his father and mother and be joined to his wife,[a] ⁸and the two shall become one flesh.' So they are no longer two, but one flesh. ⁹Therefore what God has joined together, let no one separate."

¹⁰Then in the house the disciples asked him again about this matter. ¹¹He said to them, "Whoever divorces his wife and marries another commits adultery against her; ¹²and if she divorces her husband and marries another, she commits adultery."

¹³People were bringing little children to him in order that he might touch them; and the disciples spoke sternly to them. ¹⁴But when Jesus saw this, he was indignant and said to them, "Let the little children come to me; do not stop them; for it is to such as these that the kingdom of God belongs. ¹⁵Truly I tell you, whoever does not receive the kingdom of God as a little child will never enter it." ¹⁶And he took them up in his arms, laid his hands on them, and blessed them.

[a]Other ancient authorities lack *and be joined to his wife*

Prayer Starter: Thank you, Lord, for loving me. Thank you for blessing me.

Memory Verse: Let the little children come to me; do not stop them; for it is to such as these that the kingdom of God belongs.

—*Mark 10.14*

The Passover Meal

On the first day of Unleavened Bread, when the Passover lamb is sacrificed, his disciples said to him, "Where do you want us to go and make the preparations for you to eat the Passover?" ¹³So he sent two of his disciples, saying to them, "Go into the city, and a man carrying a jar of water will meet you; follow him, ¹⁴and wherever he enters, say to the owner of the house, 'The Teacher asks, Where is my guest room where I may eat the Passover with my disciples?' ¹⁵He will show you a large room upstairs, furnished and ready. Make preparations for us there." ¹⁶So the disciples set out and went to the city, and found everything as he had told them; and they prepared the Passover meal.

¹⁷When it was evening, he came with the twelve. ¹⁸And when they had taken their places and were eating, Jesus said, "Truly I tell you, one of you will betray me, one who is eating with me." ¹⁹They began to be distressed and to say to him one after another, "Surely, not I?" ²⁰He said to them, "It is one of the twelve, one who is dipping bread*ᵃ* into the bowl*ᵇ* with me. ²¹For the Son of Man goes as it is written of him, but woe to that one by whom the Son of Man is betrayed! It would have been better for that one not to have been born."

²²While they were eating, he took a loaf of bread, and after blessing it he broke it, gave it to them, and said,

"Take; this is my body." ²³Then he took a cup, and after giving thanks he gave it to them, and all of them drank from it. ²⁴He said to them, "This is my blood of the*ᶜ* covenant, which is poured out for many. ²⁵Truly I tell you, I will never again drink of the fruit of the vine until that day when I drink it new in the kingdom of God."

²⁶When they had sung the hymn, they went out to the Mount of Olives.

*ᵃ*Gk lacks *bread*
*ᵇ*Other ancient authorities read *same bowl*
*ᶜ*Other ancient authorities add *new*

Prayer Starter: O God, thank you for giving us Jesus, your Son, through the Eucharist.

Memory Verse: The child . . .   —*Luke 1.35b*

Nail Him
to a Cross

As soon as it was morning, the chief priests held a consultation with the elders and scribes and the whole council. They bound Jesus, led him away, and handed him over to Pilate. ²Pilate asked him, "Are you the King of the Jews?" He answered him, "You say so." ³Then the chief priests accused him of many things. ⁴Pilate asked him again, "Have you no answer? See how many charges they bring against you." ⁵But Jesus made no further reply, so that Pilate was amazed.

⁶Now at the festival he used to release a prisoner for them, anyone for whom they asked. ⁷Now a man called Barabbas was in prison with the rebels who had committed murder during the insurrection. ⁸So the crowd came and began to ask Pilate to do for them according to his custom. ⁹Then he answered them, "Do you want me to release for you the

King of the Jews?" [10]For he realized that it was out of jealousy that the chief priests had handed him over. [11]But the chief priests stirred up the crowd to have him release Barabbas for them instead. [12]Pilate spoke to them again, "Then what do you wish me to do[a] with the man you call[b] the King of the Jews?" [13]They shouted back, "Crucify him!" [14]Pilate asked them, "Why, what evil has he done?" But they shouted all the more, "Crucify him!" [15]So Pilate, wishing to satisfy the crowd, released Barabbas for them; and after flogging Jesus, he handed him over to be crucified.

[a]Other ancient authorities read *what should I do*
[b]Other ancient authorities lack *the man you call*

Prayer Starter: I love you, Jesus, for suffering for me.

Memory Verse: The child to be born . . .   *—Luke 1.35b*

Soldiers Make Fun of Jesus

Then the soldiers led him [Jesus] into the courtyard of the palace (that is, the governor's headquarters[a]); and they called together the whole cohort. [17]And they clothed him in a purple cloak; and after twisting some thorns into a crown, they put it on him. [18]And they began saluting him, "Hail, King of the Jews!" [19]They struck his head with a reed, spat upon him, and knelt down in homage to him. [20]After mocking him, they stripped him of the purple cloak and put his own clothes on him. Then they led him out to crucify him.

[21]They compelled a passer-by, who was coming in from the country, to carry his cross; it was Simon of Cyrene, the father of Alexander and Rufus. [22]Then they brought Jesus[b] to the place called Golgotha (which means the place of a skull). [23]And they offered him wine mixed with myrrh; but he did not take it. [24]And they crucified him, and divided his clothes among them, casting lots to decide what each should take.

[25]It was nine o'clock in the morning when they crucified  him. [26]The inscription of the charge against him read, "The King of the Jews." [27]And with him they crucified two bandits, one on his right and one on his left.[c]

[a]Gk *the praetorium*
[b]Gk *him*
[c]Other ancient authorities add verse 28, *And the scripture was fulfilled that says, "And he was counted among the lawless."*

Prayer Starter: Thank you, Lord, thank you for Christ Jesus.

Memory Verse: The child to be born will be holy . . .   —*Luke 1.35b*

An Angel Visits Mary

In the sixth month the angel Gabriel was sent by God to a town in Galilee called Nazareth, 27to a virgin engaged to a man whose name was Joseph, of the house of David. The virgin's name was Mary. 28And he came to her and said, "Greetings, favored one! The Lord is with you."a 29But she was much perplexed by his words and pondered what sort of greeting this might be. 30The angel said to her, "Do not be afraid, Mary, for you have found favor with God. 31And now, you will conceive in your womb and bear a son, and you will name him Jesus. 32He will be great, and will be called the Son of the Most High, and the Lord God will give to him the throne of his ancestor David. 33He will reign over the house of Jacob forever, and of his kingdom there will be no end." 34Mary said to the angel, "How can this be, since I am a virgin?"b 35The angel said to her, "The Holy Spirit will come upon you, and the power of the Most High will overshadow you; therefore the child to be bornc will be holy; he will be called Son of God. 36And now, your relative Elizabeth in her old age has also conceived a son; and this is the sixth month for her who was said to be barren. 37For nothing will be impossible with God." 38Then Mary said, "Here am I, the servant of the Lord; let it be with me according to your word." Then the angel departed from her.

aOther ancient authorities add *Blessed are you among women*
bGk *I do not know a man*
cOther ancient authorities add *of you*

Prayer Starter: I am your servant, Lord. Use me.

Memory Verse: The child to be born will be holy; he will be called . . .
—*Luke 1.35b*

Mary and Elizabeth

In those days Mary set out and went with haste to a Judean town in the hill country, ⁴⁰where she entered the house of Zechariah and greeted Elizabeth. ⁴¹When Elizabeth heard Mary's greeting, the child leaped in her womb. And Elizabeth was filled with the Holy Spirit ⁴²and exclaimed with a loud cry, "Blessed are you among women, and blessed is the fruit of your womb. ⁴³And why has this happened to me, that the mother of my Lord comes to me? ⁴⁴For as soon as I heard the sound of your greeting, the child in my womb leaped for joy. ⁴⁵And blessed is she who believed that there would be*ᵃ* a fulfillment of what was spoken to her by the Lord."

⁴⁶And Mary*ᵇ* said,
"My soul magnifies the Lord,
⁴⁷   and my spirit rejoices in God my Savior,
⁴⁸ for he has looked with favor on the lowliness of his servant.
     Surely, from now on all generations will call me blessed;
⁴⁹ for the Mighty One has done great things for me,
     and holy is his name.
⁵⁰ His mercy is for those who fear him
     from generation to generation.
⁵¹ He has shown strength with his arm;
     he has scattered the proud in the thoughts of their hearts.
⁵² He has brought down the powerful from their thrones,
     and lifted up the lowly;
⁵³ he has filled the hungry with good things,
     and sent the rich away empty.
⁵⁴ He has helped his servant Israel,
     in remembrance of his mercy,
⁵⁵ according to the promise he made to our ancestors,
     to Abraham and to his descendants forever."

⁵⁶And Mary remained with her about three months and then returned to her home.

ᵃOr believed, for there will be
ᵇOther ancient authorities read Elizabeth

Prayer Starter: With all my heart, I praise the Lord.

Memory Verse: The child to be born will be holy; he will be called Son of God.
         —*Luke 1.35b*

Jesus Is Born

In those days a decree went out from Emperor Augustus that all the world should be registered. ²This was the first registration and was taken while Quirinius was governor of Syria. ³All went to their own towns to be registered. ⁴Joseph also went from the town of Nazareth in Galilee to Judea, to the city of David called Bethlehem, because he was descended from the house and family of David. ⁵He went to be registered with Mary, to whom he was engaged and who was expecting a child. ⁶While they were there, the time came for her to deliver her child. ⁷And she gave birth to her firstborn son and wrapped him in bands of cloth, and laid him in a manger, because there was no place for them in the inn.

⁸In that region there were shepherds living in the fields, keeping watch over their flock by night.

⁹Then an angel of the Lord stood before them, and the glory of the Lord shone around them, and they were terrified. ¹⁰But the angel said to them, "Do not be afraid; for see—I am bringing you good news of great joy for all the people: ¹¹to you is born this day in the city of David a Savior, who is the Messiah,ᵃ the Lord. ¹²This will be a sign for you: you will find a child wrapped in bands of cloth and lying in a manger." ¹³And suddenly there was with the angel a multitude of the heavenly host,ᵇ praising God and saying,

¹⁴ "Glory to God in the highest heaven,
   and on earth peace among those whom he favors!"ᶜ

¹⁵When the angels had left them and gone into heaven, the shepherds said to one another, "Let us go now to Bethlehem and see this thing that has taken place, which the Lord has made known to us." ¹⁶So they went with haste and found Mary and Joseph, and the child lying in the manger.

ᵃOr *the Christ*
ᵇGk *army*
ᶜOther ancient authorities read *peace, goodwill among people*

Prayer Starter: Thank you, Lord, for sending Jesus. Help me to think about him this Christmas.

Memory Verse: And Jesus increased . . .   —*Luke 2.52*

Simeon and Anna

Now there was a man in Jerusalem whose name was Simeon;[a] this man was righteous and devout, looking forward to the consolation of Israel, and the Holy Spirit rested on him. [26]It had been revealed to him by the Holy Spirit that he would not see death before he had seen the Lord's Messiah.[b] [27]Guided by the Spirit, Simeon[c] came into the temple; and when the parents brought in the child Jesus, to do for him what was customary under the law, [28]Simeon[d] took him in his arms and praised God, saying,

[29] "Master, now you are dismissing your servant[e] in peace,
according to your word;
[30] for my eyes have seen your salvation,
[31] which you have prepared in the presence of all peoples,
[32] a light for revelation to the Gentiles
and for glory to your people Israel."

[33]And the child's father and mother were amazed at what was being said about him. [34]Then Simeon[a] blessed them and said to his mother Mary, "This child is destined for the falling and the rising of many in Israel, and to be a sign that will be opposed [35]so that the inner thoughts of many will be revealed—and a sword will pierce your own soul too."

[36]There was also a prophet, Anna[f] the daughter of Phanuel, of the tribe of Asher. She was of a great age, having lived with her husband seven years after her marriage, [37]then as a widow to the age of eighty-four. She never left the temple but worshiped there with fasting and prayer night and day. [38]At that moment she came, and began to praise God and to speak about the child[g] to all who were looking for the redemption of Jerusalem.

[a]Gk *Symeon*
[b]Or *the Lord's Christ*
[c]Gk *In the Spirit, he*
[d]Gk *he*
[e]Gk *slave*
[f]Gk *Hanna*
[g]Gk *him*

Prayer Starter: Lord, your mighty power is a light for all the nations.

Memory Verse: And Jesus increased in wisdom . . .   *—Luke 2.52*

The Child Jesus

When they [Joseph and Mary] had finished everything required by the law of the Lord, they returned to Galilee, to their own town of Nazareth. ⁴⁰The child grew and became strong, filled with wisdom; and the favor of God was upon him.

⁴¹Now every year his parents went to Jerusalem for the festival of the Passover. ⁴²And when he was twelve years old, they went up as usual for the festival. ⁴³When the festival was ended and they started to return, the boy Jesus stayed behind in Jerusalem, but his parents did not know it. ⁴⁴Assuming that he was in the group of travelers, they went a day's journey. Then they started to look for him among their relatives and friends. ⁴⁵When they did not find

him, they returned to Jerusalem to search for him. ⁴⁶After three days
they found him in the temple, sitting among the teachers, listening to
them and asking them questions. ⁴⁷And all who heard him were amazed
at his understanding and his answers. ⁴⁸When his parents*ᵃ* saw him they
were astonished; and his mother said to him, "Child, why have you
treated us like this? Look, your father and I have been searching for you
in great anxiety." ⁴⁹He said to them, "Why were you searching for me?
Did you not know that I must be in my Father's house?"*ᵇ* ⁵⁰But they did
not understand what he said to them. ⁵¹Then he went down with them
and came to Nazareth, and was obedient to them. His mother treasured
all these things in her heart.

⁵²And Jesus increased in wisdom and in years,*ᶜ* and in divine and
human favor.

*ᵃ*Gk *they*
*ᵇ*Or *be about my Father's interests?*
*ᶜ*Or *in stature*

Prayer Starter: May I be like Jesus, dear Father. Make me wise and strong.

Memory Verse: And Jesus increased in wisdom and in years . . .
—*Luke 2.52*

John the Baptist

In the fifteenth year of the reign of Emperor Tiberius, when Pontius Pilate was governor of Judea, and Herod was ruler[a] of Galilee, and his brother Philip ruler[a] of the region of Ituraea and Trachonitis, and Lysanias ruler of Abilene, ²during the high priest-hood of Annas and Caiaphas, the word of God came to John son of Zechariah in the wilderness. ³He went into all the region around the Jordan, proclaiming a baptism of repentance for the forgiveness of sins, ⁴as it is written in the book of the words of the prophet Isaiah,

"The voice of one crying out in the wilderness:
'Prepare the way of the Lord,
    make his paths straight.
5   Every valley shall be filled,
        and every mountain and hill shall be made low,
    and the crooked shall be made straight,
        and the rough ways made smooth;
6   and all flesh shall see the salvation of God.'"

¹⁵As the people were filled with expectation, and all were questioning in their hearts concerning John, whether he might be the Messiah,[b] ¹⁶John answered all of them by saying, "I baptize you with water; but one who is more powerful than I is coming; I am not worthy to untie the thong of his sandals. He will baptize you with[c] the Holy Spirit and fire."

²¹Now when all the people were baptized, and when Jesus also had been baptized and was praying, the heaven was opened, ²²and the Holy Spirit descended upon him in bodily form like a dove. And a voice came from heaven, "You are my Son, the Beloved;[d] with you I am well pleased."[e]

[a]Gk *tetrarch*
[b]Or *the Christ*
[c]Or *in*
[d]Or *my beloved Son*
[e]Other ancient authorities read *You are my Son, today I have begotten you*

Prayer Starter: Lord, you are well pleased with your son Jesus. Be pleased with me, too.

Memory Verse: And Jesus increased in wisdom and in years, and in divine . . .
       —*Luke 2.52*

Jesus Heals a Servant

He [Jesus] came down with them and stood on a level place, with a great crowd of his disciples and a great multitude of people from all Judea, Jerusalem, and the coast of Tyre and Sidon. ¹⁸They had come to hear him and to be healed of their diseases.

7After Jesus*ᵃ* had finished all his sayings in the hearing of the people, he entered Capernaum. ²A centurion there had a slave whom he valued highly, and who was ill and close to death. ³When he heard about Jesus, he sent some Jewish elders to him, asking him to come and heal his slave. ⁴When they came to Jesus, they appealed to him earnestly, saying, "He is worthy of having you do this for him, ⁵for he loves our people, and it is he who built our synagogue for us." ⁶And Jesus went with them, but when he was not far from the house, the centurion sent friends to say to him, "Lord, do not trouble yourself, for I am not worthy to have you come under my roof; ⁷therefore I did not presume to come to you. But only speak the word, and let my servant be healed. ⁸For I also am a man set under authority, with soldiers under me; and I say to one, 'Go,' and he goes, and to another, 'Come,' and he comes, and to my slave, 'Do this,' and the slave does it." ⁹When Jesus heard this he was amazed at him, and turning to the crowd that followed him, he said, "I tell you, not even in Israel have I found such faith." ¹⁰When those who had been sent returned to the house, they found the slave in good health.

ᵃGk he

Prayer Starter: Give me faith like the centurion in this story, O God.

Memory Verse: And Jesus increased in wisdom and in years, and in divine and human favor.
—*Luke 2.52*

Young Man, Get Up

Soon afterwards[a] he went to a town called Nain, and his disciples and a large crowd went with him. [12]As he approached the gate of the town, a man who had died was being carried out. He was his mother's only son, and she was a widow; and with her was a large crowd from the town. [13]When the Lord saw her, he had compassion for her and said to her, "Do not weep." [14]Then he came forward and touched the bier, and the bearers stood still. And he said, "Young man, I say to you, rise!" [15]The dead man sat up and began to speak, and Jesus[b] gave him to his mother. [16]Fear seized all of them; and they glorified God, saying, "A great prophet has risen among us!" and "God has looked favorably on his people!" [17]This word about him spread throughout Judea and all the surrounding country.

[18]The disciples of John reported all these things to him. So John summoned two of his disciples[19]and sent them to the Lord to ask, "Are you the one who is to come, or are we to wait for another?"

[21]Jesus[b] had just then cured many people of diseases, plagues, and evil spirits, and had given sight to many who were blind. [22]And he answered them, "Go and tell John what you have seen and heard: the blind receive their sight, the lame walk, the lepers[c] are cleansed, the deaf hear, the dead are raised, the poor have good news brought to them. [23]And blessed is anyone who takes no offense at me."

[a]Other ancient authorities read *Next day*
[b]Gk *He*
[c]The terms *leper* and *leprosy* can refere to several diseases

Prayer Starter: Thank you, Lord, for helping those with problems.

Memory Verse: Consider the ravens . . .   —*Luke 12.24*

The Good Samaritan

Just then a lawyer stood up to test Jesus.[a] "Teacher," he said, "what must I do to inherit eternal life?" 26He said to him, "What is written in the law? What do you read there?" 27He answered, "You shall love the Lord your God with all your heart, and with all your soul, and with all your strength, and with all your mind; and your neighbor as yourself." 28And he said to him, "You have given the right answer; do this, and you will live."

29But wanting to justify himself, he asked Jesus, "And who is my neighbor?" 30Jesus replied, "A man was going down from Jerusalem to Jericho, and fell into the hands of robbers, who stripped him, beat him, and went away, leaving him half dead. 31Now by chance a priest was going down that road; and when he saw him, he passed by on the other side. 32So likewise a Levite, when he came to the place and saw him, passed by on the other side. 33But a Samaritan while traveling came near him; and when he saw him, he was moved with pity. 34He went to him and bandaged his wounds, having poured oil and wine on them. Then he put him on his own animal, brought him to an inn, and took care of him. 35The next day he took out two denarii,[b] gave them to the innkeeper, and said, 'Take care of him; and when I come back, I will repay you whatever more you spend.' 36Which of these three, do you think, was a neighbor to the man who fell into the hands of the robbers?" 37He said, "The one who showed him mercy." Jesus said to him, "Go and do likewise."

[a]Gk *him*
[b]The denarius was the usual day's wage for a laborer

Prayer Starter: Show me someone I can help this week, Lord.

Memory Verse: Consider the ravens: they neither sow nor reap . . .
—*Luke 12.24*

A Rich Fool

Someone in the crowd said to him, "Teacher, tell my brother to divide the family inheritance with me." ¹⁴But he said to him, "Friend, who set me to be a judge or arbitrator over you?" ¹⁵And he said to them, "Take care! Be on your guard against all kinds of greed; for one's life does not consist in the abundance of possessions." ¹⁶Then he told them a parable: "The land of a rich man produced abundantly. ¹⁷And he thought to himself, 'What should I do, for I have no place to store my crops?' ¹⁸Then he said, 'I will do this: I will pull down my barns and build larger ones, and there I will store all my grain and my goods. ¹⁹And I will say to my soul, 'Soul, you have ample goods laid up for many years; relax, eat, drink, be merry.' ²⁰But God said to him, 'You fool! This very night your life is being demanded of you. And the things you have prepared, whose will they be?' ²¹So it is with those who store up treasures for themselves but are not rich toward God."

Prayer Starter: Thank you for taking care of me, Lord. Help me to share what I have with others.

Memory Verse: Consider the ravens: they neither sow nor reap, they have neither . . .
—*Luke 12.24*

Now he was teaching in one of the synagogues on the sabbath. ¹¹And just then there appeared a woman with a spirit that had crippled her for eighteen years. She was bent over and was quite unable to stand up straight. ¹²When Jesus saw her, he called her over and said, "Woman, you are set free from your ailment." ¹³When he laid his hands on her, immediately she stood up straight and began praising God. ¹⁴But the leader of

the synagogue, indignant because Jesus had cured on the sabbath, kept saying to the crowd, "There are six days on which work ought to be done; come on those days and be cured, and not on the sabbath day." ¹⁵But the Lord answered him and said, "You hypocrites! Does not each of you on the sabbath untie his ox or his donkey from the manger, and lead it away to give it water? ¹⁶And ought not this woman, a daughter of Abraham whom Satan bound for eighteen long years, be set free from this bondage on the sabbath day?" ¹⁷When he said this, all his opponents were put to shame; and the entire crowd was rejoicing at all the wonderful things that he was doing.

¹⁸He said therefore, "What is the kingdom of God like? And to what

should I compare it? [19]It is like a mustard seed that someone took and sowed in the garden; it grew and became a tree, and the birds of the air made nests in its branches."

[20]And again he said, "To what should I compare the kingdom of God? [21]It is like yeast that a woman took and mixed in with[a] three measures of flour until all of it was leavened."

[a]Gk *hid in*

Prayer Starter: Lord, please help those who are sick today.

Memory Verse: Consider the ravens: they neither sow nor reap, they have neither storehouse nor barn . . . —*Luke 12.24*

Jesus' Parables

Now all the tax collectors and sinners were coming near to listen to him. ²And the Pharisees and the scribes were grumbling and saying, "This fellow welcomes sinners and eats with them."

³So he told them this parable: ⁴"Which one of you, having a hundred sheep and losing one of them, does not leave the ninety-nine in the wilderness and go after the one that is lost until he finds it? ⁵When he has found it, he lays it on his shoulders and rejoices. ⁶And when he comes home, he calls together his friends and neighbors, saying to them, 'Rejoice with me, for I have found my sheep that was lost.' ⁷Just so, I tell you, there will be more joy in heaven over one sinner who repents than over ninety-nine righteous persons who need no repentance.

⁸"Or what woman having ten silver coins,ᵃ if she loses one of them, does not light a lamp, sweep the house, and search carefully until she finds it? ⁹When she has found it, she calls together her friends and neighbors, saying, 'Rejoice with me, for I have found the coin that I had lost.' ¹⁰Just so, I tell you, there is joy in the presence of the angels of God over one sinner who repents."

ᵃGk *drachmas*, each worth about a day's wage for a laborer

Prayer Starter: May more and more people turn to you, O Lord.

Memory Verse: Consider the ravens: they neither sow nor reap, they have neither storehouse nor barn, and yet God feeds them.

—Luke 12.24

A Son Comes Home

Then Jesus*ᵃ* said, "There was a man who had two sons. ¹²The younger of them said to his father, 'Father, give me the share of the property that will belong to me.' So he divided his property between them. ¹³A few days later the younger son gathered all he had and traveled to a distant country, and there he squandered his property in dissolute living. ¹⁴When he had spent everything, a severe famine took place throughout that country, and he began to be in need. ¹⁵So he went and hired himself out to one of the citizens of that country, who sent him to his fields to feed the pigs. ¹⁶He would gladly have filled himself with*ᵇ* the pods that the pigs were eating; and no one gave him anything. ¹⁷But when he came to himself he said, 'How many of my father's hired hands have bread enough and to spare, but here I am dying of hunger! ¹⁸I will get up and go to my father, and I will say to him, "Father, I have sinned against heaven and before you; ¹⁹I am no longer worthy to be called your

son; treat me like one of your hired hands."' ²⁰So he set off and went to his father. But while he was still far off, his father saw him and was filled with compassion; he ran and put his arms around him and kissed him. ²¹Then the son said to him, 'Father, I have sinned against heaven and before you; I am no longer worthy to be called your son.'*ᶜ* ²²But the father said to his slaves, 'Quickly, bring out a robe—the best one—and put it on him; put a ring on his finger and sandals on his feet. ²³And get the fatted calf and kill it, and let us eat and celebrate; ²⁴for this son of mine was dead and is alive again; he was lost and is found!' And they began to celebrate.

²⁵"Now his elder son was in the field; and when he came and approached the house, he heard music and dancing. ²⁶He called one of the slaves and asked what was going on. ²⁷He replied, 'Your brother has come, and your father has killed the fatted calf, because he has got him back safe and sound.' ²⁸Then he became angry and refused to go in. His father came out and began to plead with him. ²⁹But he answered his father, 'Listen! For all these years I have been working like a slave for you, and I have never disobeyed your command; yet you have never given me even a young goat so that I might celebrate with my friends. ³⁰But when this son of yours came back, who has devoured your property with prostitutes, you killed the fatted calf for him!' ³¹Then the father*ᵈ* said to

him, 'Son, you are always with me, and all that is mine is yours. [32]But we had to celebrate and rejoice, because this brother of yours was dead and has come to life; he was lost and has been found.'"

[a]Gk *he*
[b]Other ancient authorities read *filled his stomach with*
[c]Other ancient authorities add *treat me as one of your hired servants*
[d]Gk *he*

Prayer Starter: Dear God, help us to love each other in our families.

Memory Verse: Thus it is written . . .   *—Luke 24.46*

A Widow and a Judge

Then Jesus[a] told them a parable about their need to pray always and not to lose heart. [2]He said, "In a certain city there was a judge who neither feared God nor had respect for people. [3]In that city there was a widow who kept coming to him and saying, 'Grant me justice against my opponent.' [4]For a while he refused; but later he said to himself, 'Though I have no fear of God and no respect for anyone, [5]yet because this widow keeps bothering me, I will grant her justice, so that she may not wear me out by continually coming.'"[b] [6]And the Lord said, "Listen to what the unjust judge says. [7]And will not God grant justice to his chosen ones who cry to him day and night? Will he delay long in helping them? [8]I tell you, he will quickly grant justice to them. And yet, when the Son of Man comes, will he find faith on earth?"

[a]Gk *he*
[b]Or *so that she may not finally come and slap me in the face*

19He [Jesus] entered Jericho and was passing through it. ²A man was there named Zacchaeus; he was a chief tax collector and was rich. ³He was trying to see who Jesus was, but on account of the crowd he could not, because he was short in stature. ⁴So he ran ahead and climbed a sycamore tree to see him, because he was going to pass that way. ⁵When Jesus came to the place, he looked up and said to him, "Zacchaeus, hurry and come down; for I must stay at your house today." ⁶So he hurried down and was happy to welcome him. ⁷All who saw it began to grumble and said, "He has gone to be the guest of one who is a sinner." ⁸Zacchaeus stood there and said to the Lord, "Look, half of my possessions, Lord, I will give to the poor; and if I have defrauded anyone of anything, I will pay back four times as much." ⁹Then Jesus said to him, "Today salvation has come to this house, because he too is a son of Abraham. ¹⁰For the Son of Man came to seek out and to save the lost."

Prayer Starter: Help me to keep on praying, Lord, and never give up.

Memory Verse: Thus it is written, that the Messiah is to suffer . . .
—*Luke 24.46*

Jesus Is Arrested

He [Jesus] came out and went, as was his custom, to the Mount of Olives; and the disciples followed him. ⁴⁰When he reached the place, he said to them, "Pray that you may not come into the time of trial."ᵃ ⁴¹Then he withdrew from them about a stone's throw, knelt down, and prayed, ⁴²"Father, if you are willing, remove this cup from me; yet, not my will but yours be done." [⁴³Then an angel from heaven appeared to him and gave him strength. ⁴⁴In his anguish he prayed more earnestly, and his sweat became like great drops of blood falling down on the ground.ᵇ] ⁴⁵When he got up from prayer, he came to the disciples and found them sleeping because of grief, ⁴⁶and he said to them, "Why are you sleeping? Get up and pray that you may not come into the time of trial."ᵃ

⁴⁷While he was still speaking, suddenly a crowd came, and the one called Judas, one of the twelve, was leading them. He approached Jesus to kiss him; ⁴⁸but Jesus said to him, "Judas, is it with a kiss that you are betraying the Son of Man?" ⁴⁹When those who were around him saw what was coming, they asked, "Lord, should we strike with the sword?" ⁵⁰Then one of them struck the slave of the high priest and cut off his right ear. ⁵¹But Jesus said, "No more of this!" And he touched his ear and healed him. ⁵²Then Jesus said to the chief priests, the officers of the temple police, and the elders who had come for him, "Have you come out with swords and clubs as if I were a bandit? ⁵³When I was with you day after day in the temple, you did not lay hands on me. But this is your hour, and the power of darkness!"

ᵃOr *into temptation*
ᵇOther ancient authorities lack verses 43 and 44

Prayer Starter: Lord, teach me to pray as Jesus did.

Memory Verse: Thus it is written, that the Messiah is to suffer and to rise . . .

—*Luke 24.46*

Travelers to Emmaus

Now on that same day two of them were going to a village called Emmaus, about seven miles from Jerusalem, [14]and talking with each other about all these things that had happened. [15]While they were talking and discussing, Jesus himself came near and went with them, [16]but their eyes were kept from recognizing him. [17]And he said to them, "What are you discussing with each other while you walk along?" They stood still, looking sad.[a] [18]Then one of them, whose name was Cleopas, answered him, "Are you the only stranger in Jerusalem who does not know the things that have taken place there in these days?" [19]He asked them, "What things?" They replied, "The things about Jesus of Nazareth,[b] who was a prophet mighty in deed and word before God and all the people, [20]and how our chief priests and leaders handed him over to be condemned to death and crucified him."

[25]Then he said to them, "Oh, how foolish you are, and how slow of heart to believe all that the prophets have declared! [26]Was it not necessary that the Messiah[c] should suffer these things and then enter into his glory?" [27]Then beginning with Moses and all the prophets, he interpreted to them the things about himself in all the scriptures.

[a]Other ancient authorities read *walk along, looking sad?"*
[b]Other ancient authorities read *Jesus the Nazorean*
[c]Or *the Christ*

Prayer Starter: I'm so glad Jesus is alive, Lord! Hallelujah!

Memory Verse: Thus it is written, that the Messiah is to suffer and to rise from the dead . . .
—*Luke 24.46*

Jesus Returns to Heaven

While they were talking about this, Jesus himself stood among them and said to them, "Peace be with you."[a] [37]They were startled and terrified, and thought that they were seeing a ghost. [38]He said to them, "Why are you frightened, and why do doubts arise in your hearts? [39]Look at my hands and my feet; see that it is I myself. Touch me and see; for a ghost does not have flesh and bones as you see that I have." [40]And when he had said this, he showed them his hands and his feet.[b] [41]While in their joy they were disbelieving and still wondering, he said to them, "Have you anything here to eat?" [42]They gave him a piece of broiled fish, [43]and he took it and ate in their presence.

[44]Then he said to them, "These are my words that I spoke to you while I was still with you— that everything written about me in the law of Moses, the prophets, and the psalms must be fulfilled." [45]Then he opened their minds to understand the scriptures, [46]and he said to them, "Thus it is written, that the Messiah[c] is to suffer and to rise from the dead on the third day, [47]and that repentance and forgiveness of sins is to be proclaimed in his name to all nations,[d] beginning from Jerusalem. [48]You are witnesses of these things. [49]And see, I am sending upon you what my Father promised; so stay here in the city until you have been clothed with power from on high."

[50]Then he led them out as far as Bethany, and, lifting up his hands, he blessed them. [51]While he was blessing them, he withdrew from them and was carried up into heaven.[e]

[a]Other ancient authorities lack *and said to them, "Peace be with you."*
[b]Other ancient authorities lack verse 40
[c]Or *the Christ*
[d]Or *nations. Beginning from Jerusalem you are witnesses*
[e]Other ancient authorities lack *and was carried up into heaven*

Prayer Starter: Dear God, help me to understand the Bible better.

Memory Verse: Thus it is written, that the Messiah is to suffer and to rise from the dead on the third day.   —*Luke 24.46*

A Wedding in Cana

On the third day there was a wedding in Cana of Galilee, and the mother of Jesus was there. ²Jesus and his disciples had also been invited to the wedding. ³When the wine gave out, the mother of Jesus said to him, "They have no wine." ⁴And Jesus said to her, "Woman, what concern is that to you and to me? My hour has not yet come." ⁵His mother said to the servants, "Do whatever he tells you." ⁶Now standing there were six stone water jars for the Jewish rites of purification, each holding twenty or thirty gallons. ⁷Jesus said to them, "Fill the jars with water." And they filled them up to the brim. ⁸He said to them, "Now draw some out, and take it to the chief steward." So they took it. ⁹When the steward tasted the water that had become wine, and did not know where it came from (though the servants who had drawn the water knew), the steward called the bridegroom ¹⁰and said to him, "Everyone serves the good wine first, and then the inferior wine after the guests have become drunk. But you have kept the good wine until now." ¹¹Jesus did this, the first of his signs, in Cana of Galilee, and revealed his glory; and his disciples believed in him.

¹²After this he went down to Capernaum with his mother, his brothers, and his disciples; and they remained there a few days.

Prayer Starter: Help me to do whatever Jesus tells me to, Lord.

Memory Verse: For God so loved the world . . .   *—John 3.16*

Nicodemus Visits Jesus

Now there was a Pharisee named Nicodemus, a leader of the Jews. [2]He came to Jesus[a] by night and said to him, "Rabbi, we know that you are a teacher who has come from God; for no one can do these signs that you do apart from the presence of God." [3]Jesus answered him, "Very truly, I tell you, no one can see the kingdom of God without being born from above."[b] [4]Nicodemus said to him, "How can anyone be born after having grown old? Can one enter a second time into the mother's womb and be born?" [5]Jesus answered, "Very truly, I tell you, no one can enter the kingdom of God without being born of water and Spirit. [6]What is born of the flesh is flesh, and what is born of the Spirit is spirit.[c] [7]Do not be astonished that I said to you, 'You[d] must be born from above.'[e] [8]The wind[c] blows where it chooses, and you hear the sound of it, but you do not know where it comes from or where it goes. So it is with everyone who is born of the Spirit." [9]Nicodemus said to him, "How can these things be?" [10]Jesus answered him, "Are you a teacher of Israel, and yet you do not understand these things?

[11]"Very truly, I tell you, we speak of what we know and testify to what we have seen; yet you[f] do not receive our testimony. [12]If I have told you about earthly things and you do not believe, how can you believe if I tell you about heavenly things?"

[a]Gk *him*
[b]Or *born anew*
[c]The same Greek word means both *wind* and *spirit*
[d]The Greek word for *you* here is plural
[e]Or *anew*
[f]The Greek word for *you* here and in verse 12 is plural.

Prayer Starter: Thank you, God, for loving the people of this world enough to give your only Son to save them.

Memory Verse: For God so loved the world that he gave his only Son . . .

—John 3.16

The Woman at the Well

He left Judea and started back to Galilee. [4]But he had to go through Samaria. [5]So he came to a Samaritan city called Sychar, near the plot of ground that Jacob had given to his son Joseph. [6]Jacob's well was there, and Jesus, tired out by his journey, was sitting by the well. It was about noon.

[7]A Samaritan woman came to draw water, and Jesus said to her, "Give me a drink." [8](His disciples had gone to the city to buy food.) [9]The Samaritan woman said to him, "How is it that you, a Jew, ask a drink of me, a woman of Samaria?" (Jews do not share things in common with Samaritans.)[a] [10]Jesus answered her, "If you knew the gift of God, and who it is that is saying to you, 'Give me a drink,' you would have asked him, and he would have given you living water." [11]The woman said to him, "Sir, you have no bucket, and the well is deep. Where do you get that living water? [12]Are you greater than our ancestor Jacob, who gave us the well, and with his sons and his flocks drank from it?" [13]Jesus said to her, "Everyone who drinks of this water will be thirsty again, [14]but those who drink of the water that I will give them will never be thirsty. The water that I will give will become in them a spring of water gushing up to eternal life."

[a]Other ancient authorities lack this sentence

Prayer Starter: You give me the water of life, Lord. Thank you.

Memory Verse: For God so loved the world that he gave his only Son, so that everyone who believes in him . . .   *—John 3.16*

Jesus' Brothers

After this Jesus went about in Galilee. He did not wish[a] to go about in Judea because the Jews were looking for an opportunity to kill him. [2]Now the Jewish festival of Booths[b] was near. [3]So his brothers said to him, "Leave here and go to Judea so that your disciples also may see the works you are doing; [4]for no one who wants[c] to be widely known acts in secret. If you do these things, show yourself to the world." [5](For not even his brothers believed in him.) [6]Jesus said to them, "My time has not yet come, but your time is always here. [7]The world cannot hate you, but it hates me because I testify against it that its works are evil. [8]Go to the festival yourselves. I am not[d] going to this festival, for my time has not yet fully come." [9]After saying this, he remained in Galilee.

[10]But after his brothers had gone to the festival, then he also went, not publicly but as it were[e] in secret. [11]The Jews were looking for him at the festival and saying, "Where is he?" [12]And there was considerable complaining about him among the crowds. While some were saying, "He is a good man," others were saying, "No, he is deceiving the crowd." [13]Yet no one would speak openly about him for fear of the Jews.

[37]On the last day of the festival, the great day, while Jesus was standing there, he cried out, "Let anyone who is thirsty come to me, [38]and let the one who believes in me drink. As[f] the scripture has said, 'Out of the believer's heart[g] shall flow rivers of living water.'" [39]Now he said this about the Spirit, which believers in him were to receive; for as yet there was no Spirit,[h] because Jesus was not yet glorified.

[a]Other ancient authorities read *was not at liberty*
[b]Or *Tabernacles*
[c]Other ancient authorities read *wants it*
[d]Other ancient authorities add *yet*
[e]Other ancient authorities lack *as it*
[f]Or *come to me and drink.*
[g]Gk *out of his belly*
[h]Other ancient authorities read *for as yet the Spirit* (others, *Holy Spirit*) *had not been given*

Prayer Starter: Father, help me to share the water of life with others.

Memory Verse: For God so loved the world that he gave his only Son, so that everyone who believes in him may not perish . . .   —*John 3.16*

The Blind Man

As he walked along, he saw a man blind from birth. [2]His disciples asked him, "Rabbi, who sinned, this man or his parents, that he was born blind?" [3]Jesus answered, "Neither this man nor his parents sinned; he was born blind so that God's works might be revealed in him. [4]We[a] must work the works of him who sent me[b] while it is day; night is coming when no one can work. [5]As long as I am in the world, I am the light of the world." [6]When he had said this, he spat on the ground and made mud with the saliva and spread the mud on the man's eyes, [7]saying to him, "Go, wash in the pool of Siloam" (which means Sent). Then he went and washed and came back able to see. [8]The neighbors and those who had seen him before as a beggar began to ask, "Is this not the man who used to sit and beg?" [9]Some were saying, "It is he." Others were saying, "No, but it is someone like him." He kept saying, "I am the man." [10]But they kept asking him, "Then how were your eyes opened?" [11]He answered, "The man called Jesus made mud, spread it on my eyes, and said to me, 'Go to Siloam and

wash.' Then I went and washed and received my sight." ¹²They said to him, "Where is he?" He said, "I do not know."

¹³They brought to the Pharisees the man who had formerly been blind. ¹⁴Now it was a sabbath day when Jesus made the mud and opened his eyes. ¹⁵Then the Pharisees also began to ask him how he had received his sight. He said to them, "He put mud on my eyes. Then I washed, and now I see." ¹⁶Some of the Pharisees said, "This man is not from God, for he does not observe the sabbath." But others said, "How can a man who is a sinner perform such signs?" And they were divided. ¹⁷So they said again to the blind man, "What do you say about him? It was your eyes he opened." He said, "He is a prophet."

²⁴So for the second time they called the man who had been blind, and they said to him, "Give glory to God! We know that this man is a sinner." ²⁵He answered, "I do not know whether he is a sinner. One thing I do know, that though I was blind, now I see."

ᵃOther ancient authorities read *I*
ᵇOther ancient authorities read *us*

Prayer Starter: I'm amazed at Jesus' power! I praise and worship him.

Memory Verse: For God so loved the world that he gave his only Son, so that everyone who believes in him may not perish but may have eternal life.
—*John 3.16*

The Good Shepherd

So again Jesus said to them, "Very truly, I tell you, I am the gate for the sheep. [8]All who came before me are thieves and bandits; but the sheep did not listen to them. [9]I am the gate. Whoever enters by me will be saved, and will come in and go out and find pasture. [10]The thief comes only to steal and kill and destroy. I came that they may have life, and have it abundantly.

[11]"I am the good shepherd. The good shepherd lays down his life for the sheep. [12]The hired hand, who is not the shepherd and does not own the sheep, sees the wolf coming and leaves the sheep and runs away—and the wolf snatches them and scatters them. [13]The hired hand runs away because a hired hand does not care for the sheep. [14]I am the good shepherd. I know my own and my own know me, [15]just as the Father knows me and I know the Father. And I lay down my life for the sheep. [16]I have other sheep that do not belong to this fold. I must bring them also, and they will listen to my voice. So there will be one flock, one shepherd."

Prayer Starter: Lord, give me life to the fullest!

Memory Verse: The thief comes only to steal . . .   *—John 10.10*

Lazarus, Come Out!

Jesus said to her, "I am the resurrection and the life.[a] Those who believe in me, even though they die, will live, 26and everyone who lives and believes in me will never die. Do you believe this?" 27She said to him, "Yes, Lord, I believe that you are the Messiah,[b] the Son of God, the one coming into the world."

28When she had said this, she went back and called her sister Mary, and told her privately, "The Teacher is here and is calling for you." 29And when she heard it, she got up quickly and went to him. 30Now Jesus had not yet come to the village, but was still at the place where Martha had met him. 31The Jews who were with her in the house, consoling her, saw Mary get up quickly and go out. They followed her because they thought that she was going to the tomb to weep there. 32When Mary came where Jesus was and saw him, she knelt at his feet and said to him, "Lord, if you had been here, my brother would not have died." 33When Jesus saw her weeping, and the Jews who came with her also weeping, he was greatly disturbed in spirit and deeply moved. 34He said, "Where have you laid him?" They said to him, "Lord, come and see." 35Jesus began to weep.

36So the Jews said, "See how he loved him!" 37But some of them said, "Could not he who opened the eyes of the blind man have kept this man from dying?"

38Then Jesus, again greatly disturbed, came to the tomb. It was a cave, and a stone was lying against it. 39Jesus said, "Take away the stone." Martha, the sister of the dead man, said to him, "Lord, already there is a stench because he has been dead four days." 40Jesus said to her, "Did I not tell you that if you believed, you would see the glory of God?" 41So they took away the stone. And Jesus looked upward and said, "Father, I thank you for having heard me. 42I knew that you always hear me, but I have said this for the sake of the crowd standing here, so that they may believe that you sent me." 43When he had said this, he cried with a loud voice, "Lazarus, come out!" 44The dead man came out, his hands and feet bound with strips of cloth, and his face wrapped in a cloth. Jesus said to them, "Unbind him, and let him go."

[a]Other ancient authorities lack *and the life*
[b]Or *the Christ*

Prayer Starter: Father, I thank you for answering my prayers.

Memory Verse: The thief comes only to steal and kill and destroy. . . .
—*John 10.10*

Washing Feet

Now before the festival of the Passover, Jesus knew that his hour had come to depart from this world and go to the Father. Having loved his own who were in the world, he loved them to the end. ²The devil had already put it into the heart of Judas son of Simon Iscariot to betray him. And during supper ³Jesus, knowing that the Father had given all things into his hands, and that he had come from God and was going to God, ⁴got up from the table,ᵃ took off his outer robe, and tied a towel around himself. ⁵Then he poured water into a basin and began to wash the disciples' feet and to wipe them with the towel that was tied around him. ⁶He came to Simon Peter, who said to him, "Lord, are you going to wash my feet?" ⁷Jesus answered, "You do not know now what I am doing, but later you will understand." ⁸Peter said to him, "You will never wash my feet." Jesus answered, "Unless I wash you, you have no share with me." ⁹Simon Peter said to him, "Lord, not my feet only but also my hands and my head!" ¹⁰Jesus said to him, "One who has bathed does not need to wash, except for the feet,ᵇ but is entirely clean. And youᶜ are clean, though not all of you." ¹¹For he knew who was to betray him; for this reason he said, "Not all of you are clean."

¹²After he had washed their feet, had put on his robe, and had returned to the table, he said to them, "Do you know what I have done to you? ¹³You call me Teacher and Lord—and you are right, for that is what I am. ¹⁴So if I, your Lord and Teacher, have washed your feet, you also ought to wash one another's feet. ¹⁵For I have set you an example, that you also should do as I have done to you. ¹⁶Very truly, I tell you, servants*d* are not greater than their master, nor are messengers greater than the one who sent them. ¹⁷If you know these things, you are blessed if you do them."

*ª*Gk *from supper*
*ᵇ*Other ancient authorities lack *except for the feet*
*ᶜ*The Greek word for *you* here is plural
*ᵈ*Gk *slaves*

Prayer Starter: Make me a humble servant, just like the Lord Jesus.

Memory Verse: The thief comes only to steal and kill and destroy. I came . . .
—John 10.10

Jesus Is Arrested

After Jesus had spoken these words, he went out with his disciples across the Kidron valley to a place where there was a garden, which he and his disciples entered. ²Now Judas, who betrayed him, also knew the place, because Jesus often met there with his disciples. ³So Judas brought a detachment of soldiers together with police from the chief priests and the Pharisees, and they came there with lanterns and torches and weapons. ⁴Then Jesus, knowing all that was to happen to him, came forward and asked them, "Whom are you looking for?" ⁵They answered, "Jesus of Nazareth."ᵃ Jesus replied, "I am he."ᵇ Judas, who betrayed him, was standing with them. ⁶When Jesusᶜ said to them, "I am he,"ᵇ

they stepped back and fell to the ground. ⁷Again he asked them, "Whom are you looking for?" And they said, "Jesus of Nazareth."ᵃ ⁸Jesus answered, "I told you that I am he.ᵇ So if you are looking for me, let these men go." ⁹This was to fulfill the word that he had spoken, "I did not lose a single one of those whom you gave me." ¹⁰Then Simon Peter, who had a sword, drew it, struck the high priest's slave, and cut off his right ear. The slave's name was Malchus. ¹¹Jesus said to Peter, "Put your sword back into its sheath. Am I not to drink the cup that the Father has given me?"

¹²So the soldiers, their officer, and the Jewish police arrested Jesus and bound him.

ᵃGk *the Nazorean*
ᵇGk *I am*
ᶜGk *he*

Prayer Starter: Help me to be patient, Lord, with people I don't like.

Memory Verse: The thief comes only to steal and kill and destroy. I came that they may have life . . .   *—John 10.10*

**King of
the Jews**

Pilate also had an inscription written and put on the cross. It read, "Jesus of Nazareth,[a] the King of the Jews." [20]Many of the Jews read this inscription, because the place where Jesus was crucified was near the city; and it was written in Hebrew,[b] in Latin, and in Greek. [21]Then the chief priests of the Jews said to Pilate, "Do not write, 'The King of the Jews,' but, 'This man said, I am King of the Jews.'" [22]Pilate answered, "What I have written I have written." [23]When the soldiers had crucified Jesus, they took his clothes and divided them into four parts, one for each soldier. They also took his tunic; now the tunic was seamless, woven in one piece from the top. [24]So they said to one another, "Let us not tear it, but cast lots for it to see who will get it." This was to fulfill what the scripture says,

"They divided my clothes among themselves,
and for my clothing they cast lots."

[25]And that is what the soldiers did.

Meanwhile, standing near the cross of Jesus were his mother, and his mother's sister, Mary the wife of Clopas, and Mary Magdalene. [26]When Jesus saw his mother and the disciple whom he loved standing beside her, he said to his mother, "Woman, here is your son." [27]Then he said to the disciple, "Here is your mother." And from that hour the disciple took her into his own home.

[28]After this, when Jesus knew that all was now finished, he said (in order to fulfill the scripture), "I am thirsty." [29]A jar full of sour wine was standing there. So they put a sponge full of the wine on a branch of hyssop and held it to his mouth. [30]When Jesus had received the wine, he said, "It is finished." Then he bowed his head and gave up his spirit.

[a]Gk *the Nazorean*
[b]That is, *Aramaic*

Prayer Starter: Help me never to forget what Jesus has done for me on the Cross.

Memory Verse: The thief comes only to steal and kill and destroy. I came that they may have life, and have it abundantly.   —*John 10.10*

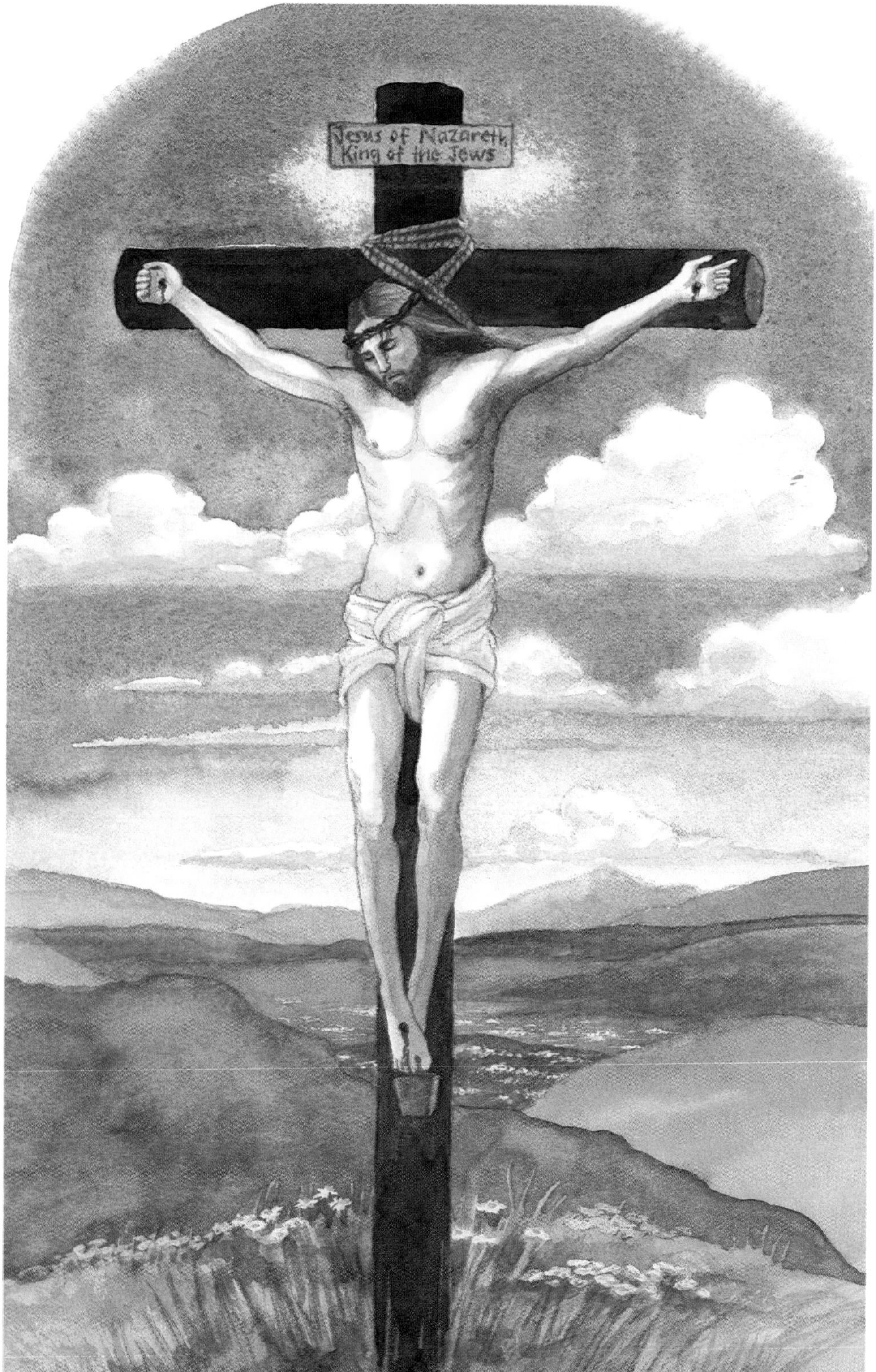
Jesus of Nazareth,
King of the Jews

The Empty Tomb

After these things, Joseph of Arimathea, who was a disciple of Jesus, though a secret one because of his fear of the Jews, asked Pilate to let him take away the body of Jesus. Pilate gave him permission; so he came and removed his body. ³⁹Nicodemus, who had at first come to Jesus by night, also came, bringing a mixture of myrrh and aloes, weighing about a hundred pounds. ⁴⁰They took the body of Jesus and wrapped it with the

spices in linen cloths, according to the burial custom of the Jews. ⁴¹Now there was a garden in the place where he was crucified, and in the garden there was a new tomb in which no one had ever been laid. ⁴²And so, because it was the Jewish day of Preparation, and the tomb was nearby, they laid Jesus there.

20 Early on the first day of the week, while it was still dark, Mary Magdalene came to the tomb and saw that the stone had been removed from the tomb. ²So she ran and went to Simon Peter and the other disciple, the one whom Jesus loved, and said to them, "They have taken the Lord out of the tomb, and we do not know where they have laid him." ³Then Peter and the other disciple set out and went

toward the tomb. ⁴The two were running together, but the other disciple outran Peter and reached the tomb first. ⁵He bent down to look in and saw the linen wrappings lying there, but he did not go in ⁶Then Simon Peter came, following him, and went into the tomb. He saw the linen wrappings lying there, ⁷and the cloth that had been on Jesus' head, not lying with the linen wrappings but rolled up in a place by itself. ⁸Then the other disciple, who reached the tomb first, also went in, and he saw and believed; ⁹for as yet they did not understand the scripture, that he must rise from the dead. ¹⁰Then the disciples returned to their homes.

Prayer Starter: Remind me each day, Lord, that Jesus is alive.

Memory Verse: But you will receive power . . .   —*Acts 1.8*

Jesus Appears to Mary

But Mary stood weeping outside the tomb. As she wept, she bent over to look*ᵃ* into the tomb; ¹²and she saw two angels in white, sitting where the body of Jesus had been lying, one at the head and the other at the feet. ¹³They said to her, "Woman, why are you weeping?" She said to them, "They have taken away my Lord, and I do not know where they have laid him." ¹⁴When she had said this, she turned around and saw Jesus standing there, but she did not know that it was Jesus. ¹⁵Jesus said to her, "Woman, why are you weeping? Whom are you looking for?" Supposing him to be the gardener, she said to him, "Sir, if you have carried him away, tell me where you have laid him, and I will take him away." ¹⁶Jesus said to her, "Mary!" She turned and said to him in Hebrew,*ᵇ* "Rabbouni!" (which means Teacher). ¹⁷Jesus said to her, "Do not hold on to me, because I have not yet ascended to the Father. But go to my brothers and say to them, 'I am ascending to my Father and your Father, to my God and your God.'" ¹⁸Mary Magdalene went and announced to the disciples, "I have seen the Lord"; and she told them that he had said these things to her.

ᵃGk lacks to look
ᵇThat is, Aramaic

Prayer Starter: Help me to tell others the good news that Jesus rose from the dead.

Memory Verse: But you will receive power when the Holy Spirit has come upon you . . .   *—Acts 1.8*

Jesus and Thomas

When it was evening on that day, the first day of the week, and the doors of the house where the disciples had met were locked for fear of the Jews, Jesus came and stood among them and said, "Peace be with you." 20After he said this, he showed them his hands and his side. Then the disciples rejoiced when they saw the Lord. 21Jesus said to them again, "Peace be with you. As the Father has sent me, so I send you." 22When he had said this, he breathed on them and said to them, "Receive the Holy Spirit. 23If you forgive the sins of any, they are forgiven them; if you retain the sins of any, they are retained."

24But Thomas (who was called the Twin*a*), one of the twelve, was not with them when Jesus came. 25So the other disciples told him, "We have seen the Lord." But he said to them, "Unless I see the mark of the nails in his hands, and put my finger in the mark of the nails and my hand in his side, I will not believe."

26A week later his disciples were again in the house, and Thomas was with them. Although the doors were shut, Jesus came and stood among them and said, "Peace be with you." 27Then he said to Thomas, "Put your finger here and see my hands. Reach out your hand and put it in my side. Do not doubt but believe." 28Thomas answered him, "My Lord and my God!"

*a*Greek *Didymus*

Prayer Starter: Thank you, heavenly Father, for Jesus who is my Lord and my God!

Memory Verse: But you will receive power when the Holy Spirit has come upon you; and you will be my witnesses in Jerusalem . . . —*Acts 1.8*

Two Men Dressed in White

After his [Jesus'] suffering he presented himself alive to them by many convincing proofs, appearing to them during forty days and speaking about the kingdom of God. ⁴While staying*ᵃ* with them, he ordered them not to leave Jerusalem, but to wait there for the promise of the Father. "This," he said, "is what you have heard from me; ⁵for John baptized with water, but you will be baptized with*ᵇ* the Holy Spirit not many days from now."

⁶So when they had come together, they asked him, "Lord, is this the time when you will restore the kingdom to Israel?" ⁷He replied, "It is not for you to know the times or periods that the Father has set by his own authority. ⁸But you will receive power when the Holy Spirit has come upon you; and you will be my witnesses in Jerusalem, in all Judea and Samaria, and to the ends of the earth." ⁹When he had said this, as they were watching, he was lifted up, and a cloud took him out of their sight. ¹⁰While he was going and they were gazing up toward heaven, suddenly two men in white robes stood by them. ¹¹They said, "Men of Galilee, why do you stand looking up toward heaven? This Jesus, who has been taken up from you into heaven, will come in the same way as you saw him go into heaven."

*ᵃ*Or *eating*
*ᵇ*Or *by*

Prayer Starter: Please hurry and come back to earth, Lord. We love you.

Memory Verse: But you will receive power when the Holy Spirit has come upon you; and you will be my witnesses in Jerusalem, in all Judea and Samaria . . .
—*Acts 1.8*

The Disciples Meet

When they had entered the city, they went to the room upstairs where they were staying, Peter, and John, and James, and Andrew, Philip and Thomas, Bartholomew and Matthew, James son of Alphaeus, and Simon the Zealot, and Judas son of[a] James. [14]All these were constantly devoting themselves to prayer, together with certain women, including Mary the mother of Jesus, as well as his brothers.

[15]In those days Peter stood up among the believers[b] (together the crowd numbered about one hundred twenty persons) and said, [16]"Friends,[c] the scripture had to be fulfilled, which the Holy Spirit through David foretold concerning Judas, who became a guide for those who arrested Jesus— [17]for he was numbered among us and was allotted his share in this ministry."

[21]"So one of the men who have accompanied us during all the time that the Lord Jesus went in and out among us, [22]beginning from the baptism of John until the day when he was taken up from us—one of these must become a witness with us to his resurrection." [23]So they proposed two, Joseph called Barsabbas, who was also known as Justus, and Matthias. [24]Then they prayed and said, "Lord, you know everyone's heart. Show us which one of these two you have chosen [25]to take the place[d] in this ministry and apostleship from which Judas turned aside to go to his own place." [26]And they cast lots for them, and the lot fell on Matthias; and he was added to the eleven apostles.

[a]Or *the brother of*
[b]Gk *brothers*
[c]Gk *Men, brothers*

Prayer Starter: Show me your choices for me, each day, O Lord.

Memory Verse: But you will receive power when the Holy Spirit has come upon you; and you will be my witnesses in Jerusalem, in all Judea and Samaria, and to the ends of the earth.
—*Acts 1.8*

The Day of Pentecost

When the day of Pentecost had come, they were all together in one place. ²And suddenly from heaven there came a sound like the rush of a violent wind, and it filled the entire house where they were sitting. ³Divided tongues, as of fire, appeared among them, and a tongue rested on each of them. ⁴All of them were filled with the Holy Spirit and began to speak in other languages, as the Spirit gave them ability.

⁵Now there were devout Jews from every nation under heaven living in Jerusalem. ⁶And at this sound the crowd gathered and was bewildered, because each one heard them speaking in the native language of each. ⁷Amazed and astonished, they asked, "Are not all these who are speaking Galileans? ⁸And how is it that we hear, each of us, in our own native language? ⁹Parthians, Medes, Elamites, and residents of Mesopotamia, Judea and Cappadocia, Pontus and Asia, ¹⁰Phrygia and Pamphylia, Egypt and the parts of Libya belonging to Cyrene, and visitors from Rome, both Jews and proselytes, ¹¹Cretans and Arabs—in our own languages we hear them speaking about God's deeds of power."

Prayer Starter: Thank you for giving me a tongue for speaking. Help me to use it to share Christ with others.

Memory Verse: There is salvation in no one else . . .   —Acts 4.12

Peter Heals a Lame Man

One day Peter and John were going up to the temple at the hour of prayer, at three o'clock in the afternoon. ²And a man lame from birth was being carried in. People would lay him daily at the gate of the temple called the Beautiful Gate so that he could ask for alms from those entering the temple. ³When he saw Peter and John about to go into the temple, he asked them for alms. ⁴Peter looked intently at him, as did John, and said, "Look at us." ⁵And he fixed his attention on them, expecting to receive something from them. ⁶But Peter said, "I have no silver or gold, but what I have I give you; in the name of Jesus Christ of Nazareth,ᵃ stand up and walk." ⁷And he took him by the right hand and raised him up; and immediately his feet and ankles were made strong. ⁸Jumping up, he stood and began to walk, and he entered the temple with them, walking and leaping and praising God. ⁹All the people saw him walking and praising God, ¹⁰and they recognized him as the one who used to sit and ask for alms at the Beautiful Gate of the temple; and they were filled with wonder and amazement at what had happened to him.

ᵃGk *the Nazorean*

Prayer Starter: Thank you for my feet and legs. Thank you for giving me energy each day.

Memory Verse: There is salvation in no one else, for there is no other name . . .
—*Acts 4.12*

**Peter and
John
Arrested**

While Peter and John[a] were speaking to the people, the priests, the captain of the temple, and the Sadducees came to them, [2]much annoyed because they were teaching the people and proclaiming that in Jesus there is the resurrection of the dead. [3]So they arrested them and put them in custody until the next day, for it was already evening. [4]But many of those who heard the word believed; and they numbered about five thousand.

[5]The next day their rulers, elders, and scribes assembled in Jerusalem, [6]with Annas the high priest, Caiaphas, John,[b] and Alexander, and all who were of the high-priestly family. [7]When they had made the prisoners[c] stand in their midst, they inquired, "By what power or by what name did you do this?" [8]Then Peter, filled with the Holy Spirit, said to them, "Rulers of the people and elders, [9]if we are questioned today because of a good deed done to someone who was sick and are asked how this man has been healed, [10]let it be known to all of you, and to all the people of Israel, that this man is standing before you in good health by the name of Jesus Christ of Nazareth,[d] whom you crucified, whom God raised from the dead. [11]This Jesus[e] is

'the stone that was rejected by you, the builders;
    it has become the cornerstone.'[f]

[12]There is salvation in no one else, for there is no other name under heaven given among mortals by which we must be saved."

[13]Now when they saw the boldness of Peter and John and realized that they were uneducated and ordinary men, they were amazed and recognized them as companions of Jesus. [14]When they saw the man who had been cured standing beside them, they had nothing to say in opposition. [15]So they ordered them to leave the council while they discussed the matter with one another.

[16]They said, "What will we do with them? For it is obvious to all who live in Jerusalem that a notable sign has been done through them; we cannot deny it. [17]But to keep it from spreading further among the people, let us warn them to speak no more to anyone in this name." [18]So they called them and ordered them not to speak or teach at all in the name of Jesus. [19]But Peter and John answered them, "Whether it is right in God's sight to listen to you rather than to God, you must judge; [20]for we cannot keep from speaking about what we have seen and heard." [21]After threatening them again, they let them go, finding no way to punish them because of the people, for all of them praised God for what had happened. [22]For the man on whom this sign of healing had been performed was more than forty years old.

[a]Gk *While they*
[b]Other ancient authorities read *Jonathan*
[c]Gk *them*
[d]Gk *the Nazorean*
[e]Gk *This*
[f]Or *keystone*

Prayer Starter: Lord, your name is the only one in all the earth that can save anyone.

Memory Verse: There is salvation in no one else, for there is no other name under heaven . . .   —*Acts 4.12*

<table>
<tr><td>Ananias
and
Sapphira</td><td></td></tr>
</table>

here was a Levite, a native of Cyprus, Joseph, to whom the apostles gave the name Barnabas (which means "son of encouragement"). [37]He sold a field that belonged to him, then brought the money, and laid it at the apostles' feet.

5 But a man named Ananias, with the consent of his wife Sapphira, sold a piece of property;

[2]with his wife's knowledge, he kept back some of the proceeds, and brought only a part and laid it at the apostles' feet. [3]"Ananias," Peter asked, "why has Satan filled your heart to lie to the Holy Spirit and to keep back part of the proceeds of the land? [4]While it remained unsold, did it not remain your own? And after it was sold, were not the proceeds at your disposal? How is it that you have contrived this deed in your heart? You did not lie to us*a* but to God!" [5]Now when Ananias heard these words, he fell down and died. And great fear seized all who heard of it. [6]The young men came and wrapped up his body,*b* then carried him out and buried him. [7]After an interval of about three hours his wife came in, not knowing what had happened. [8]Peter said to her, "Tell me whether you and your husband sold the land for such and such a price." And she said, "Yes, that was the price." [9]Then Peter said to her, "How is it that you have agreed together to put the Spirit of the Lord to the test? Look, the feet of those who have buried your husband are at the door, and they will carry you out." [10]Immediately she fell down at his feet and died. When

the young men came in they found her dead, so they carried her out and buried her beside her husband. ¹¹And great fear seized the whole church and all who heard of these things.

ᵃGk *to men*
ᵇMeaning of Gk uncertain

Prayer Starter: Help me always be honest, Lord. Keep me from cheating and lying.

Memory Verse: There is salvation in no one else, for there is no other name under heaven given among mortals . . . *—Acts 4.12*

Many Miracles

Now many signs and wonders were done among the people through the apostles. And they were all together in Solomon's Portico. ¹³None of the rest dared to join them, but the people held them in high esteem. ¹⁴Yet more than ever believers were added to the Lord, great numbers of both men and women, ¹⁵so that they even carried out the sick into the streets, and laid them on cots and mats, in order that Peter's shadow might fall

on some of them as he came by. ¹⁶A great number of people would also gather from the towns around Jerusalem, bringing the sick and those tormented by unclean spirits, and they were all cured.

¹⁷Then the high priest took action; he and all who were with him (that is, the sect of the Sadducees), being filled with jealousy, ¹⁸arrested the apostles and put them in the public prison. ¹⁹But during the night an angel of the Lord opened the prison doors, brought them out, and said, ²⁰"Go, stand in the temple and tell the people the whole message about this life." ²¹When they heard this, they entered the temple at daybreak and went on with their teaching.

When the high priest and those with him arrived, they called together the council and the whole body of the elders of Israel, and sent to the prison to have them brought. ²²But when the temple police went there, they did not find them in the prison; so they returned and reported, 23"We found the prison securely locked and the guards standing at the doors, but when we opened them, we found no one inside." 24Now when the captain of the temple and the chief priests heard these words, they were perplexed about them, wondering what might be going on. 25Then someone arrived and announced, "Look, the men whom you put in prison are standing in the temple and teaching the people!" 26Then the captain went with the temple police and brought them, but without violence, for they were afraid of being stoned by the people.

Prayer Starter: Thank you, Lord, for the angels who watch over us.

Memory Verse: There is salvation in no one else, for there is no other name under heaven given among mortals by which we must be saved.   *—Acts 4.12*

Apostles Beaten

When they had brought them, they had them stand before the council. The high priest questioned them, ²⁸saying, "We gave you strict orders not to teach in this name,ᵃ yet here you have filled Jerusalem with your teaching and you are determined to bring this man's blood on us." ²⁹But Peter and the apostles answered, "We must obey God rather than any human authority.ᵇ ³⁰The God of our ancestors raised up Jesus, whom you had killed by hanging him on a tree. ³¹God exalted him at his right hand as Leader and Savior that he might give repentance to Israel and forgiveness of sins. ³²And we are witnesses to these things, and so is the Holy Spirit whom God has given to those who obey him."

³³When they heard this, they were enraged and wanted to kill them. ³⁴But a Pharisee in the council named Gamaliel, a teacher of the law, respected by all the people, stood up and ordered the men to be put outside for a short time. ³⁵Then he said to them, "Fellow Israelites,ᶜ consider carefully what you propose to do to these men. ³⁶For some time ago Theudas rose up, claiming to be somebody, and a number of men, about four hundred, joined him; but he was killed, and all who followed him were dispersed and disappeared. ³⁷After him Judas the Galilean rose up at the time of the census and got people to follow him; he also perished, and all who followed him were scattered. ³⁸So in the present case, I tell you, keep away from these men and let them alone; because if this plan or this undertaking is of human origin, it will fail; ³⁹but if it is of God, you will not be able to overthrow them—in that case you may even be found fighting against God!"

They were convinced by him, ⁴⁰and when they had called in the apostles, they had them flogged. Then they ordered them not to speak in the name of Jesus, and let them go. ⁴¹As they left the council, they rejoiced that they were considered worthy to suffer dishonor for the sake of the name. ⁴²And every day in the temple and at homeᵈ they did not cease to teach and proclaim Jesus as the Messiah.ᵉ

ᵃOther ancient authorities read *Did we not give you strict orders not to teach in this name?*
ᵇGk *than men*
ᶜGk *Men, Israelites*
ᵈOr *from house to house*
ᵉOr *the Christ*

Prayer Starter: Lord, give me the courage to be your follower, even when it's hard.

Memory Verse: Now those . . .   —*Acts 8.4*

Stephen

And the twelve called together the whole community of the disciples and said, "It is not right that we should neglect the word of God in order to wait on tables.[a] 3Therefore, friends,[b] select from among yourselves seven men of good standing, full of the Spirit and of wisdom, whom we may appoint to this task, 4while we, for our part, will devote ourselves to prayer and to serving the word." 5What they said pleased the whole community, and they chose Stephen, a man full of faith and the Holy Spirit, together with Philip, Prochorus, Nicanor, Timon, Parmenas, and Nicolaus, a proselyte of Antioch.

8Stephen, full of grace and power, did great wonders and signs among the people. 9Then some of those who belonged to the synagogue of the Freedmen (as it was called), Cyrenians, Alexandrians, and others of those from Cilicia and Asia, stood up and argued with Stephen. 10But they could not withstand the wisdom and the Spirit[c] with which he spoke. 11Then they secretly instigated some men to say, "We have heard him speak blasphemous words against Moses and God." 12They stirred up the people as well as the elders and the scribes; then they suddenly confronted him, seized him, and brought him before the council. 13They set up false witnesses who said, "This man never stops saying things against this holy place and the law; 14for we have heard him say that this Jesus of Nazareth[d] will destroy this place and will change the customs that Moses handed on to us." 15And all who sat in the council looked intently at him, and they saw that his face was like the face of an angel.

[a]Or *keep accounts*
[b]Gk *brothers*
[c]Or *spirit*
[d]Gk *the Nazorean*

Prayer Starter: Lord, give me faith and wisdom like Stephen's.

Memory Verse: Now those who were scattered . . .

—*Acts 8.4*

Stephen Stoned to Death

When they heard these things, they became enraged and ground their teeth at Stephen.[a] [55]But filled with the Holy Spirit, he gazed into heaven and saw the glory of God and Jesus standing at the right hand of God. [56]"Look," he said, "I see the heavens opened and the Son of Man standing at the right hand of God!" [57]But they covered their ears, and with a loud shout all rushed together against him. [58]Then they dragged him out of the city and began to stone him; and the witnesses laid their coats at the feet of a young man named Saul. [59]While they were stoning Stephen, he prayed, "Lord Jesus, receive my spirit." [60]Then he knelt down and cried out in a loud voice, "Lord, do not hold this sin against them." When he had said this, he died.[b]

8And Saul approved of their killing him.

That day a severe persecution began against the church in Jerusalem, and all except the apostles were scattered throughout the countryside of Judea and Samaria. [2]Devout men buried Stephen and made loud lamentation over him. [3]But Saul was ravaging the church by entering house after house; dragging off both men and women, he committed them to prison.

⁴Now those who were scattered went from place to place, proclaiming the word. ⁵Philip went down to the city*ᶜ* of Samaria

and proclaimed the Messiah*ᵈ* to them. ⁶The crowds with one accord listened eagerly to what was said by Philip, hearing and seeing the signs that he did, ⁷for unclean spirits, crying with loud shrieks, came out of many who were possessed; and many others who were paralyzed or lame were cured. ⁸So there was great joy in that city.

*ᵃ*Gk *him*
*ᵇ*Gk *fell asleep*
*ᶜ*Other ancient authorities read *a city*
*ᵈ*Or *the Christ*

Prayer Starter: Lord, as I go from place to place, may I tell the good news.

Memory Verse: Now those who were scattered went from place to place . . .
—*Acts 8.4*

Simon

Now a certain man named Simon had previously practiced magic in the city and amazed the people of Samaria, saying that he was someone great. ¹⁰All of them, from the least to the greatest, listened to him eagerly, saying, "This man is the power of God that is called Great." ¹¹And they listened eagerly to him because for a long time he had amazed them with his magic. ¹²But when they believed Philip, who was proclaiming the good news about the kingdom of God and the name of Jesus Christ, they were baptized, both men and women. ¹³Even Simon himself believed. After being baptized, he stayed constantly with Philip and was amazed when he saw the signs and great miracles that took place.

¹⁴Now when the apostles at Jerusalem heard that Samaria had accepted the word of God, they sent Peter and John to them. ¹⁵The two went down and prayed for them that they might receive the Holy Spirit ¹⁶(for as yet the Spirit had not come*ᵃ* upon any of them; they had only been baptized in the name of the Lord Jesus). ¹⁷Then Peter and John*ᵇ* laid their hands on them, and they received the Holy Spirit. ¹⁸Now when Simon saw that the Spirit was given through the laying on of the apostles' hands, he offered them money, ¹⁹saying, "Give me also this power so that anyone on whom I lay my hands may receive the Holy Spirit." ²⁰But Peter said to him, "May your silver perish with you, because you thought you could obtain God's gift

with money! ²¹You have no part or share in this, for your heart is not right before God. ²²Repent therefore of this wickedness of yours, and pray to the Lord that, if possible, the intent of your heart may be forgiven you."

*ᵃ*Gk *fallen*
*ᵇ*Gk *they*

Prayer Starter: Lord, keep me from loving money too much.

Memory Verse: Now those who were scattered went from place to place, proclaiming . . .   *—Acts 8.4*

Philip and the Ethiopian

Then an angel of the Lord said to Philip, "Get up and go toward the south[a] to the road that goes down from Jerusalem to Gaza." (This is a wilderness road.) [27]So he got up and went. Now there was an Ethiopian eunuch, a court official of the Candace, queen of the Ethiopians, in charge of her entire treasury. He had come to Jerusalem to worship [28]and was returning home; seated in his chariot, he was reading the prophet Isaiah.

[29]Then the Spirit said to Philip, "Go over to this chariot and join it." [30]So Philip ran up to it and heard him reading the prophet Isaiah. He asked, "Do you understand what you are reading?" [31]He replied, "How can I, unless someone guides me?" And he invited Philip to get in and sit beside him. [32]Now the passage of the scripture that he was reading was this:
   "Like a sheep he was led to the slaughter,
       and like a lamb silent before its shearer,
          so he does not open his mouth.
[33] In his humiliation justice was denied him.
       Who can describe his generation?
          For his life is taken away from the earth."
[34]The eunuch asked Philip, "About whom, may I ask you, does the prophet say this, about himself or about someone else?" [35]Then Philip began to speak, and starting with this scripture, he proclaimed to him the good news about Jesus.

[a]Or *go at noon*

Prayer Starter: Lord, bless all your priests and teachers who are explaining the good news about Jesus.

Memory Verse: Now those who were scattered went from place to place, proclaiming the word.
                                                              —*Acts 8.4*

<table>
</table>

Saul Meets Jesus

Meanwhile Saul, still breathing threats and murder against the disciples of the Lord, went to the high priest ²and asked him for letters to the synagogues at Damascus, so that if he found any who belonged to the Way, men or women, he might bring them bound to Jerusalem. ³Now as he was going along and approaching Damascus, suddenly a light from heaven flashed around him. ⁴He fell to the ground and heard a voice saying to him, "Saul, Saul, why do you persecute me?" ⁵He asked, "Who are

you, Lord?" The reply came, "I am Jesus, whom you are persecuting. [6]But get up and enter the city, and you will be told what you are to do." [7]The men who were traveling with him stood speechless because they heard the voice but saw no one. [8]Saul got up from the ground, and though his eyes were open, he could see nothing; so they led him by the hand and brought him into Damascus. [9]For three days he was without sight, and neither ate nor drank.

[10]Now there was a disciple in Damascus named Ananias. The Lord said to him in a vision, "Ananias." He answered, "Here I am, Lord." [11]The Lord said to him, "Get up and go to the street called Straight, and at the house of Judas look for a man of Tarsus named Saul. At this moment he is praying, [12]and he has seen in a vision[a] a man named Ananias come in and lay his hands on him so that he might regain his sight." [13]But Ananias answered, "Lord, I have heard from many about this man, how much evil he has done to your saints in Jerusalem; [14]and here he has authority from the chief priests to bind all who invoke your name." [15]But the Lord said to him, "Go, for he is an instrument whom I have chosen to bring my name before Gentiles and kings and before the people of Israel; [16]I myself will show him how much he must suffer for the sake of my name." [17]So Ananias went and entered the house. He laid his hands on Saul[b] and said, "Brother Saul, the Lord Jesus, who appeared to you on your way here, has sent me so that you may regain your sight and be filled with the Holy Spirit." [18]And immediately something like scales fell from his eyes, and his sight was restored. Then he got up and was baptized.

[a]Other ancient authorities lack *in a vision*
[b]Gk *him*

Prayer Starter: May my friends who don't know Christ come to love and trust him.

Memory Verse: All the prophets testify about him . . . —*Acts 10.43*

Saul Escapes Damascus

For several days he was with the disciples in Damascus, ²⁰and immediately he began to proclaim Jesus in the synagogues, saying, "He is the Son of God." ²¹All who heard him were amazed and said, "Is not this the man who made havoc in Jerusalem among those who invoked this name? And has he not come here for the purpose of bringing them bound before the chief priests?" ²²Saul became increasingly more powerful and confounded the Jews who lived in Damascus by proving that Jesus*ᵃ* was the Messiah.*ᵇ*

²³After some time had passed, the Jews plotted to kill him, ²⁴but their plot became known to Saul. They were watching the gates day and night so that they might kill him; ²⁵but his disciples took him by night and let him down through an opening in the wall,*ᶜ* lowering him in a basket.

²⁶When he had come to Jerusalem, he attempted to join the disciples; and they were all afraid of him, for they did not believe that he was a disciple. ²⁷But Barnabas took him, brought him to the apostles, and described for them how on the road he had seen the Lord, who had spoken to him, and how in Damascus he had spoken boldly in the name of Jesus. ²⁸So he went in and out among them in Jerusalem, speaking boldly in the name of the Lord. ²⁹He spoke and argued with the Hellenists; but they were attempting to kill him. ³⁰When the believers*ᵈ* learned of it, they brought him down to Caesarea and sent him off to Tarsus.

³¹Meanwhile the church throughout Judea, Galilee, and Samaria had peace and was built up. Living in the fear of the Lord and in the comfort of the Holy Spirit, it increased in numbers.

*ᵃ*Gk *that this*
*ᵇ*Or *the Christ*
*ᶜ*Gk *through the wall*
*ᵈ*Gk *brothers*

Prayer Starter: Help me to speak bravely in the name of the Lord.

Memory Verse: All the prophets testify about him that everyone . . .
—*Acts 10.43*

Dorcas

Now as Peter went here and there among all the believers,[a] he came down also to the saints living in Lydda. [33]There he found a man named Aeneas, who had been bedridden for eight years, for he was paralyzed. [34]Peter said to him, "Aeneas, Jesus Christ heals you; get up and make your bed!" And immediately he got up. [35]And all the residents of Lydda and Sharon saw him and turned to the Lord.

[36]Now in Joppa there was a disciple whose name was Tabitha, which in Greek is Dorcas.[b] She was devoted to good works and acts of charity. [37]At that time she became ill and died. When they had washed her, they laid her in a room upstairs. [38]Since Lydda was near Joppa, the disciples, who heard that Peter was there, sent two men to him with the request, "Please come to us without delay." [39]So Peter got up and went with them; and when he arrived, they took him to the room upstairs. All the widows stood beside him, weeping and showing tunics and other clothing that Dorcas had made while she was with them. [40]Peter put all of them outside, and then he knelt down and prayed. He turned to the body and said, "Tabitha, get up." Then she opened her eyes, and seeing Peter, she sat

up. ⁴¹He gave her his hand and helped her up. Then calling the saints and widows, he showed her to be alive. ⁴²This became known throughout Joppa, and many believed in the Lord. ⁴³Meanwhile he stayed in Joppa for some time with a certain Simon, a tanner.

ᵃGk *all of them*
ᵇThe name Tabitha in Aramaaic and the name Dorcas in Greek mean *a gazelle*

Prayer Starter: I love to read your Bible each day, Lord. Thank you for stories like this one.

Memory Verse: All the prophets testify about him that everyone who believes in him . . .
—*Acts 10.43*

Peter's Chains Fall Off

About that time King Herod laid violent hands upon some who belonged to the church. ²He had James, the brother of John, killed with the sword. ³After he saw that it pleased the Jews, he proceeded to arrest Peter also. (This was during the festival of Unleavened Bread.) ⁴When he had seized him, he put him in prison and handed him over to four squads of soldiers to guard him, intending to bring him out to the people after the Passover. ⁵While Peter was kept in prison, the church prayed fervently to God for him.

⁶The very night before Herod was going to bring him out, Peter, bound with two chains, was sleeping between two soldiers, while guards in front of the door were keeping watch over the prison. ⁷Suddenly an angel of the Lord appeared and a light shone in the cell. He tapped Peter on the side and woke him, saying, "Get up quickly." And the chains fell off his wrists. ⁸The angel said to him, "Fasten your belt and put on your sandals." He did so. Then he said to him, "Wrap your cloak around you and follow me." ⁹Peter*ᵃ* went out and followed him; he did not realize that what was happening with the angel's help was real; he thought he was seeing a vision. ¹⁰After they had passed the first and the second guard, they came before the iron gate leading into the city. It opened for them of its own accord, and they went outside and walked along a lane, when suddenly the angel left him. ¹¹Then Peter came to himself and said, "Now I am sure that the Lord has sent his angel and rescued me from the hands of Herod and from all that the Jewish people were expecting."

¹²As soon as he realized this, he went to the house of Mary, the mother of John whose other name was Mark, where many had gathered and were praying. ¹³When he knocked at the outer gate, a maid named Rhoda came to answer. ¹⁴On recognizing Peter's voice, she was so overjoyed that, instead of opening the gate, she ran in and announced that Peter was standing at the gate. ¹⁵They said to her, "You are out of your mind!" But she insisted that it was so. They said, "It is his angel." ¹⁶Meanwhile Peter continued knocking; and when they opened the gate, they saw him and were amazed. ¹⁷He motioned to them with his hand to be silent, and described for them how the Lord had brought him out of the prison. And he added, "Tell this to James and to the believers."*ᵇ* Then he left and went to another place.

¹⁸When morning came, there was no small commotion among the soldiers over what had become of Peter. ¹⁹When Herod had searched for him and could not find him, he examined the guards and ordered them to

be put to death. Then Peter[c] went down from Judea to Caesarea and stayed there.

[a]Gk *He*
[b]Gk *brothers*
[c]Gk *he*

Prayer Starter: Send your angels to watch over me, Lord, just as they cared for Peter.

Memory Verse: All the prophets testify about him that everyone who believes in him receives forgiveness of sins . . .   —*Acts 10.43*

Elymas, Son of the Devil

Now in the church at Antioch there were prophets and teachers: Barnabas, Simeon who was called Niger, Lucius of Cyrene, Manaen a member of the court of Herod[a] the ruler, and Saul. [2]While they were worshiping the Lord and fasting, the Holy Spirit said, "Set apart for me Barnabas and Saul for the work to which I have called them." [3]Then after fasting and praying they laid their hands on them and sent them off.

[4]So, being sent out by the Holy Spirit, they went down to Seleucia; and from there they sailed to Cyprus. [5]When they arrived at Salamis, they proclaimed the word of God in the synagogues of the Jews. And they had John also to assist them. [6]When they had gone through the whole island as far as Paphos, they met a certain magician, a Jewish false prophet, named Bar-Jesus. [7]He was with the proconsul, Sergius Paulus, an intelligent man, who summoned Barnabas and Saul and wanted to hear the word of God. [8]But the magician Elymas (for that is the translation of his name) opposed them and tried to turn the proconsul away from the faith. [9]But Saul, also known as Paul, filled with the Holy Spirit, looked intently at him [10]and said, "You son of the devil, you enemy of all righteousness, full of all deceit and villainy, will you not stop making crooked the straight paths of the Lord? [11]And now listen—the hand of the Lord is against you, and you will be blind for a while, unable to see the sun." Immediately mist and darkness came over him, and he went about groping for someone to lead him by the hand. [12]When the proconsul saw what had happened, he believed, for he was astonished at the teaching about the Lord.

[a]Gk *tetrarch*

Prayer Starter: Thank you for my eyes, ears, nose, and mouth.

Memory Verse: All the prophets testify about him that everyone who believes in him receives forgiveness of sins through his name. —*Acts 10.43*

Paul and Barnabas Preach

"For David, after he had served the purpose of God in his own generation, died, was laid beside his ancestors, and experienced corruption; ³⁷but he whom God raised up experienced no corruption. ³⁸Let it be known to you therefore, my brothers, that through this man forgiveness of sins is proclaimed to you; ³⁹by this Jesus*ᵃ* everyone who believes is set free from all those sins*ᵇ* from which you could not be freed by the law of Moses. ⁴⁰Beware, therefore, that what the prophets said does not happen to you:

⁴¹ 'Look, you scoffers!
    Be amazed and perish,
for in your days I am doing a work,
    a work that you will never believe, even if someone tells you.'"

⁴²As Paul and Barnabas*ᶜ* were going out, the people urged them to speak about these things again the next sabbath. ⁴³When the meeting of the synagogue broke up, many Jews and devout converts to Judaism followed Paul and Barnabas, who spoke to them and urged them to continue in the grace of God.

⁴⁴The next sabbath almost the whole city gathered to hear the word of the Lord.*ᵈ* ⁴⁵But when the Jews saw the crowds, they were filled with jealousy; and blaspheming, they contradicted what was spoken by Paul. ⁴⁶Then both Paul and Barnabas spoke out boldly, saying, "It was necessary that the word of God should be spoken first to you. Since you reject it and judge yourselves to be unworthy of eternal life, we are now turning to the Gentiles. ⁴⁷For so the Lord has commanded us, saying,

'I have set you to be a light for the Gentiles,
    so that you may bring salvation to the ends of the earth.'"

⁴⁸When the Gentiles heard this, they were glad and praised the word of the Lord; and as many as had been destined for eternal life became believers. ⁴⁹Thus the word of the Lord spread throughout the region.

*ᵃ*Gk *this*
*ᵇ*Gk *all*
*ᶜ*Gk *they*
*ᵈ*Other ancient authorities read *God*

Prayer Starter: I want to trust you, Lord, when things seem to be going badly.

Memory Verse: Let no evil talk come out of your mouths . . .

—*Ephesians 4.29*

Paul's Stoning

In Lystra there was a man sitting who could not use his feet and had never walked, for he had been crippled from birth. 9He listened to Paul as he was speaking. And Paul, looking at him intently and seeing that he had faith to be healed, 10said in a loud voice, "Stand upright on your feet." And the man*a* sprang up and began to walk. 11When the crowds saw what Paul had done, they shouted in the Lycaonian language, "The gods have come down to us in human form!" 12Barnabas they called Zeus, and Paul they called Hermes, because he was the chief speaker. 13The priest of Zeus, whose temple was just outside the city,*b* brought oxen and garlands to the gates; he and the crowds wanted to offer sacrifice. 14When the apostles Barnabas and Paul heard of it, they tore their clothes and rushed out into the crowd, shouting, 15"Friends,*c* why are you doing this? We are mortals just like you, and we bring you good news, that you should turn from these worthless things to the living God, who made the heaven and the earth and the sea and all that is in them. 16In past generations he allowed all the nations to follow their own ways; 17yet he has not left himself without a witness in doing good—giving you rains from heaven and fruitful seasons, and filling you with food and your hearts with joy." 18Even with these words, they scarcely restrained the crowds from offering sacrifice to them.

19But Jews came there from Antioch and Iconium and won over the crowds. Then they stoned Paul and dragged him out of the city, supposing that he was dead. 20But when the disciples surrounded him, he got up and went into the city. The next day he went on with Barnabas to Derbe. 21After they had proclaimed the good news to that city and had made many disciples, they returned to Lystra, then on to Iconium and Antioch.

*a*Gk *he*
*b*Or *The priest of Zeus-Outside-the-City*

Prayer Starter: Thank you for giving us food and making our hearts glad.

Memory Verse: Let no evil talk come out of your mouths, but only what is useful for building up . . .　　　*—Ephesians 4.29*

The Jerusalem Meeting

Then certain individuals came down from Judea and were teaching the brothers, "Unless you are circumcised according to the custom of Moses, you cannot be saved." ²And after Paul and Barnabas had no small dissension and debate with them, Paul and Barnabas and some of the others were appointed to go up to Jerusalem to discuss this question with the apostles and the elders. ³So they were sent on their way by the church, and as they passed through both Phoenicia and Samaria, they reported the conversion of the Gentiles, and brought great joy to all the believers.*a* ⁴When they came to Jerusalem, they were welcomed by the church and the apostles and the elders, and they reported all that God had done with them. ⁵But some believers who belonged to the sect of the Pharisees stood up and said, "It is necessary for them to be circumcised and ordered to keep the law of Moses."

⁶The apostles and the elders met together to consider this matter. ⁷After there had been much debate, Peter stood up and said to them, "My brothers,*b* you know that in the early days God made a choice among you, that I should be the one through whom the Gentiles would hear the mes-

sage of the good news and become believers. [8]And God, who knows the human heart, testified to them by giving them the Holy Spirit, just as he did to us; [9]and in cleansing their hearts by faith he has made no distinction between them and us. [10]Now therefore why are you putting God to the test by placing on the neck of the disciples a yoke that neither our ancestors nor we have been able to bear? [11]On the contrary, we believe that we will be saved through the grace of the Lord Jesus, just as they will."

[12]The whole assembly kept silence, and listened to Barnabas and Paul as they told of all the signs and wonders that God had done through them among the Gentiles.

[a]Gk *brothers*
[b]Gk *Men, brothers*

Prayer Starter: Thank you for your church, dear Lord.

Memory Verse: Let no evil talk come out of your mouths, but only what is useful for building up, as there is need . . .   —*Ephesians 4.29*

The Apostles' Letter

Then the apostles and the elders, with the consent of the whole church, decided to choose men from among their members[a] and to send them to Antioch with Paul and Barnabas. They sent Judas called Barsabbas, and Silas, leaders among the brothers, [23]with the following letter: "The brothers, both the apostles and the elders, to the believers[b] of Gentile origin in Antioch and Syria and Cilicia, greetings. [24]Since we have heard that certain persons who have gone out from us, though with no instructions from us, have said things to disturb you and have unsettled your minds,[c] [25]we have decided unanimously to choose representatives[d] and send them to you, along with our beloved Barnabas and Paul, [26]who have risked their lives for the sake of our Lord Jesus Christ. [27]We have therefore sent Judas and Silas, who themselves will tell you the same things by word of mouth. [28]For it has seemed good to the Holy Spirit and to us to impose on you no further burden than these essentials: [29]that you abstain from what has been sacrificed to idols and from blood and from what is strangled[e] and from fornication. If you keep yourselves from these, you will do well. Farewell."

[30]So they were sent off and went down to Antioch. When they gathered the congregation together, they delivered the letter. [31]When its members[f] read it, they rejoiced at the exhortation.

[a]Gk *from among them*
[b]Gk *brothers*
[c]Other ancient authorities add *saying, 'You must be circumcised and keep the law,'*
[d]Gk *men*
[e]Other ancient authorities lack *and from what is strangled*
[f]Gk *When they*

Prayer Starter: Bless those who have gone to other nations, taking the message of Jesus.

Memory Verse: Let no evil talk come out of your mouths, but only what is useful for building up, as there is need, so that your words may give grace . . .
—*Ephesians 4.29*

Paul's Travels

Paul[a] went on also to Derbe and to Lystra, where there was a disciple named Timothy, the son of a Jewish woman who was a believer; but his father was a Greek. ²He was well spoken of by the believers[b] in Lystra and Iconium. ³Paul wanted Timothy to accompany him; and he took him and had him circumcised because of the Jews who were in those places, for they all knew that his father was a Greek. ⁴As they went from town to town, they delivered to them for observance the decisions that had been reached by the apostles and elders who were in Jerusalem. ⁵So the churches were strengthened in the faith and increased in numbers daily.

⁶They went through the region of Phrygia and Galatia, having been forbidden by the Holy Spirit to speak the word in Asia. ⁷When they had come opposite Mysia, they attempted to go into Bithynia, but the Spirit of Jesus did not allow them; ⁸so, passing by Mysia, they went down to Troas. ⁹During the night Paul had a vision: there stood a man of Macedonia pleading with him and saying, "Come over to Macedonia and help us." ¹⁰When he had seen the vision, we immediately tried to cross over to Macedonia, being convinced that God had called us to proclaim the good news to them.

[a]Gk *He*
[b]Gk *brothers*

Prayer Starter: Lead me day by day, dear Lord, just as you led the apostle Paul.

Memory Verse: Let no evil talk come out of your mouths, but only what is useful for building up, as there is need, so that your words may give grace to those who hear. —*Ephesians 4.29*

Followers in Philippi

We set sail from Troas and took a straight course to Samothrace, the following day to Neapolis, [12]and from there to Philippi, which is a leading city of the district[a] of Macedonia and a Roman colony. We remained in this city for some days. [13]On the sabbath day we went outside the gate by the river, where we supposed there was a place of prayer; and we sat down and spoke to the women who had gathered there. [14]A certain woman named Lydia, a worshiper of God, was listening to us; she was from the city of Thyatira and a dealer in purple cloth. The Lord opened her heart to listen eagerly to what was said by Paul. [15]When she and her household were baptized, she urged us, saying, "If you have judged me to be faithful to the Lord, come and stay at my home." And she prevailed upon us.

[a]Other ancient authorities read *a city of the first district*

Prayer Starter: Teach me to pray each day, to talk to you as a friend.

Memory Verse: They answered . . .   —*Acts 16.31*

A Jailer Frees Paul and Silas

The crowd joined in attacking them, and the magistrates had them stripped of their clothing and ordered them to be beaten with rods. ²³After they had given them a severe flogging, they threw them into prison and ordered the jailer to keep them securely. ²⁴Following these instructions, he put them in the innermost cell and fastened their feet in the stocks.

²⁵About midnight Paul and Silas were praying and singing hymns to God, and the prisoners were listening to them. ²⁶Suddenly there was an earthquake, so violent that the foundations of the prison were shaken; and immediately all the doors were opened and everyone's chains were unfastened. ²⁷When the jailer woke up and saw the prison doors wide open, he drew his sword and was about to kill himself, since he supposed that the prisoners had escaped. ²⁸But Paul shouted in a loud voice, "Do not harm yourself, for we are all here." ²⁹The jailer*ᵃ* called for lights, and rushing in, he fell down trembling before Paul and Silas. ³⁰Then he brought them outside and said, "Sirs, what must I do to be saved?" ³¹They answered, "Believe on the Lord Jesus, and you will be saved, you and your household." ³²They spoke the word of the Lord*ᵇ* to him and to all who were in his house. ³³At the same hour of the night he took them and washed their wounds; then he and his entire family were baptized without delay. ³⁴He brought them up into the house and set food before them; and he and his entire household rejoiced that he had become a believer in God.

*ᵃ*Gk *He*
*ᵇ*Other ancient authorities read *word of God*

Prayer Starter: Be with those in the jails and prisons, Lord, and give them the hope of the Lord Jesus.

Memory Verse: They answered, "Believe on the Lord Jesus . . ."
—*Acts 16.31*

Paul's Sermon in Athens

While Paul was waiting for them in Athens, he was deeply distressed to see that the city was full of idols. [17]So he argued in the synagogue with the Jews and the devout persons, and also in the market-place[a] every day with those who happened to be there. [18]Also some Epicurean and Stoic philosophers debated with him. Some said, "What does this babbler want to say?" Others said, "He seems to be a proclaimer of foreign divinities." (This was because he was telling the good news about Jesus and the resurrection.) [19]So they took him and brought him to the Areopagus and asked him, "May we know what this new teaching is that you are presenting? [20]It sounds rather strange to us, so we would like to know what it means." [21]Now all the Athenians and the foreigners living there would spend their time in nothing but telling or hearing something new.

[22]Then Paul stood in front of the Areopagus and said, "Athenians, I see how extremely religious you are in every way. [23]For as I went through the city and looked carefully at the objects of your worship, I found among them an altar with the inscription, 'To an unknown god.' What therefore you worship as unknown, this I proclaim to you. [24]The God who made the world and everything in it, he who is Lord of heaven and earth, does not live in shrines made by human hands, [25]nor is he served by human hands, as though he needed anything, since he himself gives to all mortals life and breath and all things. [26]From one ancestor[b] he made all nations to inhabit the whole earth, and he allotted the times of their existence and the boundaries of the places where they would live."

[a]Or *civic center*; Gk *agora*
[b]Gk *From one*; other ancient authorities read *From one blood*

Prayer Starter: Show me those I can invite to worship with me.

Memory Verse: They answered, "Believe on the Lord Jesus, and you . . ."
—*Acts 16.31*

Making Tents

After this Paul*a* left Athens and went to Corinth. *2*There he found a Jew named Aquila, a native of Pontus, who had recently come from Italy with his wife Priscilla, because Claudius had ordered all Jews to leave Rome. Paul*b* went to see them, *3*and, because he was of the same trade, he stayed with them, and they worked together—by trade they were tentmakers.

*4*Every sabbath he would argue in the synagogue and would try to convince Jews and Greeks.

*5*When Silas and Timothy arrived from Macedonia, Paul was occupied with proclaiming the word,*c* testifying to the Jews that the Messiah*d* was Jesus. *6*When they opposed and reviled him, in protest he shook the dust from his clothes*e* and said to them, "Your blood be on your own heads! I am innocent. From now on I will go to the Gentiles." *7*Then he left the synagogue*f* and went to the house of a man named Titius*g* Justus,

a worshiper of God; his house was next door to the synagogue. ⁸Crispus, the official of the synagogue, became a believer in the Lord, together with all his household; and many of the Corinthians who heard Paul became believers and were baptized.

ᵃGk *he*
ᵇGk *He*
ᶜGk *with the word*
ᵈOr *the Christ*
ᵉGk *reviled him, he shook out his clothes*
ᶠGk *left there*
ᵍOther ancient authorities read *Titus*

Prayer Starter: Give me good friends, Lord, who will help me be stronger.

Memory Verse: They answered, "Believe on the Lord Jesus, and you will be saved . . ."   —*Acts 16.31*

Paul's Stay in Corinth

One night the Lord said to Paul in a vision, "Do not be afraid, but speak and do not be silent; [10]for I am with you, and no one will lay a hand on you to harm you, for there are many in this city who are my people." [11]He stayed there a year and six months, teaching the word of God among them.

[12]But when Gallio was proconsul of Achaia, the Jews made a united attack on Paul and brought him before the tribunal. [13]They said, "This man is persuading people to worship God in ways that are contrary to the law." [14]Just as Paul was about to speak, Gallio said to the Jews, "If it were a matter of crime or serious villainy, I would be justified in accepting the complaint of you Jews; [15]but since it is a matter of questions about words and names and your own law, see to it yourselves; I do not wish to be a judge of these matters." [16]And he dismissed them from the tribunal. [17]Then all of them[a] seized Sosthenes, the official of the synagogue, and beat him in front of the tribunal. But Gallio paid no attention to any of these things.

[18]After staying there for a considerable time, Paul said farewell to the believers[b] and sailed for Syria, accompanied by Priscilla and Aquila. At Cenchreae he had his hair cut, for he was under a vow.

[a]Other ancient authorities read *all the Greeks*
[b]Gk *brothers*

Prayer Starter: Give strength to Christians around the world who are being mistreated because of their faith in you.

Memory Verse: They answered, "Believe on the Lord Jesus, and you will be saved, you and your household." —*Acts 16.31*

Priscilla, Aquila, and Apollos

When they reached Ephesus, he left them there, but first he himself went into the synagogue and had a discussion with the Jews. [20]When they asked him to stay longer, he declined; [21]but on taking leave of them, he said, "I[a] will return to you, if God wills." Then he set sail from Ephesus. [22]When he had landed at Caesarea, he went up to Jerusalem[b] and greeted the church, and then went down to Antioch. [23]After spending some time there he departed and went from place to place through the region of Galatia[c] and Phrygia, strengthening all the disciples.

[24]Now there came to Ephesus a Jew named Apollos, a native of Alexandria. He was an eloquent man, well-versed in the scriptures. [25]He had been instructed in the Way of the Lord; and he spoke with burning enthusiasm and taught accurately the things concerning Jesus, though he knew only the baptism of John. [26]He began to speak boldly in the synagogue; but when Priscilla and Aquila heard him, they took him aside and explained the Way of God to him more accurately. [27]And when he wished to cross over to Achaia, the believers[d] encouraged him and wrote to the disciples to welcome him. On his arrival he greatly helped those who through grace had become believers, [28]for he powerfully refuted the Jews in public, showing by the scriptures that the Messiah[e] is Jesus.

19 While Apollos was in Corinth, Paul passed through the interior regions and came to Ephesus, where he found some disciples. [2]He said to them, "Did you receive the Holy Spirit when you became believers?" They replied, "No, we have not even heard that there is a Holy Spirit." [3]Then he said, "Into what then were you baptized?" They answered, "Into John's baptism." [4]Paul said, "John baptized with the baptism of repentance, telling the people to believe in the one who was to come after him, that is, in Jesus." [5]On hearing this, they were baptized in the name of the Lord Jesus.

---

[a]Other ancient authorities *read I must at all costs keep the approaching festival in Jerusalem, but I*
[b]Gk *went up*
[c]Gk *the Galatian region*
[d]Gk *brothers*
[e]Or *the Christ*

Prayer Starter: You are so kind, dear Lord. Give me a kind heart, too.

Memory Verse: We must support the weak . . .   *—Acts 20.35b*

Riot at Ephesus

Now after these things had been accomplished, Paul resolved in the Spirit to go through Macedonia and Achaia, and then to go on to Jerusalem. He said, "After I have gone there, I must also see Rome." [22]So he sent two of his helpers, Timothy and Erastus, to Macedonia, while he himself stayed for some time longer in Asia.

[23]About that time no little disturbance broke out concerning the Way. [24]A man named Demetrius, a silversmith who made silver shrines of Artemis, brought no little business to the artisans. [25]These he gathered together, with the workers of the same trade, and said, "Men, you know that we get our wealth from this business. [26]You also see and hear that not only in Ephesus but in almost the whole of Asia this Paul has persuaded and drawn away a considerable number of people by saying that gods made with hands are not gods. [27]And there is danger not only that this trade of ours may come into disrepute but also that the temple of the great goddess Artemis will be scorned, and she will be deprived of her majesty that brought all Asia and the world to worship her."

[28]When they heard this, they were enraged and shouted, "Great is Artemis of the Ephesians!" [29]The city was filled with the confusion; and people[a] rushed together to the theater, dragging with them Gaius and Aristarchus, Macedonians who were Paul's travel companions. [30]Paul wished to go into the crowd, but the disciples would not let him; [31]even some officials of the province of Asia,[b] who were friendly to him, sent him a message urging him not to venture into the theater.

[a]Gk *they*
[b]Gk *some of the Asiarchs*

Prayer Starter: Comfort and encourage me today, heavenly Father.

Memory Verse: We must support the weak, remembering the words of the Lord Jesus . . .
—*Acts 20.35b*

Sleeping in Church

After the uproar had ceased, Paul sent for the disciples; and after encouraging them and saying farewell, he left for Macedonia. ²When he had gone through those regions and had given the believers*ᵃ* much encouragement, he came to Greece, ³where he stayed for three months. He was about to set sail for Syria when a plot was made against him by the Jews, and so he decided to return through Macedonia. ⁴He was accompanied by Sopater son of Pyrrhus from Beroea, by Aristarchus and Secundus from

Thessalonica, by Gaius from Derbe, and by Timothy, as well as by Tychicus and Trophimus from Asia. ⁵They went ahead and were waiting for us in Troas; ⁶but we sailed from Philippi after the days of Unleavened Bread, and in five days we joined them in Troas, where we stayed for seven days.

⁷On the first day of the week, when we met to break bread, Paul was holding a discussion with them; since he intended to leave the next day, he continued speaking until midnight. ⁸There were many lamps in the room upstairs where we were meeting. ⁹A young man named Eutychus, who was sitting in the window, began to sink off into a deep sleep while Paul talked still longer. Overcome by sleep, he fell to the ground three floors below and was picked up dead. ¹⁰But Paul went down, and bending over him took him in his arms, and said, "Do not be alarmed, for his life is in him." ¹¹Then Paul went upstairs, and after he had broken bread and eaten, he continued to converse with them until dawn; then he left. ¹²Meanwhile they had taken the boy away alive and were not a little comforted.

¹³We went ahead to the ship and set sail for Assos, intending to take Paul on board there; for he had made this arrangement, intending to go by land himself. ¹⁴When he met us in Assos, we took him on board and went to Mitylene. ¹⁵We sailed from there, and on the following day we arrived opposite Chios. The next day we touched at Samos, and*ᵇ* the day after that we came to Miletus. ¹⁶For Paul had decided to sail past Ephesus, so that he might not have to spend time in Asia; he was eager to be in Jerusalem, if possible, on the day of Pentecost.

*ᵃ*Gk *given them*
*ᵇ*Other ancient authorities add *after remaining at Trogyllium*

Prayer Starter: God, bless me when I'm at church. May I stay awake and alert as I worship you and learn about you there.

Memory Verse: We must support the weak, remembering the words of the Lord Jesus, for he himself said . . .
—*Acts 20.35b*

Paul's Speech at Ephesus

From Miletus he [Paul] sent a message to Ephesus, asking the elders of the church to meet him. [18]When they came to him, he said to them:

"You yourselves know how I lived among you the entire time from the first day that I set foot in Asia, [19]serving the Lord with all humility and with tears, enduring the trials that came to me through the plots of the Jews. [20]I did not shrink from doing anything helpful, proclaiming the message to you and teaching you publicly and from house to house, [21]as I testified to both Jews and Greeks about repentance toward God and faith toward our Lord Jesus. [22]And now, as a captive to the Spirit,[a] I am on my way to Jerusalem, not knowing what will happen to me there, [23]except that the Holy Spirit testifies to me in every city that imprisonment and persecutions are waiting for me. [24]But I do not count my life of any value to myself, if only I may finish my course and the ministry that I received from the Lord Jesus, to testify to the good news of God's grace.

²⁵"And now I know that none of you, among whom I have gone about proclaiming the kingdom, will ever see my face again. ²⁶Therefore I declare to you this day that I am not responsible for the blood of any of you, ²⁷for I did not shrink from declaring to you the whole purpose of God. ²⁸Keep watch over yourselves and over all the flock, of which the Holy Spirit has made you overseers, to shepherd the church of God*ᵇ* that he obtained with the blood of his own Son.*ᶜ* ²⁹I know that after I have gone, savage wolves will come in among you, not sparing the flock. ³⁰Some even from your own group will come distorting the truth in order to entice the disciples to follow them. ³¹Therefore be alert, remembering that for three years I did not cease night or day to warn everyone with tears. ³²And now I commend you to God and to the message of his grace, a message that is able to build you up and to give you the inheritance among all who are sanctified. ³³I coveted no one's silver or gold or clothing. ³⁴You know for yourselves that I worked with my own hands to support myself and my companions. ³⁵In all this I have given you an example that by such work we must support the weak, remembering the words of the Lord Jesus, for he himself said, 'It is more blessed to give than to receive.'"

³⁶When he had finished speaking, he knelt down with them all and prayed. ³⁷There was much weeping among them all; they embraced Paul and kissed him, ³⁸grieving especially because of what he had said, that they would not see him again. Then they brought him to the ship.

ᵃOr And now, bound in the spirit
ᵇOther ancient authorities read of the Lord
ᶜOr with his own blood; Gk with the blood of his Own

Prayer Starter: Help me remember that more blessings come from giving than receiving.

Memory Verse: We must support the weak, remembering the words of the Lord Jesus, for he himself said, "It is more blessed to give . . ."
—*Acts 20.35b*

Paul Is Warned

When we had parted from them and set sail, we came by a straight course to Cos, and the next day to Rhodes, and from there to Patara.*ᵃ* ²When we found a ship bound for Phoenicia, we went on board and set sail. ³We came in sight of Cyprus; and leaving it on our left, we sailed to Syria and landed at Tyre, because the ship was to unload its cargo there. ⁴We looked up the disciples and stayed there for seven days. Through the Spirit they told Paul not to go on to Jerusalem. ⁵When our days there were ended, we left and proceeded on our journey; and all of them, with wives and children, escorted us outside the city. There we knelt down on the beach and prayed ⁶and said farewell to one another. Then we went on board the ship, and they returned home.

⁷When we had finished*ᵇ* the voyage from Tyre, we arrived at Ptolemais; and we greeted the believers*ᶜ* and stayed with them for one day. ⁸The next day we left and came to Caesarea; and we went into the house of Philip the evangelist, one of the seven, and stayed with him. ⁹He had four unmarried daughters*ᵈ* who had the gift of prophecy. ¹⁰While we were staying there for several days, a prophet named Agabus came down from Judea. ¹¹He came to us and took Paul's belt, bound his own feet and hands with it, and said, "Thus says the Holy Spirit, 'This is the way the Jews in Jerusalem will bind the man who owns this belt and will hand him over to the Gentiles.'" ¹²When we heard this, we and the people there urged him not to go up to Jerusalem. ¹³Then Paul answered, "What are you doing, weeping and breaking my heart? For I am ready not only to be bound but even to die in Jerusalem for the name of the Lord Jesus." ¹⁴Since he would not be persuaded, we remained silent except to say, "The Lord's will be done."

ᵃOther ancient authorities add and Myra
ᵇOr continued
ᶜGk brothers
ᵈGk four daughters, virgins

Prayer Starter: Dear God, help more and more people to place their faith in Jesus Christ.

Memory Verse: We must support the weak, remembering the words of the Lord Jesus, for he himself said, "It is more blessed to give than to receive."
—*Acts 20.35b*

Paul Speaks Out

When he [the tribune] had given him permission, Paul stood on the steps and motioned to the people for silence; and when there was a great hush, he addressed them in the Hebrew[a] language, saying:

22 "Brothers and fathers, listen to the defense that I now make before you."

2When they heard him addressing them in Hebrew,[a] they became even more quiet. Then he said:

3"I am a Jew, born in Tarsus in Cilicia, but brought up in this city at the feet of Gamaliel, educated strictly according to our ancestral law, being zealous for God, just as all of you are today. 4I persecuted this Way up to the point of death by binding both men and women and putting them in prison, 5as the high priest and the whole council of elders can testify about me. From them I also received letters to the brothers in Damascus, and I went there in order to bind those who were there and to bring them back to Jerusalem for punishment.

6"While I was on my way and approaching Damascus, about noon a great light from heaven suddenly shone about me. 7I fell to the ground and heard a voice saying to me, 'Saul, Saul, why are you persecuting me?' 8I answered, 'Who are you, Lord?' Then he said to me, 'I am Jesus of Nazareth.'"[b]

[a]That is, *Aramaic*
[b]Gk *the Nazorean*

Prayer Starter: Please protect the men and women in the armed forces who protect our country.

Memory Verse: So keep up . . .   —*Acts 27.25*

The Plot Against Paul

In the morning the Jews joined in a conspiracy and bound themselves by an oath neither to eat nor drink until they had killed Paul. ¹³There were more than forty who joined in this conspiracy. ¹⁴They went to the chief priests and elders and said, "We have strictly bound ourselves by an oath to taste no food until we have killed Paul. ¹⁵Now then, you and the council must notify the tribune to bring him down to you, on the pretext that you want to make a more thorough examination of his case. And we are ready to do away with him before he arrives."

¹⁶Now the son of Paul's sister heard about the ambush; so he went and gained entrance to the barracks and told Paul. ¹⁷Paul called one of the centurions and said, "Take this young man to the tribune, for he has something to report to him." ¹⁸So he took him, brought him to the tribune, and said, "The prisoner Paul called me and asked me to bring this young man to you; he has something to tell you." ¹⁹The tribune took him by the hand, drew him aside privately, and asked, "What is it that you have to report to me?" ²⁰He answered, "The Jews have agreed to ask you to bring Paul down to the council tomorrow, as though they were going to inquire more thoroughly into his case. ²¹But do not be persuaded by them, for more than forty of their men are lying in ambush for him. They have bound themselves by an oath neither to eat nor drink until they kill him. They are ready now and are waiting for your consent." ²²So the tribune dismissed the young man, ordering him, "Tell no one that you have informed me of this."

Prayer Starter: Protect me from all evil.

Agrippa
and
Bernice

So on the next day Agrippa and Bernice came with great pomp, and they entered the audience hall with the military tribunes and the prominent men of the city. Then Festus gave the order and Paul was brought in. ²⁴And Festus said, "King Agrippa and all here present with us, you see this man about whom the whole Jewish community petitioned me, both in Jerusalem and here, shouting that he ought not to live any longer. ²⁵But I found that he had done nothing deserving death; and when he appealed to his Imperial Majesty, I decided to send him."

26Agrippa said to Paul, "You have permission to speak for yourself." Then Paul stretched out his hand and began to defend himself:

²"I consider myself fortunate that it is before you, King Agrippa, I am to make my defense today against all the accusations of the Jews, ³because you are especially familiar with all the customs and controversies of the Jews; therefore I beg of you to listen to me patiently."

Prayer Starter: May the leaders of this world bow down and worship you.

Memory Verse: So keep up your courage, men, for I have faith in God . . .
—*Acts 27.25*

Storm on the Mediterranean

When a moderate south wind began to blow, they thought they could achieve their purpose; so they weighed anchor and began to sail past Crete, close to the shore. [14]But soon a violent wind, called the northeaster, rushed down from Crete.[a] [15]Since the ship was caught and could not be turned head-on into the wind, we gave way to it and were driven. [16]By running under the lee of a small island called Cauda[b] we were scarcely able to get the ship's boat under control. [17]After hoisting it up they took measures[c] to undergird the ship; then, fearing that they would run on the Syrtis, they lowered the sea anchor and so were driven. [18]We were being pounded by the storm so violently that on the next day they began to throw the cargo overboard, [19]and on the third day with their own hands they threw the ship's tackle overboard. [20]When neither sun nor stars appeared for many days, and no small tempest raged, all hope of our being saved was at last abandoned.

[21]Since they had been without food for a long time, Paul then stood up among them and said, "Men, you should have listened to me and not have set sail from Crete and thereby avoided this damage and loss. [22]I urge you now to keep up your courage, for there will be no loss of life among you, but only of the ship. [23]For last night there stood by me an angel of the God to whom I belong and whom I worship, [24]and he said, 'Do not be afraid, Paul; you must stand before the emperor; and indeed, God has granted safety to all those who are sailing with you.' [25]So keep up your courage, men, for I have faith in God that it will be exactly as I have been told. [26]But we will have to run aground on some island."

[29]Fearing that we might run on the rocks, they let down four anchors from the stern and prayed for day to come.

[a]Gk *it*
[b]Other ancient authorities read *Clauda*
[c]Gk *helps*

Prayer Starter: Lord, help me to believe you will do all you have promised.

Memory Verse: So keep up your courage, men, for I have faith in God that it will be exactly . . .   —*Acts 27.25*

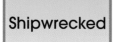

Shipwrecked

B ut when the sailors tried to escape from the ship and had lowered the boat into the sea, on the pretext of putting out anchors from the bow, ³¹Paul said to the centurion and the soldiers, "Unless these men stay in the ship, you cannot be saved." ³²Then the soldiers cut away the ropes of the boat and set it adrift.

³³Just before daybreak, Paul urged all of them to take some food, saying, "Today is the fourteenth day that you have been in suspense and remaining without food, having eaten nothing. ³⁴Therefore I urge you to take some food, for it will help you survive; for none of you will lose a hair from your heads." ³⁵After he had said this, he took bread; and giving thanks to God in the presence of all, he broke it and

began to eat. ³⁶Then all of them were encouraged and took food for themselves. ³⁷(We were in all two hundred seventy-six*ᵃ* persons in the ship.) ³⁸After they had satisfied their hunger, they lightened the ship by throwing the wheat into the sea.

³⁹In the morning they did not recognize the land, but they noticed a bay with a beach, on which they planned to run the ship ashore, if they could. ⁴⁰So they cast off the anchors and left them in the sea. At the same time they loosened the ropes that tied the steering-oars; then hoisting the foresail to the wind, they made for the beach. ⁴¹But striking a reef,*ᵇ* they ran the ship aground; the bow stuck and remained immovable, but the stern was being broken up by the force of the waves. ⁴²The soldiers'

plan was to kill the prisoners, so that none might swim away and escape; [43]but the centurion, wishing to save Paul, kept them from carrying out their plan. He ordered those who could swim to jump overboard first and make for the land, [44]and the rest to follow, some on planks and others on pieces of the ship. And so it was that all were brought safely to land.

28After we had reached safety, we then learned that the island was called Malta.

[a]Other ancient authorities read *seventy-six*; others, *about seventy-six*
[b]Gk *place of two seas*

Prayer Starter: Thank you for helping us when we are in danger.

Memory Verse: So keep up your courage, men, for I have faith in God that it will be exactly as I have been told.   —*Acts 27.25*

No Harm from a Snake

The natives showed us unusual kindness. Since it had begun to rain and was cold, they kindled a fire and welcomed all of us around it. ³Paul had gathered a bundle of brushwood and was putting it on the fire, when a viper, driven out by the heat, fastened itself on his hand. ⁴When the natives saw the creature hanging from his hand, they said to one another, "This man must be a murderer; though he has escaped from the sea, justice has not allowed him to live." ⁵He, however, shook off the creature into the fire and suffered no harm. ⁶They were expecting him to swell up or drop dead, but after they had waited a long time and saw that nothing unusual had happened to him, they changed their minds and began to say that he was a god.

¹¹Three months later we set sail on a ship that had wintered at the island, an Alexandrian ship with the Twin Brothers as its figurehead. ¹²We put in at Syracuse and stayed there for three days; ¹³then we weighed anchor and came to Rhegium. After one day there a south wind sprang up, and on the second day we came to Puteoli. ¹⁴There we found believers*ᵃ* and were invited to stay with them for seven days. And so we came to Rome.

ᵃGk brothers

Prayer Starter: Thank you for fish and birds, for reptiles and insects.

Memory Verse: For I am not ashamed . . . *—Romans 1.16a*

**Paul
in Rome**

The believers from there, when they heard of us, came as far as the Forum of Appius and Three Taverns to meet us. On seeing them, Paul thanked God and took courage.

¹⁶When we came into Rome, Paul was allowed to live by himself, with the soldier who was guarding him.

¹⁷Three days later he called together the local leaders of the Jews. When they had assembled, he said to them, "Brothers, though I had done nothing against our people or the customs of our ancestors, yet I was arrested in Jerusalem and handed over to the Romans. ¹⁸When they had examined me, the Romans*ª* wanted to release me, because there was no reason for the death penalty in my case. ¹⁹But when the Jews objected, I was compelled to appeal to the emperor—even though I had no charge to bring against my nation. ²⁰For this reason

therefore I have asked to see you and speak with you,*ᵇ* since it is for the sake of the hope of Israel that I am bound with this chain." ²¹They replied, "We have received no letters from Judea about you, and none of the brothers coming here has reported or spoken anything evil about you.

²²But we would like to hear from you what you think, for with regard to this sect we know that everywhere it is spoken against."

²³After they had set a day to meet with him, they came to him at his lodgings in great numbers. From morning until evening he explained the matter to them, testifying to the kingdom of God and trying to convince them about Jesus both from the law of Moses and from the prophets.

³⁰He lived there two whole years at his own expense*ᶜ* and welcomed all who came to him, ³¹proclaiming the kingdom of God and teaching about the Lord Jesus Christ with all boldness and without hindrance.

ᵃGk they
ᵇOr I have asked you to see me and speak with me
ᶜOr in his own hired dwelling

Prayer Starter: Dear God, help me to be an encouraging friend.

Memory Verse: For I am not ashamed of the gospel . . .
—*Romans 1.16a*

To All God's Beloved in Rome

Paul, a servant*a* of Jesus Christ, called to be an apostle, set apart for the gospel of God, ²which he promised beforehand through his prophets in the holy scriptures, ³the gospel concerning his Son, who was descended from David according to the flesh ⁴and was declared to be Son of God with power according to the spirit*b* of holiness by resurrection from the dead, Jesus Christ our Lord, ⁵through whom we have received grace and apostleship to bring about the obedience of faith among all the Gentiles for the sake of his name, ⁶including yourselves who are called to belong to Jesus Christ,

⁷To all God's beloved in Rome, who are called to be saints:

Grace to you and peace from God our Father and the Lord Jesus Christ.

⁸First, I thank my God through Jesus Christ for all of you, because your faith is proclaimed throughout the world. ⁹For God, whom I serve with my spirit by announcing the gospel*c* of his Son, is my witness that without ceasing I remember you always in my prayers, ¹⁰asking that by God's will I may somehow at last succeed in coming to you. ¹¹For I am longing to see you so that I may share with you some spiritual gift to strengthen you—¹²or rather so that we may be mutually encouraged by each other's faith, both yours and mine. ¹³I want you to know, brothers and sisters,*d* that I have often intended to come to you (but thus far have been prevented), in order that I may reap some harvest among you as I

have among the rest of the Gentiles. ¹⁴I am a debtor both to Greeks and to barbarians, both to the wise and to the foolish ¹⁵—hence my eagerness to proclaim the gospel to you also who are in Rome.

¹⁶For I am not ashamed of the gospel; it is the power of God for salvation to everyone who has faith, to the Jew first and also to the Greek. ¹⁷For in it the righteousness of God is revealed through faith for faith; as it is written, "The one who is righteous will live by faith."*ᵉ*

ᵃGk slave
ᵇOr Spirit
ᶜGk my spirit in the gospel
ᵈGk brothers
ᵉOr The one who is righteous through faith will live

Prayer Starter: Make me proud of the good news about Jesus, dear God.

Memory Verse: For I am not ashamed of the gospel; it is the power of God . . .   *—Romans 1.16a*

This Is My Body

For I received from the Lord what I also handed on to you, that the Lord Jesus on the night when he was betrayed took a loaf of bread, [24]and when he had given thanks, he broke it and said, "This is my body that is for[a] you. Do this in remembrance of me." [25]In the same way he took the cup also,

after supper, saying, "This cup is the new covenant in my blood. Do this, as often as you drink it, in remembrance of me." [26]For as often as you eat this bread and drink the cup, you proclaim the Lord's death until he comes.

[27]Whoever, therefore, eats the bread or drinks the cup of the Lord in an unworthy manner will be answerable for the body and blood of the Lord. [28]Examine yourselves, and only then eat of the bread and drink of the cup.

[33]So then, my brothers and sisters,[b] when you come together to eat, wait for one another. [34]If you are hungry, eat at home, so that when you come together, it will not be for your condemnation. About the other things I will give instructions when I come.

[a]Other ancient authorities read *is broken for*
[b]Gk *brothers*

Prayer Starter: Help me be well behaved in church and school, Lord. Help me to respect my teachers.

Memory Verse: For I am not ashamed of the gospel; it is the power of God for salvation to everyone . . .   —*Romans 1.16a*

Paul Corrects Peter

hen James and Cephas and John, who were acknowledged pillars, recognized the grace that had been given to me, they gave to Barnabas and me the right hand of fellowship, agreeing that we should go to the Gentiles and they to the circumcised. ¹⁰They asked only one thing, that we remember the poor, which was actually what I was*ᵃ* eager to do.

¹¹But when Cephas came to Antioch, I opposed him to his face, because he stood self-condemned; ¹²for until certain people came from James, he used to eat with the Gentiles. But after they came, he drew back and kept himself separate for fear of the circumcision faction. ¹³And the other Jews joined him in this hypocrisy, so that even Barnabas was led astray by their hypocrisy. ¹⁴But when I saw that they were not acting consistently with the truth of the gospel, I said to Cephas before them all, "If you, though a Jew, live like a Gentile and not like a Jew, how can you compel the Gentiles to live like Jews?"*ᵇ*

¹⁵We ourselves are Jews by birth and not Gentile sinners; ¹⁶yet we

know that a person is justified[c] not by the works of the law but through faith in Jesus Christ.[d] And we have come to believe in Christ Jesus, so that we might be justified by faith in Christ,[e] and not by doing the works of the law, because no one will be justified by the works of the law. [17]But if, in our effort to be justified in Christ, we ourselves have been found to be sinners, is Christ then a servant of sin? Certainly not! [18]But if I build up again the very things that I once tore down, then I demonstrate that I am a transgressor. [19]For through the law I died to the law, so that I might live to God. I have been crucified with Christ; [20]and it is no longer I who live, but it is Christ who lives in me. And the life I now live in the flesh I live by faith in the Son of God,[f] who loved me and gave himself for me.

[a]Or *had been*
[b]Some interpreters hold that the quotation extends into the following paragraph
[c]Or *reckoned as righteous*; and so elsewhere
[d]Or *the faith of Jesus Christ*
[e]Or *the faith of Christ*
[f]Or *by the faith of the Son of God*

Prayer Starter: Give me wisdom, Lord, to know when to tell others that they are wrong.

Memory Verse: For I am not ashamed of the gospel; it is the power of God for salvation to everyone who has faith. —*Romans 1.16a*

Christ Brings Spiritual Blessings

Paul, an apostle of Christ Jesus by the will of God,

To the saints who are in Ephesus and are faithful*a* in Christ Jesus:

²Grace to you and peace from God our Father and the Lord Jesus Christ.

³Blessed be the God and Father of our Lord Jesus Christ, who has blessed us in Christ with every spiritual blessing in the heavenly places, ⁴just as he chose us in Christ*b* before the foundation of the world to be holy and blameless before him in love. ⁵He destined us for adoption as his children through Jesus Christ, according to the good pleasure of his will, ⁶to the praise of his glorious grace that he freely bestowed on us in the Beloved. ⁷In him we have redemption through his

blood, the forgiveness of our trespasses, according to the riches of his grace [8]that he lavished on us. With all wisdom and insight [9]he has made known to us the mystery of his will, according to his good pleasure that he set forth in Christ, [10]as a plan for the fullness of time, to gather up all things in him, things in heaven and things on earth. [11]In Christ we have also obtained an inheritance,[c] having been destined according to the purpose of him who accomplishes all things according to his counsel and will, [12]so that we, who were the first to set our hope on Christ, might live for the praise of his glory. [13]In him you also, when you had heard the word of truth, the gospel of your salvation, and had believed in him, were marked with the seal of the promised Holy Spirit; [14]this[d] is the pledge of our inheritance toward redemption as God's own people, to the praise of his glory.

[15]I have heard of your faith in the Lord Jesus and your love[e] toward all the saints, and for this reason [16]I do not cease to give thanks for you as I remember you in my prayers. [17]I pray that the God of our Lord Jesus Christ, the Father of glory, may give you a spirit of wisdom and revelation as you come to know him, [18]so that, with the eyes of your heart enlightened, you may know what is the hope to which he has called you, what are the riches of his glorious inheritance among the saints.

[a]Other ancient authorities lack *in Ephesus*, reading *saints who are also faithful*
[b]Gk *in him*
[c]Or *been made a heritage*
[d]Other ancient authorities read *who*
[e]Other ancient authorities lack *and your love*

Prayer Starter: I praise you, Father, for the spiritual blessings Christ brought from above.

Memory Verse: Do not worry about anything . . .   —*Philippians 4.6*

The Armor That God Gives

Finally, be strong in the Lord and in the strength of his power. ¹¹Put on the whole armor of God, so that you may be able to stand against the wiles of the devil. ¹²For our*ᵃ* struggle is not against enemies of blood and flesh, but against the rulers, against the authorities, against the cosmic powers of this present darkness, against the spiritual forces of evil in the heavenly places. ¹³Therefore take up the whole armor of God, so that you may be able to withstand on that evil day, and having done everything, to

stand firm. [14]Stand therefore, and fasten the belt of truth around your waist, and put on the breastplate of righteousness. [15]As shoes for your feet put on whatever will make you ready to proclaim the gospel of peace. [16]With all of these,[b] take the shield of faith, with which you will be able to quench all the flaming arrows of the evil one. [17]Take the helmet of salvation, and the sword of the Spirit, which is the word of God.

[18]Pray in the Spirit at all times in every prayer and supplication. To that end keep alert and always persevere in supplication for all the saints. [19]Pray also for me, so that when I speak, a message may be given to me to make known with boldness the mystery of the gospel,[c] [20]for which I am an ambassador in chains. Pray that I may declare it boldly, as I must speak.

[21]So that you also may know how I am and what I am doing, Tychicus will tell you everything. He is a dear brother and a faithful minister in the Lord.

[22]I am sending him to you for this very purpose, to let you know how we are, and to encourage your hearts.

[23]Peace be to the whole community,[d] and love with faith, from God the Father and the Lord Jesus Christ. [24]Grace be with all who have an undying love for our Lord Jesus Christ.[e]

[a]Other ancient authorities read *your*
[b]Or *In all circumstances*
[c]Other ancient authorities lack *of the gospel*
[d]Gk *to the brothers*
[e]Other ancient authorities add *Amen*

Prayer Starter: Help me to stay alert, Lord, and to keep praying for your people.

Memory Verse: Do not worry about anything, but in everything by prayer . . .
                                                        —*Philippians 4.6*

Timothy and Epaphroditus

Therefore, my beloved, just as you have always obeyed me, not only in my presence, but much more now in my absence, work out your own salvation with fear and trembling; ¹³for it is God who is at work in you, enabling you both to will and to work for his good pleasure.

¹⁴Do all things without murmuring and arguing, ¹⁵so that you may be blameless and innocent, children of God without blemish in the midst of a crooked and perverse generation, in which you shine like stars in the world. ¹⁶It is by your holding fast to the word of life that I can boast on the day of Christ that I did not run in vain or labor in vain. ¹⁷But even if I am being poured out as a libation over the sacrifice and the offering of your faith, I am glad and rejoice with all of you—¹⁸and in the same way you also must be glad and rejoice with me.

[19]I hope in the Lord Jesus to send Timothy to you soon, so that I may be cheered by news of you. [20]I have no one like him who will be genuinely concerned for your welfare. [21]All of them are seeking their own interests, not those of Jesus Christ. [22]But Timothy's[a] worth you know, how like a son with a father he has served with me in the work of the gospel. [23]I hope therefore to send him as soon as I see how things go with me; [24]and I trust in the Lord that I will also come soon.

[25]Still, I think it necessary to send to you Epaphroditus—my brother and co-worker and fellow soldier, your messenger[b] and minister to my need; [26]for he has been longing for[c] all of you, and has been distressed because you heard that he was ill. [27]He was indeed so ill that he nearly died. But God had mercy on him, and not only on him but on me also, so that I would not have one sorrow after another. [28]I am the more eager to send him, therefore, in order that you may rejoice at seeing him again, and that I may be less anxious. [29]Welcome him then in the Lord with all joy, and honor such people, [30]because he came close to death for the work of Christ,[d] risking his life to make up for those services that you could not give me.

[a]Gk *his*
[b]Gk *apostle*
[c]Other ancient authorities read *longing to see*
[d]Other ancient authorities read *of the Lord*

Prayer Starter: Please help those who are sick, Lord, and keep us well.

Memory Verse: Do not worry about anything, but in everything by prayer and supplication with thanksgiving . . .   —*Philippians 4.6*

Press on for the Prize

For his sake I have suffered the loss of all things, and I regard them as rubbish, in order that I may gain Christ ⁹and be found in him, not having a righteousness of my own that comes from the law, but one that comes through faith in Christ,ᵃ the righteousness from God based on faith. ¹⁰I want to know Christᵇ and the power of his resurrection and the sharing of his sufferings by becoming like him in his death, ¹¹if somehow I may attain the resurrection from the dead.

¹²Not that I have already obtained this or have already reached the goal;ᶜ but I press on to make it my own, because Christ Jesus has made me his own. ¹³Beloved,ᵈ I do not consider that I have made it my own;ᵉ but this one thing I do: forgetting what lies behind and straining forward to what lies ahead, ¹⁴I press on toward the goal for the prize of the heavenlyᶠ call of God in Christ Jesus. ¹⁵Let those of us then who are mature be of the same mind; and if you think differently about anything, this too God will reveal to you. ¹⁶Only let us hold fast to what we have attained.

¹⁷Brothers and sisters,ᵈ join in imitating me, and observe those who live according to the example you have in us.

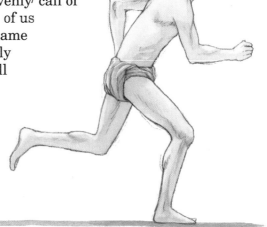

ᵃOr *through the faith of Christ*
ᵇGk *him*
ᶜOr *have already been made perfect*
ᵈGk *Brothers*
ᵉOther ancient authorities read *my own yet*
ᶠGk *upward*

Prayer Starter: Lord, I can hardly wait for the Lord Jesus Christ who is coming again from heaven.

Memory Verse: Do not worry about anything, but in everything by prayer and supplication with thanksgiving let your requests . . .
—*Philippians 4.6*

Stand Firm in the Lord

Therefore, my brothers and sisters,[a] whom I love and long for, my joy and crown, stand firm in the Lord in this way, my beloved. [2]I urge Euodia and I urge Syntyche to be of the same mind in the Lord. [3]Yes, and I ask you also, my loyal companion,[b] help these women, for they have struggled beside me in the work of the gospel, together with Clement and the rest of my co-workers, whose names are in the book of life.

[4]Rejoice[c] in the Lord always; again I will say, Rejoice.[c] [5]Let your gentleness be known to everyone. The Lord is near. [6]Do not worry about anything, but in everything by prayer and supplication with thanksgiving let your requests be made known to God. [7]And the peace of God, which surpasses all understanding, will guard your hearts and your minds in Christ Jesus.

[8]Finally, beloved,[d] whatever is true, whatever is honorable, whatever is just, whatever is pure, whatever is pleasing, whatever is commendable, if there is any excellence and if there is anything worthy of praise, think about[e] these things. [9]Keep on doing the things that you have learned and received and heard and seen in me, and the God of peace will be with you.

[a]Gk *my brothers*
[b]Or *loyal Syzygus*
[c]Or *Farewell*
[d]Gk *brothers*
[e]Gk *take account of*

Prayer Starter: Help me not to worry about anything, but to pray about everything.

Memory Verse: Do not worry about anything, but in everything by prayer and supplication with thanksgiving let your requests be made known to God.
—*Philippians 4.6*

**The Lord
Will Return**

But we do not want you to be uninformed, brothers and sisters,*ᵃ* about those who have died,*ᵇ* so that you may not grieve as others do who have no hope. ¹⁴For since we believe that Jesus died and rose again, even so, through Jesus, God will bring with him those who have died.*ᵇ* ¹⁵For this we declare to you by the word of the Lord, that we who are alive, who are left until the coming of the Lord, will by no means precede those who have died.*ᵇ* ¹⁶For the Lord himself, with a cry of command, with the archangel's call and with the sound of God's trumpet, will descend from heaven, and the dead in Christ will rise first. ¹⁷Then we who are alive, who are left, will

be caught up in the clouds together with them to meet the Lord in the air; and so we will be with the Lord forever. ¹⁸Therefore encourage one another with these words.

5 Now concerning the times and the seasons, brothers and sisters,*ᵃ* you do not need to have anything written to you. ²For you yourselves know very well that the day of the Lord will come like a thief in the night.

*ᵃ*Gk *brothers*
*ᵇ*Gk *fallen asleep*

Prayer Starter: Thank you, Lord, for all your promises about the future.

Memory Verse: For you yourselves . . .   —*1 Thessalonians 5.2*

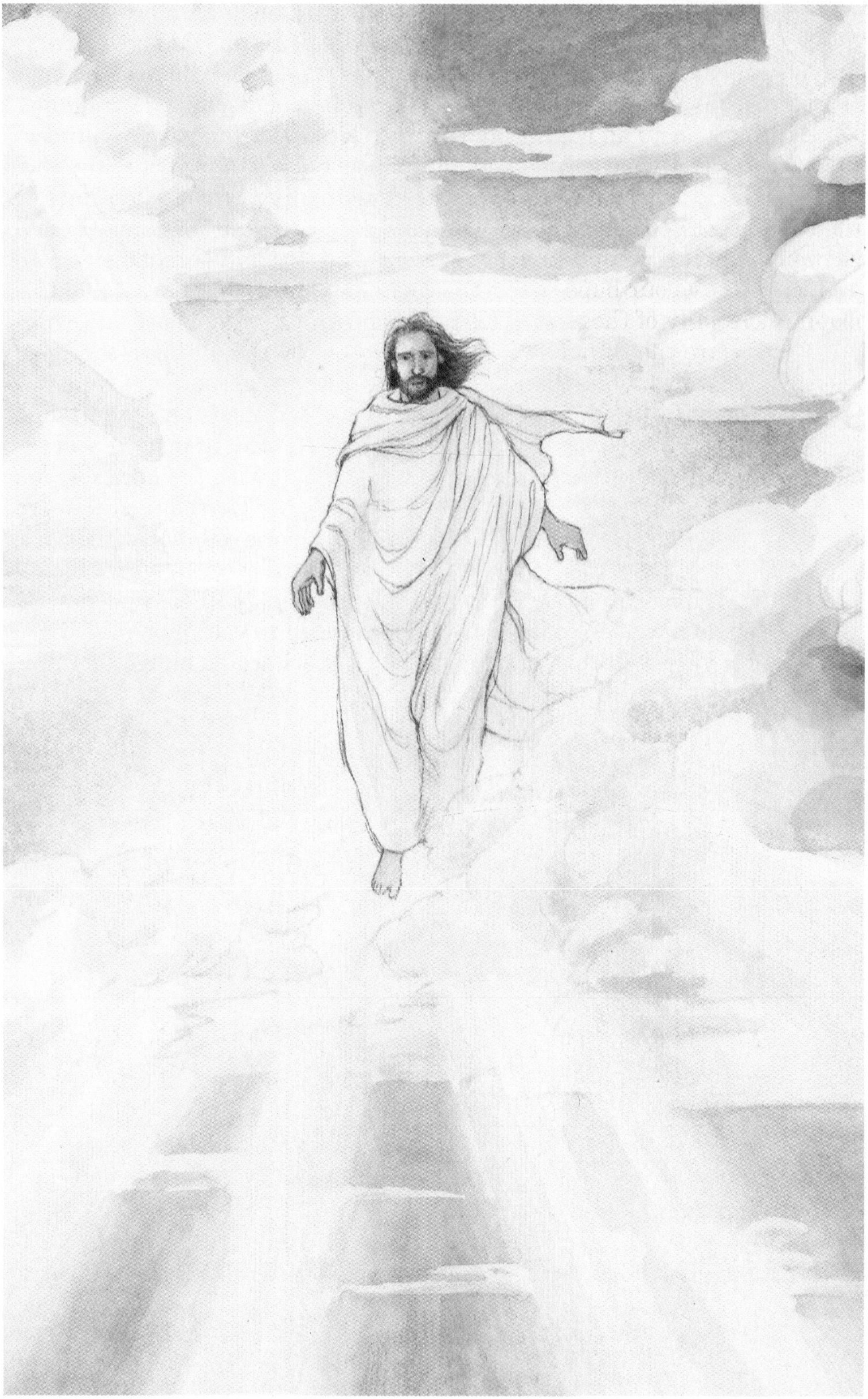

Teach These Things

If you put these instructions before the brothers and sisters,*ᵃ* you will be a good servant*ᵇ* of Christ Jesus, nourished on the words of the faith and of the sound teaching that you have followed. ⁷Have nothing to do with profane myths and old wives' tales. Train yourself in godliness, ⁸for, while physical training is of some value, godliness is valuable in every way, holding promise for both the present life and the life to come. ⁹The saying is sure and worthy of full acceptance. ¹⁰For to this end we toil and struggle,*ᶜ* because we have our hope set on the living God, who is the Savior of all people, especially of those who believe.

¹¹These are the things you must insist on and teach. ¹²Let no one despise your youth, but set the believers an example in speech and conduct, in love, in faith, in purity. ¹³Until I arrive, give attention to the public reading of scripture,*ᵈ* to exhorting, to teaching. ¹⁴Do not neglect the

gift that is in you, which was given to you through prophecy with the laying on of hands by the council of elders.*e* ¹⁵Put these things into practice, devote yourself to them, so that all may see your progress. ¹⁶Pay close attention to yourself and to your teaching; continue in these things, for in doing this you will save both yourself and your hearers.

5 Do not speak harshly to an older man,*f* but speak to him as to a father, to younger men as brothers, ²to older women as mothers, to younger women as sisters—with absolute purity.

*a*Gk *brothers*
*b*Or *deacon*
*c*Other ancient authorities read *suffer reproach*
*d*Gk *to the reading*
*e*Gk *by the presbytery*
*f*Or *an elder*, or *a presbyter*

Prayer Starter: Help me, Lord, to respect and be kind to older people.

Memory Verse: For you yourselves know very well . . .

—1 Thessalonians 5.2

Eunice and Lois

Paul, an apostle of Christ Jesus by the will of God, for the sake of the promise of life that is in Christ Jesus,

²To Timothy, my beloved child:

Grace, mercy, and peace from God the Father and Christ Jesus our Lord.

³I am grateful to God—whom I worship with a clear conscience, as my ancestors did—when I remember you constantly in my prayers night and day. ⁴Recalling your tears, I long to see you so that I may be filled with joy. ⁵I am reminded of your sincere faith, a faith that lived first in your grandmother Lois and your mother Eunice and now, I am sure, lives in you. ⁶For this reason I remind you to rekindle the gift of God that is within you through the laying on of my hands; ⁷for God did not give us a spirit of cowardice, but rather a spirit of power and of love and of self-discipline.

⁸Do not be ashamed, then, of the testimony about our Lord or of me his prisoner, but join with me in suffering for the gospel, relying on the

power of God, [9]who saved us and called us with a holy calling, not according to our works but according to his own purpose and grace. This grace was given to us in Christ Jesus before the ages began, [10]but it has now been revealed through the appearing of our Savior Christ Jesus, who abolished death and brought life and immortality to light through the gospel. [11]For this gospel I was appointed a herald and an apostle and a teacher,[a] [12]and for this reason I suffer as I do. But I am not ashamed, for I know the one in whom I have put my trust, and I am sure that he is able to guard until that day what I have entrusted to him.[b] [13]Hold to the standard of sound teaching that you have heard from me, in the faith and love that are in Christ Jesus. [14]Guard the good treasure entrusted to you, with the help of the Holy Spirit living in us.

[a]Other ancient authorities add *of the Gentiles*
[b]Or *what has been entrusted to me*

Prayer Starter: Thank you, God, for all the people who love me.

Memory Verse: For you yourselves know very well that the day of the Lord . . .
—*1 Thessalonians 5.2*

Philemon

When I remember you[a] in my prayers, I always thank my God [5]because I hear of your love for all the saints and your faith toward the Lord Jesus. [6]I pray that the sharing of your faith may become effective when you perceive all the good that we[b] may do for Christ. [7]I have indeed received much joy and encouragement from your love, because the hearts of the saints have been refreshed through you, my brother.

[8]For this reason, though I am bold enough in Christ to command you to do your duty, [9]yet I would rather appeal to you on the basis of love—and I, Paul, do this as an old man, and now also as a prisoner of Christ Jesus.[c] [10]I am appealing to you for my child, Onesimus, whose father I have become during my imprisonment. [11]Formerly he was useless to you, but now he is indeed useful[d] both to you and to me. [12]I am sending him, that is, my own heart, back to you. [13]I wanted to keep him with me, so that he might be of service to me in your place during my imprisonment for the gospel; [14]but I preferred to do nothing without your consent, in order that your good deed might be voluntary and not something forced. [15]Perhaps this is the reason he was separated from you for a while, so that you might have him back forever, [16]no longer as a slave but more than a slave, a beloved brother—especially to me but how much more to you, both in the flesh and in the Lord.

[17]So if you consider me your partner, welcome him as you would welcome me. [18]If he has wronged you in any way, or owes you anything, charge that to my account. [19]I, Paul, am writing this with my own hand: I will repay it. I say nothing about your owing me even your own self.

[a]From verse 4 through verse 21, *you* is singular
[b]Other ancient authorities read *you* (plural)
[c]Or *as an ambassador of Christ Jesus, and now also his prisoner*
[d]The name Onesimus means *useful* or (compare verse 20) *beneficial*

Prayer Starter: Lord, use my love to make others happy.

Memory Verse: For you yourselves know very well that the day of the Lord will come . . .   —*1 Thessalonians 5.2*

Faith

By faith Enoch was taken so that he did not experience death; and "he was not found, because God had taken him." For it was attested before he was taken away that "he had pleased God." ⁶And without faith it is impossible to please God, for whoever would approach him must believe that he exists and that he rewards those who seek him. ⁷By faith Noah, warned by God about events as yet unseen, respected the warning and built an ark to save his household; by this he condemned the world and became an heir to the righteousness that is in accordance with faith.

⁸By faith Abraham obeyed when he was called to set out for a place that he was to receive as an inheritance; and he set out, not knowing where he was going. ⁹By faith he stayed for a time in the land he had been promised, as in a foreign land, living in tents, as did Isaac and Jacob, who were heirs with him of the same promise. ¹⁰For he looked forward to the city that has foundations, whose architect and builder is God.

¹³All of these died in faith without having received the promises, but from a distance they saw and greeted them. They confessed that they were strangers and foreigners on the earth, ¹⁴for people who speak in this way make it clear that they are seeking a homeland. ¹⁵If they had been thinking of the land that they had left behind, they would have had opportunity to return. ¹⁶But as it is, they desire a better country, that is, a heavenly one. Therefore God is not ashamed to be called their God; indeed, he has prepared a city for them.

Prayer Starter: Increase my faith, Lord. Help me believe that you are real and that you reward those who seek you.

Memory Verse: For you yourselves know very well that the day of the Lord will come like a thief in the night.   —*1 Thessalonians 5.2*

**Religion That
Pleases God**

B: ut be doers of the word, and not merely hearers who deceive themselves. ²³For if any are hearers of the word and not doers, they are like those who look at themselves^a in a mirror; ²⁴for they look at themselves and, on going away, immediately forget what they were like. ²⁵But those who look into the perfect law, the law of liberty, and persevere, being not hearers who forget but doers who act—they will be blessed in their doing.

²⁶If any think they are religious, and do not bridle their tongues but deceive their hearts, their religion is worthless. ²⁷Religion that is pure and undefiled before God, the Father, is this: to care for orphans and widows in their distress, and to keep oneself unstained by the world.

2 My brothers and sisters,^b do you with your acts of favoritism really believe in our glorious Lord Jesus Christ?^c ²For if a person with gold rings and in fine clothes comes into your assembly, and if a poor person in dirty clothes also comes in, ³and if you take notice of the one wearing the fine clothes and say, "Have a seat here, please," while to the one who is poor you say, "Stand there," or, "Sit at my feet,"^d ⁴have you not made distinctions among yourselves, and become judges with evil thoughts? ⁵Listen, my beloved brothers and sisters.^e Has not God chosen

the poor in the world to be rich in faith and to be heirs of the kingdom that he has promised to those who love him? [6]But you have dishonored the poor. Is it not the rich who oppress you? Is it not they who drag you into court? [7]Is it not they who blaspheme the excellent name that was invoked over you?

[a]Gk *at the face of his birth*
[b]Gk *My brothers*
[c]Or *hold the faith of our glorious Lord Jesus Christ without acts of favoritism*
[d]Gk *Sit under my footstool*
[e]Gk *brothers*

Prayer Starter: Give me love and concern for those who don't have as much as I have.

Memory Verse: If we confess our sins . . .   —*1 John 1.9*

Pray for One
Another

Be patient, therefore, beloved,[a] until the coming of the Lord. The farmer waits for the precious crop from the earth, being patient with it until it receives the early and the late rains. [8]You also must be patient. Strengthen your hearts, for the coming of the Lord is near.[b] [9]Beloved,[c] do not grumble against one another, so that you may not be judged. See, the Judge is standing at the doors! [10]As an example of suffering and patience, beloved,[a] take the prophets who spoke in the name of the Lord. [11]Indeed we call blessed those who showed endurance. You have heard of the endurance of Job, and you have seen the purpose of the Lord, how the Lord is compassionate and merciful.

[12]Above all, my beloved,[a] do not swear, either by heaven or by earth or by any other oath, but let your "Yes" be yes and your "No" be no, so that you may not fall under condemnation.

[13]Are any among you suffering? They should pray. Are any cheerful? They should sing songs of praise. [14]Are any among you sick? They should

call for the elders of the church and have them pray over them, anointing them with oil in the name of the Lord. [15]The prayer of faith will save the sick, and the Lord will raise them up; and anyone who has committed sins will be forgiven. [16]Therefore confess your sins to one another, and pray for one another, so that you may be healed. The prayer of the righteous is powerful and effective. [17]Elijah was a human being like us, and he prayed fervently that it might not rain, and for three years and six months it did not rain on the earth. [18]Then he prayed again, and the heaven gave rain and the earth yielded its harvest.

[19]My brothers and sisters,[d] if anyone among you wanders from the truth and is brought back by another, [20]you should know that whoever brings back a sinner from wandering will save the sinner's[e] soul from death and will cover a multitude of sins.

[a]Gk *brothers*
[b]Or *is at hand*
[c]Gk *Brothers*
[d]Gk *My brothers*
[e]Gk *his*

Prayer Starter: Teach me to sing praises to you, Lord, especially when I am feeling good.

Memory Verse: If we confess our sins, he who is faithful and just . . .
—*1 John 1.9*

A Message for Church Leaders

Now as an elder myself and a witness of the sufferings of Christ, as well as one who shares in the glory to be revealed, I exhort the elders among you [2]to tend the flock of God that is in your charge, exercising the oversight,[a] not under compulsion but willingly, as God would have you do it[b] —not for sordid gain but eagerly. [3]Do not lord it over those in your charge, but be examples to the flock. [4]And when the chief shepherd appears, you will win the crown of glory that never fades away. [5]In the same way, you who are younger must accept the authority of the elders.[c] And all of you must clothe yourselves with humility in your dealings with one another, for

"God opposes the proud,
  but gives grace to the humble."

[6]Humble yourselves therefore under the mighty hand of God, so that he may exalt you in due time. [7]Cast all your anxiety on him, because he cares for you. [8]Discipline yourselves, keep alert.[d] Like a roaring lion your adversary the devil prowls around, looking for someone to devour. [9]Resist him, steadfast in your faith, for you know that your brothers and sisters[e] in all the world are undergoing the same kinds of suffering. [10]And after you have suffered for a little while, the God of all grace, who has called you to his eternal glory in Christ, will himself restore, support, strengthen, and establish you. [11]To him be the power forever and ever. Amen.

[a]Other ancient authorities lack *exercising the oversight*
[b]Other ancient authorities lack *as God would have you do it*
[c]Or *of those who are older*
[d]Or *be vigilant*
[e]Gk *your brotherhood*

Prayer Starter: Bless and encourage the priests of my church, dear Lord.

Memory Verse: If we confess our sins, he who is faithful and just will forgive us our sins . . .   —1 John 1.9

God Is Light

We declare to you what was from the beginning, what we have heard, what we have seen with our eyes, what we have looked at and touched with our hands, concerning the word of life— ²this life was revealed, and we have seen it and testify to it, and declare to you the eternal life that was with the Father and was revealed to us—³we declare to you what we have seen and heard so that you also may have fellowship with us; and truly our fellowship is with the Father and with his Son Jesus Christ. ⁴We are writing these things so that our*ª* joy may be complete.

⁵This is the message we have heard from him and proclaim to you, that God is light and in him there is no darkness at all. ⁶If we say that we have fellowship with him while we are walking in darkness, we lie and do not do what is true; ⁷but if we walk in the light as he himself is in the light, we have fellowship with one another, and the blood of Jesus his Son cleanses us from all sin. ⁸If we say that we have no sin, we deceive ourselves, and the truth is not in us. ⁹If we confess our sins, he who is faithful and just will forgive us our sins and cleanse us from all unrigh-

teousness. ¹⁰If we say that we have not sinned, we make him a liar, and his word is not in us.

ᵃOther ancient authorities read *your*

Prayer Starter: Show me when I sin, Father, so that I can ask for your forgiveness.

Memory Verse: If we confess our sins, he who is faithful and just will forgive us our sins and cleanse us . . .   *—1 John 1.9*

On Patmos Island

I, John, your brother who share with you in Jesus the persecution and the kingdom and the patient endurance, was on the island called Patmos because of the word of God and the testimony of Jesus.[a] 10I was in the spirit[b] on the Lord's day, and I heard behind me a loud voice like a trumpet 11saying, "Write in a book what you see and send it to the seven churches, to Ephesus, to Smyrna, to Pergamum, to Thyatira, to Sardis, to Philadelphia, and to Laodicea."

12Then I turned to see whose voice it was that spoke to me, and on turning I saw seven golden lampstands, 13and in the midst of the lampstands I saw one like the Son of Man, clothed with a long robe and with a golden sash across his chest. 14His head and his hair were white as white wool, white as snow; his eyes were like a flame of fire, 15his feet were like burnished bronze, refined as in a furnace, and his voice was like the sound of many waters. 16In his right hand he held seven stars, and from his mouth came a sharp, two-edged sword, and his face was like the sun shining with full force.

17When I saw him, I fell at his feet as though dead. But he placed his right hand on me, saying, "Do not be afraid; I am the first and the last, 18and the living one. I was dead, and see, I am alive forever and ever; and I have the keys of Death and of Hades."

[a]Or *testimony to Jesus*
[b]Or *in the Spirit*

Prayer Starter: Help me realize how glorious Jesus Christ really is.

Memory Verse: If we confess our sins, he who is faithful and just will forgive us our sins and cleanse us from all unrighteousness. *—1 John 1.9*

Listen and Be Ready

" And to the angel of the church in Laodicea write: The words of the Amen, the faithful and true witness, the origin*a* of God's creation:

¹⁵"I know your works; you are neither cold nor hot. I wish that you were either cold or hot. ¹⁶So, because you are lukewarm, and neither cold nor hot, I am about to spit you out of my mouth. ¹⁷For you say, 'I am rich, I have prospered, and I need nothing.' You do not realize that you are wretched, pitiable, poor, blind, and naked. ¹⁸Therefore I counsel you to buy from me gold refined by fire so that you may be rich; and white robes to clothe you and to keep the shame of your nakedness from being seen;

and salve to anoint your eyes so that you may see. [19]I reprove and discipline those whom I love. Be earnest, therefore, and repent. [20]Listen! I am standing at the door, knocking; if you hear my voice and open the door, I will come in to you and eat with you, and you with me. [21]To the one who conquers I will give a place with me on my throne, just as I myself conquered and sat down with my Father on his throne. [22]Let anyone who has an ear listen to what the Spirit is saying to the churches."

[a]Or *beginning*

Prayer Starter: Keep me from being lukewarm about you, dear God.

Memory Verse: The one who testifies . . .

—*Revelation 22.20*

The Lamb

Then I saw in the right hand of the one seated on the throne a scroll written on the inside and on the back, sealed[a] with seven seals; [2]and I saw a mighty angel proclaiming with a loud voice, "Who is worthy to open the scroll and break its seals?" [3]And no one in heaven or on earth or under the earth was able to open the scroll or to look into it. [4]And I began to weep bitterly because no one was found worthy to open the scroll or to look into it. [5]Then one of the elders said to me, "Do not weep. See, the Lion of the tribe of Judah, the Root of David, has conquered, so that he can open the scroll and its seven seals."

[6]Then I saw between the throne and the four living creatures and among the elders a Lamb standing as if it had been slaughtered, having seven horns and seven eyes, which are the seven spirits of God sent out into all the earth. [7]He went and took the scroll from the right hand of the one who was seated on the throne. [8]When he had taken the scroll, the four living creatures and the twenty-four elders fell before the Lamb, each holding a harp and golden bowls full of incense, which are the prayers of the saints. [9]They sing a new song:

> "You are worthy to take the scroll
> and to open its seals,
> for you were slaughtered and by your blood you ransomed for God
> saints from[b] every tribe and language and people and nation."

[a]Or *written on the inside, and sealed on the back*
[b]Gk *ransomed for God from*

Prayer Starter: You, Lord, are worthy of all my love and worship.

Memory Verse: The one who testifies to these things says . . .
—*Revelation 22.20*

Worship in Heaven

After this I looked, and there was a great multitude that no one could count, from every nation, from all tribes and peoples and languages, standing before the throne and before the Lamb, robed in white, with palm branches in their hands. ¹⁰They cried out in a loud voice, saying,

"Salvation belongs to our God
who is seated on the throne, and to the Lamb!"

¹¹And all the angels stood around the throne and around the elders and the four living creatures, and they fell on their faces before the throne and worshiped God, ¹²singing,

"Amen! Blessing and glory and wisdom
and thanksgiving and honor
and power and might
be to our God forever and ever!
Amen."

¹³Then one of the elders addressed me, saying, "Who are these, robed in white, and where have they come from?" ¹⁴I said to him, "Sir, you are the one that knows." Then he said to me, "These are they who have come out of the great ordeal; they have washed their robes and made them white in the blood of the Lamb."

Prayer Starter: Praise, glory, wisdom, thanks, and strength belong to our God forever and ever! Amen!

Memory Verse: The one who testifies to these things says, "Surely I am coming soon." . . .
—*Revelation 22.20*

| King
of Kings |
|---|

Then I saw heaven opened, and there was a white horse! Its rider is called Faithful and True, and in righteousness he judges and makes war. [12]His eyes are like a flame of fire, and on his head are many diadems; and he has a name inscribed that no one knows but himself. [13]He is clothed in a robe dipped in[a] blood, and his name is called The Word of God.

[14]And the armies of heaven, wearing fine linen, white and pure, were following him on white horses. [15]From his mouth comes a sharp sword with which to strike down the nations, and he will rule[b] them with a rod of iron; he will tread the wine press of the fury of the wrath of God the Almighty. [16]On his robe and on his thigh he has a name inscribed, "King of kings and Lord of lords."

[17]Then I saw an angel standing in the sun, and with a loud voice he called to all the birds that fly in midheaven, "Come, gather for the great supper of God, [18]to eat the flesh of kings, the flesh of captains, the flesh of the mighty, the flesh of horses and their riders—flesh of all, both free and slave, both small and great." [19]Then I saw the beast and the kings of the earth with their armies gathered to make war against the rider on the horse and against his army. [20]And the beast was captured, and with it the false prophet who had performed in its presence the signs by which he deceived those who had received the mark of the beast and those who worshiped its image.

[a]Other ancient authorities read *sprinkled with*
[b]Or *will shepherd*

Prayer Starter: You, O Lord God, are King of kings and Lord of lords.

Memory Verse: The one who testifies to these things says, "Surely I am coming soon." Amen. . . .
—*Revelation 22.20*

I Am Coming Soon

Then I saw a new heaven and a new earth; for the first heaven and the first earth had passed away, and the sea was no more. ²And I saw the holy city, the new Jerusalem, coming down out of heaven from God, prepared as a bride adorned for her husband. ³And I heard a loud voice from the throne saying,

"See the home*ᵃ* of God is among mortals.
He will dwell*ᵃ* with them as their God;*ᵇ*
they will be his peoples,*ᶜ*
and God himself will be with them;*ᵈ*
⁴ he will wipe every tear from their eyes.
Death will be no more;
mourning and crying and pain will be no more,
for the first things have passed away."

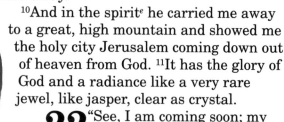

¹⁰And in the spirit*ᵉ* he carried me away to a great, high mountain and showed me the holy city Jerusalem coming down out of heaven from God. ¹¹It has the glory of God and a radiance like a very rare jewel, like jasper, clear as crystal.

22"See, I am coming soon; my reward is with me, to repay according to everyone's work. ¹³I am the Alpha and the Omega, the first and the last, the beginning and the end."

¹⁶"It is I, Jesus, who sent my angel to you with this testimony for the churches. I am the root and the descendant of David, the bright morning star."

¹⁷ The Spirit and the bride say, "Come."
And let everyone who hears say, "Come."
And let everyone who is thirsty come.
Let anyone who wishes take the water of life as a gift.
²⁰The one who testifies to these things says, "Surely I am coming soon." Amen. Come, Lord Jesus!
²¹The grace of the Lord Jesus be with all the saints. Amen.*ᶠ*

ᵃGk tabernacle
ᵇOther ancient authorities lack as their God
ᶜOther ancient authorities read people
ᵈOther ancient authorities add and be their God
ᵉOr in the Spirit
ᶠOther ancient authorities lack all; others lack the saints; others lack Amen

Prayer Starter: Lord Jesus, thank you that you make your home with us.

Memory Verse: The one who testifies to these things says, "Surely I am coming soon." Amen. Come, Lord Jesus!   —*Revelation 22.20*

Subject List